THE GOOD CITIZEN

Using applied political theory, JoAnne Myers presents five markers by which citizens become second-class citizens—property, productivity, participation, patriotism, and reproduction. Citizenship is a highly contested status since it grants members political rights and responsibilities. It is contextualized by cultural, political, historical, economic, situational, and place. In the United States, we think of citizenship in principle as an equal status, but citizenship is not just a binary status: norms, policies, and laws can mark some citizens as "other."

In *The Good Citizen: The Markers of Privilege in America*, Myers argues that being marked as not having or achieving these markers is how citizenship is controlled and regulated. To illustrate this argument, each chapter begins with a practical question or myth to ease the reader into the marker being examined. She later articulates the ways in which law and norms and biopower regulates and controls citizens in three policy areas.

Myers moves beyond theories of citizen marginalization based on identity politics and intersectionality to provide a new understanding of citizenship practice. *The Good Citizen* will be of interest to scholars and researchers of politics, sociology, or legal studies of citizenship, and anyone concerned with distributive justice.

JoAnne Myers is associate professor of political science and co-founder the Women, Gender and Sexuality Program at Marist College, Poughkeepsie, NY. As an applied political philosopher, her research interrogates the relationship between citizen, non-citizen, and the state in the modern liberal state, focusing on human rights.

"In *The Good Citizen*, Professor JoAnne Myers makes us think seriously and critically about the ever contested concept and practices of liberal-democratic citizenship. Informed by history both American and comparative, she challenges us to see the realities of American belonging, the lived experience of citizenship, the elevation of some and the marginalization of others, in terms of five markers outlined. This is a most timely book. A book that will help us, all of us, not only scholars and students, better understand and address the manifold crises we confront."

Harvey J. Kaye
Director, Center for History and Social Change,
University of Wisconsin-Green Bay

THE GOOD CITIZEN

The Markers of Privilege in America

JoAnne Myers

Routledge
Taylor & Francis Group
NEW YORK AND LONDON

First published 2020
by Routledge
52 Vanderbilt Avenue, New York, NY 10017

and by Routledge
2 Park Square, Milton Park, Abingdon, Oxon, OX14 4RN

Routledge is an imprint of the Taylor & Francis Group, an informa business

Library of Congress Cataloging-in-Publication Data
Names: Myers, JoAnne, 1954- author.
Title: The good citizen : the markers of privilege in America / JoAnne Myers.
Description: 1. | New York, NY : Routledge, 2020. | Includes bibliographical references and index.
Identifiers: LCCN 2019016240 (print) | LCCN 2019980739 (ebook) | ISBN 9781138543508 (hardback) | ISBN 9781138543515 (paperback) | ISBN 9781351006675 (mobi) | ISBN 9781351006705 (ebook) | ISBN 9781351006699 (pdf) | ISBN 9781351006682 (epub)
Subjects: LCSH: Citizenship--Social aspects--United States. | Political participation--Social aspects--United States. | Privilege (Social psychology)--United States. | Social structure--United States. | Distributive justice--United States.
Classification: LCC JK1759 .M955 2020 (print) | LCC JK1759 (ebook) | DDC 323.6/50973--dc23
LC record available at https://lccn.loc.gov/2019016240
LC ebook record available at https://lccn.loc.gov/2019980739

ISBN: 978-1-138-54350-8 (hbk)
ISBN: 978-1-138-54351-5 (pbk)
ISBN: 978-1-351-00670-5 (ebk)

Typeset in Bembo
by Lumina Datamatics Limited

To Evan, Logan, and Cameron

Rights are not a zero sum game.

CONTENTS

PROLOGUE

Citizenship is not just a binary status.

1. Around the country from New York to Colorado, county sheriffs do not ask if someone is a citizen, but only inquire where they were born. The sheriffs say people know where they were born, they do not know if they are citizens. A non-American birthplace becomes the marker by which the deputies determine immigration status, even though there are many foreign-born American citizens, green card holders, visitors, and visa holders. Immigration and Customs Enforcement (ICE) is notified of every foreign-born person in custody.

   State and local governments and their officials are not required to enforce federal laws, such as in this case, sharing information regarding citizenship status with Immigration and Custom Enforcement. For many municipalities, public safety trumps notifying ICE, and they would rather people contact the police and fire departments for assistance regardless of their immigration or citizenship status.

   The number of municipalities that are calling themselves Sanctuary or Welcoming Cities or towns has increased. President Trump issued Executive Order 13768[1] on 25 January 2017, which withheld federal funding from these municipalities to coerce them into being compliant with his agenda of a politics of fear of immigrants. The president also uses the rhetoric of public safety—in this case, keeping citizens safe from immigrants; he paints the immigrants as criminals, lazy. On 1 August 2018, the US Circuit Court of Appeals for the Ninth Circuit declared that the Executive Order was unconstitutional because of the Supreme Court decision in Printz v. United States, 521 U.S. 898 (1997) stated that, because of the Tenth Amendment of the Constitution, the US government cannot engage in "commandeering of state governments."

2. US Customs and Border Protection (CBP), may, as per the Immigration and Nationality Act 287(a)(3) and copied in 8 Code of Federal Regulations (CFR) 287 (a)(3), without a warrant, "within a reasonable distance from any external boundary of the United States … board and search for aliens in any vessel within the territorial waters of the United States and any railcar, aircraft, conveyance, or vehicle. 8 CFR 287 (a)(1) defines reasonable distance as 100 air miles from the border."

   One hundred air miles of the border of the United States includes all of Florida, Maine, Michigan, and New Hampshire, all of Chicago, Los Angeles and New York City; in fact, almost two-thirds of the population of the United States resides within this border zone jurisdiction.

   This past year in New York State, CBP agents have boarded western-bound trains in Syracuse and set up checkpoints on the Northway (the main highway between Albany and Montreal Canada). CBP agents have also boarded Greyhound buses between Spokane, Washington, and Portland, Oregon, removing passengers and asking for their papers (proof of citizenship). American citizens do not have to carry their proof of citizenship, but naturalized citizens have taken to carrying their proof. CBP has the right to set up checkpoints and ask people about their immigration status, even if they have no suspicion that the person illegally entered the country or overstayed their visa (the dominant means of becoming an undocumented alien).

3. Prove right now you are a citizen.

   US citizens do not have to carry proof of citizenship in the country, though if they are traveling domestically, they need to carry government-issued photo identification such as a driver's license. If you have immigration documents (visas and green cards), you need to carry these on your person if you are over the age of 18.

   Proof of citizenship is a passport or a birth certificate. Only 42% of Americans hold passports. Thus, they must prove their citizenship with their birth certificates. If you are like most people, you will never diet back to your birth weight.

4. Can you pass the US Naturalization test?

   /www.uscis.gov/us-citizenship/naturalization-test

5. Game of Privilege using the five markers of citizenship laid out in this book—Patriotism, Property Ownership, Participation, Productivity, and Reproductivity (with apologies to Peggy Macintosh). If you do this with a

group, take one step forward if you have a positive answer, a step backwards if negative, and remain in place if the question does not pertain to you. If you do the game by yourself, just check off the ones that pertain to you.

- Are you registered for selective service?
- To further your education, or to gain a skill did you enlisted in the military?
- Did one of your parents enlisted in the military to gain a skill or to further their education?
- Did you grow up in a single-family home?
- Did you go to vote with your parents?
- Did you have an allowance when you were a child?
- Do you lock the doors while driving in certain neighborhoods?
- When you are pulled over for a traffic stop, do you immediately start reaching for your license, registration and insurance card as the officer is walking towards you?
- Are you paid the same rate as all others at your level doing your job?
- Do you make at least 25% of what the CEO makes?
- Do you have health insurance through your work?
- Are you a citizen of the country you were born in?
- If you are stopped by law enforcement, would you be questioned about your citizenship?
- Can you move wherever you want?
- Can you move whenever you want?
- Do you think twice about hanging out in Starbucks or at the local mall?
- If practicing sex, do you think about (and have control over) protection from venereal diseases and/or pregnancy?
- Do you expect to have in the next 10 years, or currently have:
  - Your own home?
  - A post graduate professional degree?
  - A six plus figure salary?
  - A nine-to-five job?
  - Be politically involved in your hometown from attending public meetings to running for office.
- Do you agree or disagree that
  - Women should work.
  - Two income families are necessary.

- If you are arrested, can you make bail or be released on your own cognizance?
- Do you have good credit?
- Do you live paycheck to paycheck?

Now analyze the results. Why are some of your group further ahead, or if you are alone, why did you end up with the number of checks you did? Come up with a theory, an explanation, and write it down. After finishing this book, is your answer substantiated?

This book sets forth how citizenship is not just a binary status.

Note

1 www.whitehouse.gov/presidential-actions/executive-order-enhancing-public-safety-interior-united-states/

ACKNOWLEDGMENTS

I would like to thank my family, my friends, my colleagues, and my students for their patience, good humor, and support, and my editor for her faith in me.

The first very rough concept of this book was delivered as a paper at the Human Rights conference held in Wheeling, West Virginia. Certain parts of the chapters have been delivered at the Law and Society Association annual meetings, the Sociology of Law meetings, and the Western Political Science Association meetings.

1

INTRODUCTION

Being a citizen in the United States of America, as in other nations/states, is a position that grants political rights and representation, agency, empowerment, and autonomy. For all our liberal ideals and virtues, and our political values of equality and fairness, being a citizen is imbued with status, rights, and responsibilities that are made explicit by law, policy, and practice. Normative political theory looks at good citizenship from three intersecting perspectives: obedience to the rule of law; providing and caring for oneself and family; and contributing to and promoting the public good. Citizenship is the hegemonic means for both defining who gets to be included as part of the (nation) state and maintaining (enforcing) order in society. What happens when there are citizens who may not reach the ideal of good citizen? Are they not worthy of rights, responsibilities, and entitlements?

There are others who, while citizens by birth or naturalization, do not enjoy full citizenship—they are second-class citizens. These second-class citizens are controlled and regulated, and they are put in order and kept in their place by law, policy, and social practice. What this book tries to make explicit is this entrenching of second-class citizenship. As feminists have known: if you can name the problem, you are on the way to fixing it. The existence and entrenchment of second-class citizens is problematic if equality, one of America's ideals, is to be truly attainable.

We see people who have citizenship but are unable to access all their rights, and for many, they are blamed for their situation and for not being able to access all their rights; a true Catch-22. Hurricane Katrina in 2005 was a perfect storm hitting the Gulf Coast at the end of the month when people who rely on monthly payments from social security or pensions, and/or social welfare programs had no available funds to use to vacate the lowlands, and nowhere to go.

This situation gets repeated for every subsequent hurricane from Sandy in 2012 to the hurricanes in 2017 Harvey in Texas; Maria's devastation left on Puerto Rico and other islands still remains years after. People may have full citizenship but they are not able to access their rights or pubic services because of the double whammy of poverty and disaster or because social norms relegate some to outsider status (same sex couples in some states may not adopt children).

> We the People of the United States, in Order to form a more perfect Union, establish Justice, insure domestic Tranquility, provide for the common defence, promote the general Welfare, and secure the Blessings of Liberty ourselves and our Posterity, do ordain and establish this Constitution of the United States of America.

So begins our Constitution[1] written in 1789, setting forth the role of government. But who are "We the people"? The Constitution remained silent not defining the people as citizens until the Fourteenth Amendment (1868), yet clearly articulating that the Constitution and its amendments cover all people, for example: the First Amendment "the right of the people" to petition the government and assemble peacefully; the Second Amendment, right to bear arms, the Fourth Amendment against unreasonable searches and seizures; the last two of the so-called Bill of Rights, the Ninth and Tenth Amendments reserve the unenumerated rights and powers "to the people." Two Supreme Court cases articulate that this phrase refers to "persons who are part of the national community": United States v. Verdugo-Urquidez, 494 U.S. 259 (1990) and District of Columbia v. Heller, 128 S.Ct.2783 (2008) "the people" refers to all members of the political community.

And, thus, this book begins with this puzzle of who are "We the people?" Do we just have some sort of relationship with the national community? What sort of relationship is it? Are we members of the political community, voters? Though voting is a right, not an obligation, and even some citizens might lose their right to vote—felons in prison, for example, others who are not eligible due to their young age, or those who have not exercised the right to vote and registered to do so appropriately.

But then we need to double back to the Constitution, and we realize that representation is of *all* persons, regardless of whether they are citizens and/or noncitizens. Hence, Congress was empowered to undertake a census (Article 1, section 2) to *count* all people in the country, which it has done so every 10 years since 1790. This accounting of all the people is to ensure equal representation of all and for states to equally size (apportion) congressional districts. It is the apportionment of representation, we are a republic[2] after all, and that is why we now consider as racist the Three-Fifths Compromise, which counted male slaves as three-fifths a person. People who are serving prison sentences are counted as residents of the district in which the prison is located, adding representatives to the rural areas where most prisons are located and undercounts the incarcerated persons' home districts. The over/undercounting of persons also effects allocations of funds and services. This accounting is how the majority in power is really a demographic minority: males are only 49% of the total population. The minority in power keeps the majority in check, and that, my friends, is what this book will try to make evident. Demographic predictions state that by 2030 immigration, rather than birth rate, will be the source of our new population; by 2045 non-Hispanic whites will no longer be the majority population in the United States (Klein, 2018). For those white males in power, this browning of America by people with Black, Hispanic, Asian, or mixed heritage is troubling. Non-whites make up 37% of our population, currently; the perception is that this percentage is higher—49%. We have seen the impact of gender inequality and misogyny on our politics and culture—women who comprise 51% of our population only received the vote in 1919, and though the Equal Pay Act was passed in 1963, women still earn substantially less than males in 2019.

And, as we head into another census taking period, the current administration wants to add a question regarding citizenship. We know this because, as per the statute codifying the census, Title 13, U.S. Code (1954), the Census Bureau must notify Congress of general census subjects (demographics) and the specific questions that will be asked three and two years, respectively, prior to the actual census. If this question stands, it marks a chasm between "We the People" and those members of the national community who are citizens. This will be the first time in 50 plus years that such a question has been asked and, doing so, underscores citizenship as a valued status. The administration is claiming that it needs this information to enforce the Voting Rights Act, yet registering to vote is a state function. Many claim that asking this question is an anti-immigrant tool and will suppress participation resulting in a significant undercount of persons who are not citizens.

This question on the 2020 census appears to be aimed at the immigrant community to lower their response. In turn, it would potentially impact the electoral strength of not only these communities, but the states as well since lower population numbers could result in fewer Congressional representation (seats) while also reducing potential federal (and state) funding and strategic planning based on demographics. The number of people that would be undercounted has been estimated at 24 million. This case went to the United States District Court Southern District, a ruling which Judge Jesse Furman issued on 15 January 2019 and found that the Commerce Secretary's "decision to add a citizenship question to the 2020 Census—even if it did not violate the Constitution itself—was unlawful for a multitude of independent reasons and must be set aside." The ruling was appealed by the Department of Commerce to the Supreme Court, evidence provided indicate that the Trump administration knew that adding the question would also help Republicans and harm Democrats and Latino communities when it comes to redistricting based on the results of the 2020 census count. The Supreme Court decision in Department of Commerce v. New York (588 U.S. ______, 27 June 2019) effectively blocked the question from the 2020 census because the administration did not provide a legitimate justification for including it.

The most cursory definition of citizen is that of being a member of the country. Belonging or not belonging, as if this binary denotes that all citizens are equal. But we know that not all citizens are equal. Paying attention to the news informs us that while the economy and stock market has recovered from the 2008 housing bubble and ensuing financial collapse, the cost of living has increased and many people have not seen a substantive increase in their pay, and their budgets are suffering from the increased cost of food, fuel, and health care. We also are made aware that persons of color are treated unequally—they are presumed guilty and may be summarily shot by police, yet at the same time, white men who commit serial killings are usually apprehended alive if they do not commit suicide by cop. Not to mention that women's words are not given as much weight as men's words, as many reported anecdotes from both academic and business meetings indicate. But, even with these blatant discrepancies, this book does not use race, class, and gender, instead this book delves deeper into the essence of citizenship using a more nuanced lens of the hegemonic norm of a good citizen. This norm articulates five markers of citizenship that, because of both policy and practice, these are invisible to the naked eye.

Citizen is a contested position. American citizenship is considered an equal status, but norms, policies, and laws mark some citizens as others. This book uncovers five markers of good citizenship—property, productivity, participation, patriotism, and reproduction—by which citizens who do not hit these markers are regulated. These regulated citizens are entrenched in a second-class citizenship from which they cannot easily recover, nor can they practice all the rights afforded full citizens.

The goal of our democracy is to be a nation of good productive citizens. But citizen is not just a binary status: citizen or noncitizen; some are second-class (othered) citizens, and still others, failed citizens—the incarcerated—and others are aspirational citizens, those who will be transitioning to citizen either as they age (children) or if they are successful in the naturalization process. *If* we think of the othered citizens, we see them as deserving their unequal status. We practice democratic Calvinism: if citizens are not virtuous good citizens, we tolerate them, treating them differently; their status becomes entrenched. Could these citizens be regulated into non-citizenship? Who would notice? Who would care?

This book looks at the potential endgame: articulating why equality is important. The objective is not only to make visible the entrenchment, but to develop a path to counter this, for without correction this attitude shifts quickly from tolerance to a politics of disgust and aversion.

This book looks at the unseen in most laws, policies, and norms that constrain many in the second-class position and maintain the status quo. Is this justice and liberty for all?

The book does not use race, class, and gender as the markers for citizenship, because while the government limits who enters the country by using some categories of race, class (it costs a lot of money to emigrate), religion (for example, today prohibiting some who are from Muslim majority countries, but not all Muslim majority countries), and gender (escaping from domestic violence or because of one's sexual orientation or presentation is persecuted in one's home country)—this book examines how we limit persons who are already citizens. And, while race, class, and gender are used to regulate citizens by what Michelle Alexander labels as the New Jim Crow laws, by misogynistic policies and norms, or by limiting access based on ability to pay—it is even more nuanced than that. Some of our myths and norms maintain the status quo—tolerance, for instance.

The purpose of this book is to set forth a working paradigm to use citizenship theory and cultural and public policy to identify how citizens get subjugated into second-class citizenship and perhaps further into denaturalization, what Hannah Arendt called a "hole of oblivion" (1951, pp. 430, 437) without the majority citizens taking notice or, worse yet, caring (empathy). It is the small almost imperceivable microaggressions and regulations that become normalized. If microaggressions and regulations do not affect you directly, it is easy to carry on with your life. It is this carrying on that becomes the willful ignorance of the policies that entrap; it is cultural norms that secure.

The first goal is to understand, and the second is to be able to recover to allow us to reach our aspirational goals of equality for all. These aspirational democratic values equality, justice, liberty, and understanding how and why we fall short of reaching them may be the booby prize. It is only the booby prize if nothing is done to correct or change the outcome.

It is the language of the politics of disgust—as Martha Nussbaum has defined it: "a fundamental refusal of another person's full humanity" (Nussbaum, 2010, p. xiii)—which have allowed for norms, policies and laws that enable the average person to not notice, overlook, disregard, in order to carry on with their own lives. As a German philologist described life in Germany after 1933, "To live in this process is absolutely not to be able to notice it.... Each step was so small, so inconsequential... one no more saw it developing from day to day than a farmer in his field sees the corn growing. One day it is over his head." (Mayer, 2017, p. 167). In fact, a lot was happening and has been happening, so the basic concept of normal already is skewed against the common citizen; the average worker. This book is meant to help understand the policies that entrench some and empower others.

Overview

Chapter 1 presents an overview of political modernity: Liberal theory. Liberalism as a political theory—a set of theories that burst forward from the enlightenment and from which the founders of the United States of America based this country on—is a combination of rationalism and individualism, including what we call capitalism, and a theory of natural rights from which we aspire to progressive egalitarianism that allows for equality and justice for all. Our founders did not articulate a definition of citizen, leaving that up to the states to decide based on their own rubric of residency, property, and gender. We have been taught our political history as part of our socialization using this lens of liberalism, and it might be a distorted vision viewing our politics from the position of those who rule and those who make our laws.

Providing a snapshot of those in power, political, economic, and social power at all levels, we see predominately white Christian heterosexual propertied males. If these are the only people at the proverbial table are we even shocked that our laws and norms change at glacial speed—incrementally. We hardly learn or recognize the story of all the peoples of America; we do not question how liberalism maintains the power structure allowing the minority to rule as a powerful and oppressive majority over the true demographic majority.

Citizenship theory emerged from the mid-twentieth-century World War II alongside the Universal Declaration of Human Rights. What rights do people need, politically, socially, and economically to thrive? Chapter three thus goes on to explain these theories and their relation to American political culture and policy. What does it mean to be a citizen, and especially an American citizen, with our aspirations of liberty, equality, and justice? Are all citizens equal or is Citizenship a privileged status? What makes one a good, virtuous citizen?

Citizenship is not only contested, it is contextualized, constricted, and controlled in such a way that most people are unaware of how they are controlled. The overarching thesis of this book is that citizens are controlled and constricted by laws and norms that maintain the category of virtuous citizen: patriotism, property, production, participation, and reproduction. Each subsequent five chapters will articulate how citizens get marked by not achieving fully one or more of these markers. How getting marked as not being a virtuous citizen, they become less than full citizens and as such they are controlled and constricted; they even become deprived of their basic rights. For most of the rest of the population, we do not see the control or deprivation of rights as something oppressive but as something that maintains the public good, the status quo, if we are even notice.

For example, chapter eight focuses on reproduction. How citizenship is controlled as it is reproduced—asking those difficult questions: who can reproduce, and how? This is the chapter that looks at both the most private of all decisions and some of the most public declarations—from marriage to children, from immigration to chained immigration.

The final chapter will look at what not correcting for the creation of second-class citizens, what does entrenchment in this second class mean, is there is no hope of recovery. Placing second-class citizens in an historic context. Historically, second-class citizens have fallen out of the status of citizen entirely and then may be treated as unworthy humans, as nonhuman (see Jews in Germany 1933, or the Tutsi in Rwanda in the early 1990s); dehumanization is one of the stages of genocide. This last chapter of this book will (hopefully) propose a workable liberatory path to move liberal democracy truly forward toward equality.

I am writing this as the current American federal administration is separating families at the border and transporting children a thousand miles away from their parents and as the Muslim travel ban is upheld held by the Supreme Court. All of this did not happen overnight, and none of this is "new" except to those who are recently "woke." Referring to other people as vermin, who will infest, parasites, animals, or some type of criminal is dehumanizing. This language was used by Hitler and Stalin in the mid-twentieth century and by the Hutus against the Tutsis in Rwanda, and today, the language is being used as part of state sanctioned apartheid of the Rohingya in Myanmar; to name a few examples. This is alarming because this language of dehumanization is one of the first stages of genocide that Dr. Gregory Stanton of genocidewatch.net has identified. This language is finding a welcomed foothold in the United States and Europe in the second decade of the twenty-first century. It is the language that is allowing for the poor to be blamed for their circumstances; for those without the means to make bail to be imprisoned for years before their trial; for refugees seeking asylum to be imprisoned or turned back. For example, the language allows the Danish government to force assimilation, labeling 25 low-income predominantly Muslim immigrant urban areas as ghettos and proscribing laws that regulate their lives, demanding assimilation (Barry and Sorenson, *New York Times*, 7/1/18).

Notes

1 The Constitution was the second, but lasting attempt at establishing the US government. The first compact, The Articles of Confederation mentions citizens in Article Four: "the free inhabitants of each of these states, paupers, vagabonds and fugitives from justice excepted, shall be entitled to all privileges and immunities of free citizens in the several states."

2 A republic is a form of a liberal democracy with a representative government and a president as head of state.

References

Arendt, Hannah (1951) *Origins of Totalitarianism*. New York: Harcourt.

Arendt, Hannah (1958) *The Human Condition*. Chicago, IL: Chicago University Press.

Barry, Ellen and Martin Selsoe Sorenson (1 July 2018) "In Denmark, Harsh New Laws for Immigrant 'Ghettos'." *New York Times*. Accessed 25 July 2019, www.nytimes.com/2019/07/01/world/europe/denmark-immigrant-ghettos.html.

Klein, Ezra (30 July 2018) "White Threat in a Browning America: How Demographic Change Is Fracturing Our Politics." www.vox.com/policy-and-politics/2018/7/30/17505406/trump-obama-race-politics-immigration, 8/10/18.

Mayer, Milton ([1955] 2017) *They Thought They Were Free: The Germans, 1933–45*. Chicago, IL: University of Chicago Press.

Nussbaum, Martha (2010) *From Disgust to Humanity: Sexual Orientation and Constitutional Law.* New York: Oxford University Press.

2

CITIZEN AND POLITICAL THEORY IN AMERICA (AN OVERVIEW)

In today's world, acknowledging citizenship is made much more significant with the number of refugees from wars and environmental disasters, immigrants and migrants seeking a better quality of life, asylum seekers escaping from political persecution and violence, and other displaced people. Citizenship is very much in the headlines. There are the undocumented people who come into the United States on a visa and overstay; there are children whose parents brought them into the United States—the dreamers who know no other home but the United States. These dreamers, who are trying to achieve the American Dream, number roughly 800,000 and are in school or legally working under the Deferred Action for Childhood Arrivals program. There are people who cross into the United States without documentation seeking work, a better life, or both. We read about securing our borders from those who either flock or flee to our border controls. We understand the most simplistic definition of citizenship: who belongs and who does not. But citizenship is much more complicated than this, and that complication is what this book begins to lay bare.

The basics of citizenship theory will be laid forth in this chapter, from the most basic definition and theory of citizenship to the most complicated and contested, and how they have been historically applied in the United States. There are three areas of debate in citizenship theory: the traditional legal status of belonging, and the rights and responsibility granted by this status; multiculturalism—the impact of diversity and assimilation; and the nature of social citizenship (Isin, 2013)—the relationships we have in civil society.

American hegemonic citizenship is articulated by the dominant social political and economic (DSPE) paradigm—white, heterosexual Christian male property owner—and ingrained in the American Dream of material consumption—the house with the white picket fence and all its suburban trappings including the stay-at-home wife/mother. It is the combined power of the DSPE and the American Dream that manifests in public policies such as those that push home ownership and in the hegemonic preferencing of property owners over non-property owners. The hegemonic norm also influences the laws and policies by which those others are controlled and regulated. The values that Americans hold dear, articulated in the Declaration of Independence and in the Pledge of Allegiance, are liberty, freedom, the right to private property, the importance of the free market (capitalist) system, justice, and equality. Our founders and politicians from our founding forward have articulated and justified policies using these values. Slogans such as "No taxation without representation" or "Land of the free" and beliefs such as anyone can grow up to be president—that we are politically socialized with re-enforce these values. These become the hegemonic norms that operate in the background of American life. The principles of liberal democratic theory seemingly are built on these values, yet unarticulated is that, for the most part, these values are only for a few—wealthy white men who are among the power elite.

Citizenship is at once an important concept, as Hannah Arendt succinctly put it: citizenship is "the right to have rights," yet at the same time, it is a concept that most people do not think about unless they are outside the hegemonic norm and have had their rights restricted or denied. This book is about thinking about that space in the political world and in civil society in which citizens have their rights curtailed, and the consequences thereof. A citizen of the United States may vote and serve on a jury and as an elected official (though only natural born citizens may serve as President). Citizenship, then, is a valuable yet, for many who are citizens, it is an invisible concept.

In the United States, citizens do not carry around the official documents that identify themselves as citizens—a birth certificate (and trust me, I am not recognizable by my birth certificate: I will never be able to diet down to my original weight of 6 pounds, 1 ounce, and I am much taller than 21 inches); nor carry around their passport—as of 2016, only 36% of Americans even hold passports (passports cost $130 dollars, not counting the cost of the photograph, and more time and money is incurred if you need to get a copy of your birth certificate). There are enhanced driver's licenses that allow people who live near, and regularly cross, the borders of Canada or Mexico and the United States to have an expedited passage between the countries (these usually cost only $30 more than a regular license might); and as of Fall 2020, domestic airline passengers will be required to have either enhanced drivers licenses or passports, courtesy of the REAL ID Act of 2005.

Overview

It would be easy if we could say that people were either citizens or non-citizens. This is the most basic definition of citizenship, being a recognized member of a state. This basic status of belonging is the underpinnings of who makes up a state. It was not until the French Revolution that the French solved for "the Jewish Question"[1] that all persons within the sovereign boundaries of in this case, France, became citizens by virtue of being within the territorial boundaries. The Jewish People had been seen as outsiders and separate from the other Europeans because of their religious practices and their strong cultural practices. When the Jewish people were extended legal and political rights, they began to assimilate, casting aside some of their own cultural practices to belong to the citizenry. This very acculturation lead to a backlash in which some thought the Jews would subvert the existing culture. This existing anti-Semitism, coupled with the harsh economics after World War I, set the stage for what we know now as the Holocaust. I came to this project trying to understand how the Jewish people of Germany who were citizens, thought of themselves as Germans, and contributed to the Germany society and polity slid down a slippery slope into non-citizenship.

While most people mark *Kristallnacht*, 9–10 November 1938—Night of Broken Glass—as the beginning of the Jewish Holocaust in Nazi Germany, it started much earlier with the first anti-Semitic law to pass in Nazi Germany in what would become the Nuremberg Laws.[2] This law, an anti-kosher butchering law, was passed on 21 April 1933, less than one month after the Enabling Act that gave the Nazis power in Germany (23 March 1933).

While Germany had toyed with regulating animal slaughter since the late nineteenth century, no regulation of kosher butchering had been implemented, In fact, the Reichstag had amended the criminal code in 1911 to read "State regulations which interfere with the ritual prescriptions of any religious groups in the matter of animal slaughtering are not allowable" (Article 360, 1911). When the National Socialist Party was gaining a foothold in Germany in 1926, they proposed a law that would prohibit animals being conscious when slaughtered, arguing that kosher butchering as cruelty to animals, and by extension, the Jewish People were cruel to animals. In 1926, Bavaria passed such a law, but since it violated Article 360, it was never implemented.

But on 21 April 1933, the first anti-kosher butchering act, called an animal rights law, while it did not mention kosher butchering, it did require that animals being used for food needed to be stunned before being killed. Kosher butchering requires that, for the meat to be kosher, the animal must be conscious. This law only affected Jewish people, and while the rabbis and butchers tried to find a work around, there was none. Soon the importation of kosher food was prohibited. By 1938, kosher meat was virtually unattainable in Germany because of government restrictions or its prohibitive costs; Jewish Germans were eating a meatless diet. Since this only affected the Jewish population that kept kosher, other citizens did not take notice. The 1 April national boycott of all Jewish businesses took place, and it was easy to see that the German people as a whole could, without much recourse, destroy Jewish economic life. The laws that followed shrank Jewish public life, from limiting the number of students to the professions Jewish people may ply. These laws built on the existing anti-Semitism and the politics of prejudice and disgust.

It is the language of the politics of disgust—as Martha Nussbaum has defined it: "a fundamental refusal of another person's full humanity" (Nussbaum, 2010, p. xiii)—which have allowed for norms, policies, and laws that allow for the average person to not notice, overlook, disregard, and carry on with their own lives. As Mayer ([1955] 2017) and others have noted the laws that allowed Jews and others to be dehumanized were legal, and more importantly they only affected the "other." The normalization of policies are unseen by most of us because they do not affect us directly; we are allowed to carry on our daily lives thinking we are (all) free and equal, as we mark our place, and some fall further away from the aspirational liberal democracy.

Laws are not always just, ethical, or moral—we need to be reminded that the Holocaust was legal. The people who helped the Jews and hid the Jews were the ones breaking the law, and in the same way that slavery was legal, and the subsequent Jim Crow laws were also legal. The norms that allow for this intolerance to exist, that some people are not deserving as others, also allows for the those who are entrenched to bear the blame, and those who are full citizens not to acknowledge their privilege or guilt.

Only in hindsight do we see the slippery slope that flushed Jewish Germans away from citizenship into non-citizenship. The purpose of this book is to shed light on the norms and policies that entrench people in second-class citizenship, so we may help all achieve full citizenship. This book is meant to help understand the policies that entrench some and empower others, to shine the light on those policies and social norms that allow us not to grant full citizenship to others. It is important to note that today, in 2019, there are a growing number of anti-kosher and anti-Halal butchering laws being implemented in modern European states, such as Belgium, and The Netherlands which has been seen as the pinnacle of religious tolerance. Once again these laws are couched in protecting animals from being cruelly butchered, but in effect, are a means of expressing anti-immigration, anti-Semitic, and anti-Muslim sentiments.

It is the goal of liberal democracy with a liberal economic system to be a nation of good productive citizens. In today's neoliberal world, we think of citizenship in principle as democratic. Citizen is a title, and for most of us, we think of that as one that denotes a form of equality. All citizens are created equal. This principle implies that citizens are equal in status, having the same access to social justice and opportunities. But citizen is not just an equal binary status: citizen or noncitizen; norms, policies, and laws mark some citizens as other, as second-class citizens, and still others as failed citizens, not to mention the non-citizens and the aspirational citizens.

We, the enfranchised and empowered people, our officials, and representatives tend to think, if we think of the othered citizens at all, as citizens deserving of their unequal status. In the American neoliberal republic, we practice a form of democratic Calvinism predetermining the treatment of citizens. They are considered virtuous citizens, who attain the markers of citizenship, who are property owners, productive, participatory, patriotic, and reproducing more citizens, then they are citizens deserving all rights and privileges. If the citizen is marked by not attaining one (or more) of the markers, for example, living in public housing, they are not deserving of all the rights and privileges guaranteed by the government.

Thus, if citizens are not seen as virtuous good citizens, we not only tolerate them, we treat them differently—we control and regulate them via social norms, policies, and laws. While there is the rhetoric of recoverable and attainable equality, it is individualized to a fault (i.e. if only they worked harder, they would have more access to material goods). Their status as second-class citizens becomes entrenched. From this entrenched position, could these citizens be regulated into non-citizenship? Who would notice? who would care? How do these invisible constraints and the web of laws and practices conspire to keep individuals in place, without the possibility of achieving equality, thus, maintaining the status quo.

The steadfast ideas about our democratic principles, which we repeated every morning of elementary school in the Pledge of Allegiance "with liberty and justice for all," are the ideas—freedom, justice, and equal political participation—that we find in our founding documents. "All men are created equal" to "We the people" are ideals not reality. The reality is institutionalized in laws and social norms for reasons of security and stability or predictability (Cohen, 2009, p. 12).

The category Citizen is extremely contested and contextualized by cultural, political, historical, economic, situational, and place. Based on citizenship theory and public policy as public good, and good citizenship as the goal of liberal democracy, there are five markers of good citizenship—patriotism, property ownership, productivity, (re)production/procreativity, and participation. People who do not attain these markers are negatively marked, thus, do not enjoy equality or all the rights of a full citizen. These citizens are restricted by public policy, societal norms, and laws. This book is meant to help understand the policies that entrench some and empower others. A good citizen hits all these marks without being marked.

Each subsequent chapter will articulate the ways in which law, norms, and biopower regulates and controls citizens marked by the markers.

Citizenship is entwined with the concept of sovereignty—one needs to be a citizen of a nation. Since the Treaty of Westphalia in 1648, the Western world has recognized the power of the nation-state to control not only its territory, but its citizens. But until the French Revolution, citizenship was not given to all who resided within the nation's borders, and still today, nations that do not recognize all residents as being citizens makes implementing basic human rights complex.[3] The study of human rights shows us that rights are not universal but government granted. And, not all governments, even those who presumably accept the concept of universal natural rights, such as the United States, have signed on to the majority of universal human rights documents.

The very basis of citizenship theory is the legal recognition of belonging, it confers other political, social, or economic rights, or not. Yet over the course of our history, Americans have excluded some even from this basic form of recognition—certain immigrant group such as the Chinese and the Irish, for instance. Native Americans and slaves have been excluded also. Such exclusions make evident that citizenship is a status that bestows benefits. This is the contested site of refugee rights and human rights, of those persons who are citizen wannabes—children and immigrants, for example. The second part of this first debate is comprised of what those political, social, economic, and cultural rights and responsibilities exercised by various members of a polity are. Who can take part in the public discourse, who governs, who may exercise their political right to participate, and how may they participate? One hears the echoes of Hegel's statement that laws are made to protect the haves from the have-nots.

The third working definition of citizenship operates in the vernacular as per T.H. Marshall and has been the norm in citizenship theory since the mid-twentieth century—those who both are considered and consider themselves to be members of the polity, who share the moral, cultural, and de facto norms of the hegemonic polity, and who benefit from belonging. These concepts can be distilled into the notions of hegemony, community, and institutional benefits. The last definition of citizenship is the contested site between the ideal of equality and the actual legal and cultural practices of citizenship. It is in this space that one finds the concepts that privilege and expand the political, social, and economic citizen. It is here where Hannah Arendt further distilled the idea of citizenship as "the right to have rights." It is the realization that one does not belong, and the benefit from belonging becomes the catalyst driving social political movements; for example, the movement to reintegrate former felons—considered to be failed citizens—back into the public.

The modern political theorists' concept of civil citizenship as individual and civil rights in the polity were expanded during the nineteenth century and early twentieth century to mean political citizen—participation in the democratic processes. The latter half of the twentieth century saw citizenship morph into that of social citizenship based on benefits and entitlements. Thus, as we move toward inclusion and equality, there is slippage down the slope of who deserves all the rights, responsibilities, and benefits of citizenship. It is here that we find what Foucault called "biopower"—the cultural practices and interactions, legal, institutional, and political (re)constructions that organize thought and governmentality practice around the concept of full and good citizen. It is the confluence of the legal and institutional constructs with cultural and societal norms. Think about a baby—if it is female, someone will say, "Oh, she will make a pretty bride." The cultural goal of a white (expensive) wedding and marriage are visited on this baby—being a bride is her ultimate goal along with being one-half of a married couple. Society will push her down this path. Our laws will reward the married couple—there will be tax incentives and privileges for the couple. The male baby is not so shackled; he can be anything he dreams about being. But to be deemed stable and successful, he to, when matured, will take a partner.

A brief history of citizenship in the United States finds it a contested category as far back as our founding. In the United States, legal citizenship is a product of birth or naturalization. But the underlying context of full citizenship can be found in the concept entering into the social contract by one's own choice, the question is: Do we all have that choice? The ability to enter into a contract and to be bound by said contract is the basis of not only our polity, but our economy. The rationale is that the good, virtuous citizen should contribute to justice, economic prosperity, and social stability. The citizens who do not so contribute are considered less than, and the concept of the democratic Calvinism is then in place. Democratic Calvinism is this author's construct of the use of the morality of law to keep certain people in their presumed deserved place—either they are full, thus, good citizens and have access to all their rights, responsibilities, and opportunities, or they are less than full citizens and thus do not deserve all the rights and privileges good citizens enjoy. This concept is based on the Calvinistic principle, predetermination.

Citizenship Theory

Liberal theory is built on the assumption that the concept of citizen is both universal and neutral. The dominant paradigm and normative discourse about citizenship in the United States, and Western society, historically considers the white-propertied heterosexual, Christian male as the norm and backgrounds these assumptions, thus building the claim of universality gender neutral citizen on a questionable foundation (see Myers and Tronto, 1998). That the citizen is gendered, classed (propertied), and raced can be traced back to the Ancient Greece democracies. Two thousand plus years ago, Citizen was both a status and responsibility given only to men over the age of 20, who had been publicly recognized at birth by their citizen fathers, and who had the ability to be warriors, masters, and patriarchs. Women, children, immigrants, and slaves were excluded from citizenship. Aristotle in Book III of *Politics* states that the citizen is responsible for ruling (it does not matter if his decisions are good or bad, just that he rules), actively participating in public life and decision-making, as well as being ruled. This ancient underpinning has become so backgrounded that we do not notice it when it affects those who are fully enfranchised today and who have the opportunities to succeed. More than that, we blame those who do not assimilate to this norm, individualizing the problem and the solution while not looking at the institutional, political, and social structures that maintain the status quo.

The Classical Liberal Meaning of Citizen

Citizen has three meanings according to T.H. Marshall. The first meaning of citizen is that of a member—it is belonging. The second meaning of citizenship is one that is comprised of those political, social, economic, and cultural rights exercised by members of a polity. Who has the ability to take part in the public discourse, who governs, who may exercise their political right to participate, and how may they participate? It is having these rights that our Founders made explicit for all, attempting to implement the concept of natural rights.

The third working definition of citizenship operates in the vernacular—those who both are considered and consider themselves to be members of the polity, who share the moral, cultural, and de facto norms of the hegemonic polity, and who benefit from belonging.

The two overarching models of citizenship for a democracy have been either that of republicanism or liberalism. The republican model emphasizes the civic responsibility of self-rule; civic republicanism acting in the best public interest, or what Rousseau called the general will. The liberal model is that of a legal identity, a status that does not require political agency, but focuses on individual, private rights. When we think of citizenship today, we may think of a combined model, or we may preference that of a stronger private individualistic mode when we take part in public decision making, voting.

Citizenship is more than just a legal status of belonging or not to a community or, in the wider sense, to belong to a sovereign nation as more than a subject upon which laws and norms are acted upon, without the subject's agency or control. To be a citizen is to be able to self-govern—to be what the modern political thinkers have called an individual. An individual who can self-govern has control over their body, thoughts, and labor. John Locke in the *Second Treatise on Government*, Chapter 5 "On Property" sets forth this concept of individual and the ability to own oneself, and thus self-govern:

> 27. Though men as a whole own the earth and all inferior creatures, every individual man has a property in his own person [= "owns himself"]; this is something that nobody else has any right to. The labour of his body

> and the work of his hands, we may say, are strictly his. So when he takes something from the state that nature has provided and left it in, he mixes his labour with it, thus joining to it something that is his own; and in that way he makes it his property. He has removed the item from the common state that nature has placed it in, and through this labour the item has had annexed to it something that excludes the common right of other men: for this labour is unquestionably the property of the labourer, so no other man can have a right to anything the labour is joined to—at least where there is enough, and as good, left in common for others.

This individual has agency over his own self—no laws can be made on their body, nor does anyone else have a right to their body or the products there of. This individual has personal and bodily autonomy. All others are not capable of self governing, self ownership or agency, nor do they have bodily autonomy. Laws may be written on their bodies.

This definition does not stray too far from the ideas of Aristotle—that a citizen is a male over the age of majority, who is a patriarch, self-sufficient, and a warrior, who is the son of another citizen, who can participate in public life, who governs, and is governed, who deliberates in public rulemaking and be ruled in turn. A citizen, according to Aristotle, is deeply and intrinsically involved in the polity from sitting on a jury to holding office. For Aristotle, all others are just inhabitants of the city-state. He does make the citizen an active participant, who must take his turn at ruling, but the citizen does not have to be a good ruler (*Politics*, Book III).

Jean-Jacques Rousseau moves the idea of citizen to one who is also a better participant in the sovereign state, one who can make decisions based on what he calls the general will, or the best interests of all citizens, not just himself. But like the philosophers before him, the citizen is male and excludes not only women but also children, foreigners, and slaves. Women are critical only for inheritance, which includes property and the title of citizen. Aristotle had a similar requirement, a citizen could only be born to a resident of the city-state who herself who had been acknowledged by her citizen father as his. Women were not full participants in the social contract, and their role was limited to the private sphere of the family. A woman was defined solely by her reproductive role; she was virtuous, passive, responsible for control of the nursery (maternal), and thus could then raise future citizens Familial paternity had to be guaranteed. She answered to her patriarch—first her father, then her husband; she was property. Rousseau considered the family the stable anchor of the polity. The male, then as citizen, could be understood to be independent, equal to fellow citizens, and able to participate in the public sphere and in public discourse and deliberation.

These various definitions of citizen—as an individual who has self-governance and agency, who can participate and make decisions in the larger project that is self-governance in a liberal democracy—are entrenched in our conception of good citizen.

Most male thinkers such as Hegel and others relegate women to the private sphere where their life is constricted to reproducing and to maintaining the family. Women are not part of civil society or the political contract. Simone de Beauvoir noted that women are made by society; they are not born. Carole Pateman and other feminists put forth that the social contract[4] is very much a sexual contract since the male philosophers did not acknowledge that women had the same capabilities as males, and as women, they have been treated as chattel, property, and have laws written on their bodies. Women do not enjoy the same status as men—either in the polity, in civil society, or in the workplace. We can further subdivide those who have been othered—by race, ethnicity, class, and other markers of oppression as not equal to the male citizen. Hannah Arendt, on the other hand, maintained that one's self-identity—i.e. racial, ethnic, or religious—was irrelevant to their identity as citizen; their active membership in the political community.

Somewhere in between all of these definitions of citizen lie a fuller definition of citizenship; one that encompasses all who are both political actors and politically acted upon. It is making this visible, and once made visible, we can start to reach for truly equal citizenry with all the rights and responsibilities thereof. That is the purpose of this book to understand the contested position of citizen.

Citizenship Theory and the United States

In the United States, we have birthright citizenship—by virtue of being native born, born on the nation's soil—*jus soli*, the Latin for right of soil—(which includes foreign military bases and territories of the United States such as Guam or Puerto Rico), born of a mother (and with DNA and blood tests this possibility is extended to the father) who is a American, or being legally recognized as having been naturalized. A recent Supreme Court Case, Sessions v. Morales held that a child born out of wedlock to one American Citizen parent and the other a foreign national requires that the American parent had been a resident in the United States for at least five years after they turned 14, and prior to the birth of the child. Some other nations confer citizenship by blood—*jus sanguinis*, the Latin for the right of blood—in some countries you need to have at least one grandparent (and in some cases only a grandfather) who was a citizen to be recognized as a citizen—Jordan, India, Ireland, for example. Lithuania requires that your relative, parent or grandparent, held Lithuanian citizenship prior to 15 June 1940, the date when the Soviet Union annexed the country. The United States has a similar provision that allows for a child under 18, who has a grandparent who is US citizen, to become naturalized as a citizen without a residency requirement, though the child has to be in the United States for the naturalization (Child Citizenship Act of 2000). We will revisit how citizens are reproduced in Chapter 8.

This type of citizenship—legal membership citizenship or nationality—is the legal recognition of belonging. It confers no other political, social, or economic rights. Yet over the course of our history, Americans have excluded some even from this basic form of recognition—certain immigrant groups such as the Chinese and the Irish, for instance. Native Americans and slaves have been excluded also. Such exclusions make evident that citizenship is a status. Our founders were proponents of the concept of the Enlightenment thinkers' natural rights, which we find first in John Locke's *Second Treatise on Government*—life, liberty, and property (he did include health, oh well)—that we find echoing in The Declaration of Independence, then fleshed out for all in the Bill of Rights. Today, we expect government to put into action Locke's ideas regarding not only citizenship, but also government. The role of government reinforces the rights of citizens; a citizen expects the government's power to preserve his property. Property in his own person and, as Cheryl Harris (1993) constructs, whiteness has become a property right in our laws and in his possessions. The citizen for Locke was male (hence, the male pronoun) also looks to political power to protect his right to speech and other liberties. Thus, when we look at our laws, what they do, and whom they protect or act on, we see the effect of Locke's construction of the individual and the importance of property.

One of the first citizenship theorists, T.H. Marshall, in the mid-twentieth century described and situated three types of citizenship into the development of liberal theory over the course of the three centuries. The first, legal membership also gives those citizens civil rights. Marshall called this "the civil element...composed of the rights necessary for individual freedom—the liberty of the person, freedom of speech, thought, and faith, the right to own property and to conclude valid contracts, and the right to justice" (Marshall, 1965, p. 78).

Marshall's second meaning of citizenship is one that has the "political elements in the exercise of political power, as a member of a body invested with political authority or as an elector of the members of such a body" (Ibid., p. 78). These are the rights to political agency, and the right to participate is comprised of those political, social, economic, and cultural rights exercised by members of a polity. Who has the ability to take part in the public discourse, who governs, who may exercise their political right to participate, and how may they participate? This exercise of political rights we see take root in the practices of the nineteenth century as the definition of who may be a citizen begins to be expanded.

His third working definition of citizenship operates in the vernacular—what he calls "a social element [including] the right to a modicum of economic welfare and security to the right to share to the full in the social heritage and to live the life of a civilized being according to the standards prevailing in the society" (Ibid., p. 78). These social rights follow the hegemonic norms of society. The hegemonic norms of both civil society and the polity are embedded in cultural and economic expectations and values.

It is Marshall's final definition of citizenship that has witnessed the modern political theorists' expansion of the concept of civil citizenship as individual and civil rights during the nineteenth century and in the early twentieth century to mean political citizen—participation in the democratic processes. The latter half of the twentieth century saw citizenship morph into that of social citizenship based on benefits and entitlements. Thus, as we move toward inclusion and equality, there is slippage down the slope of who deserves all the rights, responsibilities and benefits of citizenship. It is here that we find what Foucault called "biopower"—the cultural practices and interactions, legal, institutional and political (re)constructions that organize thought and practice around the concept of full and good citizen. It is at this juncture of citizenship that we locate the social cohesion of the political community, that gives citizens their source of identity, or what some might say is the focus of what all need to assimilate toward.

Who is a citizen is extremely contested and contextualized by cultural, political, historical, economic, situational, and place. Foucault's definition of biopower is apparent with the cultural practices and interactions, legal, institutional, and political (re)constructions that organize thought and practice around the concept of full and good citizen. Thus, there are markers that render people unfit citizens. In the United States, these markers include race, gender, class, age (maturity), property ownership, sexuality, patriotism, and the right to privacy (read as "control over one's mind, body and labor") among others. These markers fall into five basic categories that this book will uncover for the reader: patriotism, participation, productivity, property, and reproductivity.

A brief history of citizenship in the United States finds it a contested category as far back as our founding. In the United States, legal citizenship is a product of birth, or naturalization. But the underlying context of full citizenship can be found in the concept entering into the social contract by one's own choice. The ability to enter into a contract and to be bound by said contract is the basis of not only our polity but our economy. The key "by one's own choice" is the concept of agency, and it is this concept that gives rise to the concept of individual. Who may be an individual is key to understanding the concept of citizen? John Locke gave us the true meaning in his chapter "On Property" (Chapter 5, section 27):

> Though the earth, and all inferior creature, be common to all men, yet every man has a property in his own person: this no body has any right to but himself. The labor of his body, and the work of his hands, we may say, are properly his.

If we examine this closely, we will see that only man has agency to have property, to control his body, and labor. Having this agency, allows one to be an individual—all others have laws that get written on their bodies, and they do not have control over their bodies or labor. Only individuals get full citizenship. For example, can one have agency if one cannot control their own body because of laws made on one's body? Feminist theorists have noted that in the patriarchal world, women have been excluded from decision-making, while those decisions affect them significantly. We may think back to the room full of men gathered in Congress, for instance, writing the GOP health bill, limiting women's access to affordable reproductive health care. The universalist model, (Myers and Tronto, 1998, p. 808) while purporting to be what Iris Marion Young called "difference-blind," (1990) was not since it did not take into account differences of identity such as race and class as laws were formulated and implemented.

John Rawls tried to give us a way to make empirical decisions using a normative frame with his veil of ignorance. His concept was that if we had a vision of what we wanted society to be, and understood the institutions, constraints, and biases, we could make pluralistic policy-making fair for all. "Justice as fairness," as he stated, is understanding that "the natural distribution [of human traits and characteristics] is neither just or unjust; nor is it unjust that persons are born into society at some particular position. These are simply natural facts. What is just and unjust is the way that institutions deal with these facts."[5] Rawls' theory that we can start from a position of neutrality and make good policy that everyone would benefit from assumes that policy-making is not going to be incremental and full of compromises; it is hypothetical at best as it tries to attain equality.

What we can take away from liberal theory and social contract theory from Locke to Rawls and beyond is that, in Western democracy, the hegemonic theory is that liberalism entails liberty as the "perfect freedom for one's actions."[6] The underlying concept is that all are considered full individuals; thus, full citizens, when in truth, they are not.

These critiques gave rise to a multicultural or heterogeneous theory of citizenship where citizens from wherever they are situated can deliberate as part of a public to achieve a reasonable solution to public problems (Young, 1990, p. 267). Will Kymlicka and Wayne Norman (2000) developed these ideas more fully to address temporary special representational rights—affirmative action, for example—for disadvantaged groups such as the non-abled bodied or persons of color who have been historically marginalized. They further looked at multicultural rights which would cover immigrants and religious groups to allow these all these people access into the political community that maintain their cultural uniqueness through legal exemption from practices (laws) which would allow within reason the maintenance of cultural or religious practices, allowing the wearing of the Sikh turban or kosher or halal butchering practices, for example. Since 11 September 2001, there has been a backlash against multicultural practices. We have seen this most recently with the Trump executive orders banning visitors or immigrants from certain Muslim majority countries;

in France, there have been bans on the wearing of religious clothing such as hijabs and burkas in public institutions (*see* Joan Wallach Scott). Theorists have also taken multiculturalism to task claiming that focusing on policies that maintain cultural heritage distract from the greater public project of achieving full-throated justice (Carens, 2002).

What all of the citizenship theories have in common is that they are rights-based, and the rights emanate from the nation-state, even though they might be deemed "natural" human rights (see Universal Declaration of Human Rights). Globalization and the more recent diasporas that have been caused by civil unrest, political discrimination (asylum seekers), environmental crises (water shortages, earthquakes, etc.), wars, or the quest for a better economic situation are challenging these ideas. Seyla Benhabib (2011) and Thomas Pogge (2002), among others, have shown that this type of rights model one in which rights are government (state) granted do not work for any of the refugee groups. Benhabib and Pogge encourage open borders and portable rights. But this cosmopolitanism, while a very vital and current debate is not the issue of this book. Or, put another way, we need to start local before we think global. But the local does need to be grounded in human rights not just legal or civil rights.

What this book does is look at what is the virtuous good citizen, and what happens if a citizen is, or a group of citizens are, not seen as virtuous good or does not attain this status. Do we see them as citizens, or do we make it their fault that they are not full citizens, so we limit their access to privileges and opportunities. This book does not look at the failed citizen who has lost their agency, their rights, even temporarily, or the aspirational citizen, such as immigrants who are on the path to citizenship and children who will grow up to become citizens.

This book identified five markers of citizenship, and if one is marked as not achieving one of these markers, one is then not a good citizen. Thus that citizen becomes restricted, they do not enjoy or have access to the full range of rights, responsibilities, and privileges of other citizens. The virtuous citizen is one who is a patriot and a property owner, who has political agency, who is a productive citizen, and who can freely reproduce citizens. Most of us do not even notice these markers and restrictions; they have become part of the structure that maintains our American hegemonic norms. The laws and social practices that make up these structures are invisible to the naked eye unless we are affected or we are taught to see. This book will make this more explicit, but first we must look at the values and myths that hold us together as a nation.

In the early twentieth century citizen took on the meaning of political citizen, one who could participate in public decision making. We see this in the three times enfranchisement was extended to others after the Constitution had been ratified—with black men, then women, then the 18–21-year-olds. Native Americans were granted citizenship in 1924, but some states barred them from voting until 1957.

The latter half of the twentieth century saw citizenship morph into that of social citizenship based on benefits and entitlements. As we move toward inclusion and equality, there is slippage down the slope of who deserves all the rights, responsibilities and benefits of citizenship. The same public definition of, concept of, and rights of (full) citizens and aliens in the United States in the first decade of the twenty-first century mirror those of the last decade of the eighteenth century with the US Patriot Act and the Military Commissions Act. The current public discourse on same-sex marriage, the Supreme Court ruling on eminent domain, political speech of minors versus that of corporations, and with the racism, poverty, and ageism that Hurricane Katrina uncovered in the Gulf Coast seem to indicate that citizenship is contracting in America. But in reality, the concept of the American Citizen has been expanding—*de jure* via Constitutional amendments and contracting via public policy laws, such as The Personal Responsibility Act of 1996, and *de facto* via social practices over the course of our history.

American hegemonic citizenship is articulated by the dominant social, political, and economic paradigm of what a good citizen is supposed to be and reinforced by the aspirational American Dream. It is the combined power of both which underpin public policies and norms such as not providing adequate social welfare programs, because one is supposed to be that rugged individual who can pull themselves up by the bootstraps.

The power of hegemony is that it is unspoken, it is considered the norm, it is the goal to which we must fully assimilate. We only identify the person who is othered—the non-white, the female, the homeless, the poor, the homosexual, the non-Christian. It is this articulation of this othering that allows us to distinguish between citizens in a normative fashion that limits and entrenches citizenship.

Citizenship has its boundaries which are defined by both exclusion and inclusion. We define citizen in the vernacular—as the productive, the reproductive, the patriotic, the propertied, and the participatory citizens. Thus, certain people, homosexuals, for instance, are essentialized by society by their sexual orientation, even if they are not sexually active. They have been and, in some cases, continue to be managed by public policy that mark and entrench them in a second-class citizenship from which they cannot easily recover. The marked transgender person cannot, at this point, serve openly in the American military and, thus, cannot be seen as patriotic, while a foreign national may serve, and may become an American citizen because of such service. Sexual minorities may be discriminated against in employment, thus may not be as productive a citizen. In some states, they are prohibited from adopting children. Same-sex partners, even those who are married, may not sponsor their foreign-born partner for citizenship. Without the legal right to adopt children or sponsor their partners, same-sex people are not seen as reproductive citizens.

Liberal Theory

Contemporary liberal theory continues to be tweaked as principles and concepts are critiqued and practiced. Liberal theory, in its original and current form, stresses equality—it strives to break down the subordination of one group, made into the other, to the ideal. The focus of liberal democratic theory is on individual rights as if we all are homogeneous and have full self-determination. While we might all agree that we may not be homogeneous, as there is no universal identity that we all fit into, and identity, as per Judith Butler, may just be performative depending on context and place. The concept of self-determination, or freedom of choice, is a hypothetical choice—do we always choose or are some choices by default—such as what birth place, citizenship, culture, and religion? Zizek (2007) points out that

> liberalism…shows intolerance when individuals of other cultures are not given freedom of choice (clitoridectomy, child brideship, infanticide, polygamy, family rape…); however, it ignores the tremendous pressure which, for example, compels women in our liberal society to undergo plastic surgery, cosmetic implants, Botox injections, etc., in order to remain competitive on the sex market. (p. 3)

Reliance on these two concepts that gird the principle of individualism detract us from cultural, gender, and ethnic identities that mark people; such marking is, for the most part, immutable, which does not allow for full assimilation or conformity to the dominant culture and practices. It also distracts us from the role that government(s) and society play in maintaining the hegemony.

Liberal theory is about political equality in the public sphere, which has been translated into the concept of tolerance of others. In a multicultural nation, tolerance has become problematic; it can mean that one avoids the other—the live and let live mantra, or that the privileged ones have the power over the othered to tolerate them. We can see the potential illiberal results of toleration in liberal states such as The Netherlands where the Muslim immigrants are not integrated into the liberal society but have been allowed to develop their own pillar of society, parallel to but insulated from the full rights and responsibilities of liberal citizenship.

However, integration strategies are not always successful; witness for example Black Americans (and women) and the practice of affirmative action. While the liberal state is obligated to ensure equality, the means and practices come up against cultural and political practices. For example, is affirmative action desirable and does it realistically address the problem of racial inequality?

The question becomes what can a liberal state demand of its citizens in their relations with other citizens? Liberal theory has fallen back on the public/private split—that is how one is treated in the public sphere must be without discrimination. Liberal theory thus fails in achieving its primary goals if all citizens are not equal, and if some people can be subjugated and treated as second-class citizens.

Feminism uncovered the fallacy of the public/private distinction—the other were not granted the full realm of self-determination necessary to be considered full citizens; public policies and practices subjugate and subordinate the other. Citizenship has had a privileged and male bias. The not gender-neutral laws and policies diminish self-determination, individual, and bodily autonomy. Laws control the bodies and actions of the others—the otherly gendered, the otherly raced, religion or ethnicity, or the otherly classed—where they would dare not control those of the privileged. Women's reproductive choices are subjected to public policies, persons of color or different religions are suspect, people living in poverty are required to leave their children and to work, persons living in public housing have their Fourth Amendment rights to illegal searches and seizures waived, and so on. We tend to vilify those on welfare, the poor (if they only worked harder…) yet at the same time, we benefit from middle-class welfare—the mortgage interest deductions, corporate welfare, and so on.

Hegel and Marx claimed that those in power protect the haves from the have-nots, and these protections are reinforced by the cultural practices that Foucault called biopower. For instance, since we measure the worth of a citizen by their earning power, this allows employed and well-compensated citizens to claim that those who are poor are poor because they are just not working hard enough, pointing to the exceptions who have escaped poverty. Full citizens do not see the effect of public policies keeping the poor, poor—minimum wage, lack of health care, lack of affordable childcare, inadequate housing.

A lot of the writing on liberal theory and diverse groups looks at those group identities, which are seemingly voluntary—religious groups as with Jeff Spinner's 1995 examination of Amish and Hasidic identity in America. These religious groups separate themselves from the rest of American polity, having negotiated their position—what Spinner (1995) calls their public recognition as a group with the state (vis-a-vis education and military service, for instance). But Spinner is quick to note that such public recognition as a distinct group is not viable for most Jews, for instance, and we can extrapolate this to now include most Muslims as well when looking at how people are treated in society. Most Jewish people and Muslims practice their religions in private and go about their public business. It is only when orthodox Jews or Muslims, or for that matter Jehovah Witnesses, are put in situations in which their religious practices contradict the dominant practices that we see them as members of a group. The military does not draft, recruit, or allow religious practices to challenge the set norms.

Communitarian theory built upon the republican idea of civic participation, and the ideal citizen must be actively engaged in the polity. This perspective critiques the liberal individualism that allows the alienation of the citizen from their government and from their fellow citizens. It is the citizens' identification with their political community that provides their identity (see Oldfield in Shafir). Oldfield argues that modern communities need to allow for alternative definitions of "the good life," reflecting both individualism and diversity, which leads us back to the liberal Rawls' premise of justice as fairness.

The tension between liberal theory, culture, and identity has been identified in feminist and legal theory. Susan Moller Okin (1999) noted that most ideologies and cultures are patriarchies, and by extension, most states are so too. She finds that most cultural requirements disadvantage women, while men benefit, and the more powerful men even more so. While this raised a lot of debate and gave rise to a form of misrepresentation that allowed for the continued oppression of women in the name of respecting multiculturalism, it did not allow for women (and others) to have agency to choose and to change. It also gave rise to use the oppression of women (and others) as a means to perpetuate cultural stereotypes but to a justification to literally attack those cultures (see for example, the many US State Department reports on the Taliban and women issued after 9/11). Anne Phillips (2007) puts forth a view of culture that allows for gender equality to be achieved within and among different cultures, because she presents a picture of culture that is neither a static nor a monolithic one. Uma Narayan (1997) investigates how cultures change to keep up with the demands of modernity.

Liberal theory needs to be flexible, just as cultures change to keep up with the demands of modern life. Young (1990) and Myers and Tronto (1998), along with Marxist theorists, have noted that the so-called universality of citizens is a "specifically male experience," and we may even go further and race, class, and heterosexualize this experience. Zizek (2007) points to

> The sexualized division of labor [which] still predominates which confers a male twist on basic liberal categories (autonomy, public activity, competition), and relegates women to the private sphere of family solidarity, etc., liberalism itself, in its opposition of private and public, harbors male dominance. Furthermore, it is only the modern Western capitalist culture for which autonomy, individual freedom, etc., stand higher than collective solidarity, connection, responsibility for dependent others, the duty to respect the customs of one's community—again, liberalism itself privileges a certain culture, the modern Western one.

Acknowledging such allows us to develop liberal theory and practice more fully and accept all citizens as potential equals.

Liberal theory has the potential to create the means for all to gain equality—to participate in the political arena arguing for their rights against the discriminatory legal and cultural practices. It is in these spaces that change can happen.

Liberal theory is built on the assumption that the concept of citizen is universal, submerging the racial and the gendered aspects. Historically, the dominant paradigmatic discourse of citizenship is white male, despite the claim of universality gender neutral citizen (see Myers and Tronto, 1998).

Elizabeth Anderson (2019) views equality as the basis of freedom, and it is this freedom that allows the civil society to work: its members able to function (food, shelter, health—think Maslow's basic hierarchy of needs), to be productive members (education fair-value wages opportunity), to act as citizens (participate), and to move and be in civil society.

This book articulates how, as Hegel puts it, the haves are protected by the have-nots or the full citizens with all the rights and privileges versus the others, though still citizens, but who do not have all those rights and privileges. But these differences are not noticed because the laws, policies and norms are not questioned, they are invisible to the naked eye unless one is looking for them. We tolerate these different states of rights and privileges because those, who do not have them, do not have them because they have not hit all the right markers of citizenship and this has been normalized.

Much of the discrimination is ingrained and hegemonic. Zizek calls this the "obscene underground of habits," which he pessimistically says "is really difficult to change" (2007, p. 25). We (the generic we) see differentness from the norm and other the other. Wendy Brown (2006) explores this concept in her book *Regulating Aversion: Tolerance in the Age of Identity and Empire*. It is the Western assumptions about liberalism that Zizek critiques. There is another concern because even correcting for her assumptions, she would still arrive at her same conclusion: that liberalism promotes the toleration of difference, and it is this difference that is essentialized and, thus, depoliticized. It is very politicized.

Her work is grounded in both Herbert Marcuse and Michel Foucault. Marcuse's essay "Repressive Tolerance" (1964) claims that tolerance is, or the conditions of tolerance are, "loaded." He differentiates between "constitutional equality" (legal or procedural equality) and the inequalities that are a consequence of the institutions of privilege, discrimination, and inherited wealth. These inequalities remain in place unseen by the legal system and unchanged by society.

From Michel Foucault's (1978) *The History of Sexuality*, Wendy Brown draws on the concept of biopower, those societal mores that control as much as law. She critiques the concept of tolerance by stating that differences are produced by tolerance that produces a status quo politics based on the assumption that difference cannot be negotiated—since it is naturalized—but only managed. Difference becomes a cultural divide—that is just how they are because of their fill-in-the-blank difference from the norm. If it is their nature, it reduces political motivations to essentialized culture.[7] Essentialization legitimizes intolerance.

This is reminiscent of the turn of the twentieth-century debate between nativist and assimilation lists over immigration—nativists stating that immigrants would taint Anglo-Saxon stock, and assimilation lists stating that everyone can become American. Horace Kallen (1924) stated that ethnic identity cannot be ignored or assimilated—their ties are to their ancestors—to be Americanized then was to be free of the stigma foreigner, America must allow difference, cultural pluralism.

While Marcuse argued that there was good (left) and bad (right) objects of tolerance, Brown's argument is that difference is both essentialized and privatized and thus depoliticized. She comes at this from the perspective of biopower or civil society.

In her argument, one hears echoes of Hegel's concept of full worth of rights; whose rights are more respected based on valuation and membership in a corporation, of work as a measure of a person (Hegel). This idea of valuing a person based on their productivity is well-accepted in a capitalist society.

Difference *is* being essentialized, and this essentialism is further essentialized and managed via public policy that mark and entrench certain peoples in a second-class citizenship from which they cannot easily recover. The state is not a neutral entity but works to maintain the status of the majority, who are the citizens who empower the State and thus define public good. Thus, civil society is not separate from civil society as Hegel proposed. In fact, he even wrote that the corporations adhere to the policies set by the state, because the policies of the state are the work of the corporations—as represented by the legislature (p. 189). "The corporation mind ... is ... inwardly converted into the mind of the state... [manifesting in the] ... secret of patriotism" (p. 189).

If the state has constructed a rubric of second-class citizens, the state is not, nor does it have to be, that Lockean neutral umpire securing and protecting the rights of all—because all people are not citizens and citizens are not equal. Once a government legitimizes intolerance, abridging rights of certain people's, liberal democracy ceases as the government becomes authoritarian.

How It Happens Here...

The state's (read: the government, both politicians and the public administrators who implement the laws and policies) purpose is to not only maintain and sustain the nation, but to grow it—to make it productive, wealthy, and powerful. There is a tension between the state and democracy, or to put it simply, a tension between the state and its citizens—the state needs to control its citizens so that it can achieve its goals, and in a liberal democracy, the citizens are not only theoretically the government, but the government exists so that the citizens can reach their full potential. This tension manifests itself in the access to political participation in the public sphere, and how those in power control this access and, thus, the ensuing rights of those without power.

We witness then not only the public policies that limit access to the public sphere, but also the social constraints that encourage passivity and define the good citizen as one who obeys the laws and does not question, nor do they have time or resources to question the state.

We can see the power of cultural norms when we look at political participation or voting as a chief marker of citizenship. Americans want to be seen as model citizens. We all claim to vote, yet of the 100% of the population who can register to vote, less than 80% are registered, and of those 80%, we are ecstatic when over 50% show up at the polls—so in reality less than 36.5% of Americans vote. This claiming to vote, yet in reality not voting, is problematic for pollsters, who want to get accurate results; pollsters ask about voting behavior in many ways in order to ascertain who will vote for whom.

Yet at the same time, we make voting a right that is an exercise—registering in most states 30 days prior to an election and then getting oneself to the polls—which may be open for some elections only from noon until 7 p.m., cutting out a huge segment of the working and commuting population. Or, making it difficult for college students to vote where they spend ten months a year and many dollars. Or, if one moves or is deployed during elections, one can be removed from the voting registers. If one has the name of a felon, one may find their name removed (Berman, 2015). And, if one is educated to be a good test taker, and not a problem solver or critical thinker, one learns not to question, and thus, one might not have the skills to participate in public discourse.

We are aware of the particular ideal citizen and can name the qualities of such if we look at the dominant political, economic, and social paradigms (DSPE) of our culture. The DSPE helps define who has power; those that closely fit this paradigm are more powerful than those who do not. In the United States, the dominant social paradigm is the heterosexual, white male property owner. It is this DSPE that leads us to think that white males are the majority, even though if we look at the actual census numbers we find males to be in the minority: there are more females in America than males (roughly 147,103,000–141,275,000), and there are will be more people of color than white people within the next ten years. As of 2016, there were slightly more babies of color being borne, 50.2%, than non-Hispanic, white babies according to the Census Bureau.

A citizen is a status category that grants the person political rights and representation, agency, empowerment, and autonomy. For all the liberal civic ideals and virtues, our political values of equality and fairness, being a citizen is imbued with status, rights, and responsibilities that are made explicit by law and practice. These laws and practices also entrench second-class citizens. This book will look at the laws, policies, and practices that keep some people privileged and others entrenched in a second-class citizenship, and what that means for a liberal democracy.

A VERY Brief History of Citizenship in the United States

What is now considered the United States of America has been a nation of immigrants since the first indigenous people walked across the Beringia, what is now the Bering Strait, roughly 12,000 years ago. Some of these first immigrants continued on to what is now Central and South America, those who remained on the coast and plains of what is now the United States survived, and even thrived, until the next wave of immigrants arrived (see Zinn, 2015). The European settlers from the first in what is now Virginia to the those who settled in Massachusetts after a brief period of cooperation with the native peoples took the Natives' land. Governor John Winthrop declared that "the area [was] legally a 'vacuum.' The Native Americans, had not 'subdued' the land, and therefore had only a 'natural' right to it, but not a 'civil right.' A 'natural right' did not have legal standing." Coupled with a religious justification from the Bible, Romans 13:2: "Whosoever therefore resisteth the power, resisteth the ordinance of God: and they that resist shall receive to themselves damnation."—the settlers took forceful possession of the land (Zinn). Thus, began years of pushing the Native Americans westward (inland) and killing them off via disease, warfare, or starvation.

Besides the first European settlers in search of fortune or religious liberty, the other group that came to the Colonies were criminals. Under the British Transportation Act of 1717 and through the American Revolution, criminals were shipped to the colonies to be indentured servants.

The first ratified American national government in 1781 was under the Articles of Confederation, which existed for a decade. Not only did the Articles name the United States of America, it set up a confederacy that allowed the states (the former colonies) to retain most of their powers (Article 2) and, at the same time, respect the citizens of the other states (Article 4); what we know now as the "Full Faith and Credit Clause." The Articles of Confederation was ineffectual for numerous reasons, from the specificity of needing the original nine states to agree to cooperate on all new states or declaring war (and then all the states to do so), to the lack of enforcement of its laws, and to actually raise the funds necessary to pay off the debts of the colonies (Article 12). Each state had their own requirements for citizenship—from either a property or tax payment, to residencies (either within the state or nation—or, in some cases, none, such as Connecticut, New Hampshire, and Rhode Island); to male or freeman (except for Connecticut, Delaware, New Jersey, and Rhode Island), only three of the original states had race as a requirement: Georgia, South Carolina, and Virginia all citizens to be white (Keyssar, 2009, pp. 306–307). People were citizens of their states, first. Notice the parallel between the citizens of the Greek city-states and the United States of America.

The failing of the Articles of Confederation was discussed in Annapolis in September of 1786, which gave way to the Constitutional Convention in Philadelphia in 1787. Secret discussions ensued about representation—from the Virginia plan (big state) to the New Jersey plan (small state), to the ultimate compromise that gave us the House of Representatives (representation based on population) and Senate (equal representation of each state, which retained the concept of state sovereignty). The concept of citizenship and suffrage was wrought—while most delegates upheld the concepts of liberty and equality, they were still within the mold of their state's concepts of suffrage, i.e. male property owners. The delegates could not come to an agreement on citizenship, so left that to the states to decide. Citizenship was not raised again until the Fourteenth Amendment, which declared a birthright for citizenship. But perhaps the most negative mark on the Constitution was the Three-Fifths Compromise—the counting of slaves as three-fifths a person for purposes of representation and taxation. That, along with a fugitive slave clause, "Person held to Service or Labour in one State ... [and] escaping into another, ... shall be delivered up on Claim of the Party to whom such Service or Labour may be due," enshrined slavery without mentioning the term.

The Constitution of the United States did not address citizenship. The Constitution also enshrined the concept of democracy in the opening words of the Preamble, "We the people," which was adopted on 21 June 1788. The first ten amendments, known as the Bill of Rights, was ratified and adopted on 15 December 1791. The importance of the Bill of Rights is that they were meant for all people, not just citizens, on US territory.

The first two laws that were adopted by the new country concerning citizenship were the Naturalization Acts of 1790 and 1795. These laws limited naturalization to free white men (and their children), if they were of good moral character, non-criminals, and non-drunkards who had resided in the country for two years in the 1790 version and revised to five years residency in 1795. Indigenous people, women, free black men, slaves, and indentured servants were excluded (more on immigration as a way to increase citizens in Chapter 8, "Reproducing Citizens").

Citizenship is extended to children through birth—being born on United States soil (the concept of *jus soli* means literally the "right of the soil"), or *jus sanguinis* the "right of blood" born to parents who are United States citizens. This is except for slaves, as per the Dred Scott v. Sandford, 60 U.S. 393 (1857) decision in which Chief Justice Roger Taney wrote in the majority opinion that Americans of African descent, free or enslaved, were not American Citizens and thus did not have the right (standing) to sue in federal court. Dred Scott was a slave in Missouri, but since he had resided for ten years in a free state (Illinois) and in the Louisiana Territory where slavery was prohibited as per the Missouri Compromise, he sued upon return to Missouri that decade in a state and territory made him a free man. This ruling stood until the Thirteenth

Amendment, ratified in 1865, abolished slavery, and the Fourteenth amendment to the Constitution, adopted in 1868, was the first mention of citizenship. Section 1 of the amendment reads as follows:

> All persons born or naturalized in the United States, and subject to the jurisdiction thereof, are citizens of the United States and of the state wherein they reside. No state shall make or enforce any law which shall abridge the privileges or immunities of citizens of the United States; nor shall any state deprive any person of life, liberty, or property, without due process of law; nor deny to any person within its jurisdiction the equal protection of the laws.

Thus, birthright citizenship, and naturalization were seen as paths to citizenship, and such citizenship gave citizens equal protection of the laws (the equal protection clause) and prohibited states from abridging the rights and privileges of citizens.

Importance of the Public Square

As much as people idealize the notion of the public square, especially how Habermas (1991) had articulated the public sphere where private persons gather to discuss matters of public concern and common interest, access to public sphere is controlled by the state. As Habermas stated in 1984, modernization, led by the forces of economic and administrative rationalization based on the duel logic of efficiency and control, capitalism, and mass consumption, have limited the access to the public sphere.

Democracy is messy. This messiness is an anathema to the state since the purpose of governmental states is to efficiently control its sovereign public. It is this public that this book addresses—the multiethnic, intersectional[8] body of people that comprise the social, civil, and political communities. If one believes in the idealized concepts of equality and participation in liberal democracies, how one can achieve such ideals when the state controls, via public policy, access to full citizenship?

One of the most hotly contested debates in contemporary democracy revolves around issues of political presence, and whether the fair representation of disadvantaged groups requires their presence in elected assemblies to have their needs addressed or can others address their needs, in other words, is there a politics of ideas rather than identities? The idea of political presence might be reducing people to one essentialized identity disregarding the intersectional of other (cultural) identities. For instance, not all women are feminists, nor all feminists women. Anne Phillips (1998) addresses this debate by stating that there needs to be a balance of representation, accountability, and autonomy.

Yet in a representative democracy, the United States is a republic, not a parliamentary government with a winner takes all majority rule. The question becomes are those members of minorities truly represented? Or, are their bodies just counted for purposes of the Census and the divvying up of political seats, and their issues and needs discounted, so that the majority's interest may be maintained?

Democratic public life only thrives where institutions enable citizens to debate matters of public importance. Habermas (1991) describes an ideal speech situation, where actors are equally endowed with the capacities of discourse, recognize each other's basic social equality, and in which their speech is completely undistorted by ideology or misrecognition.

Habermas is and has been optimistic about the possibility of the revival of the public sphere. He sees hope for the future in the new era of political community that transcends the national state based on ethnic and cultural likeness for one based on the equal rights and obligations of legally vested citizens.

This discursive theory of democracy requires that the political community can collectively define its political will. This political system requires an activist public sphere, where matters of common interest and political issues can be discussed, and the force of public opinion can influence the decision-making process. That mass media is homogenizing since the ownership of the media is in the hands of the few, and thus, information is controlled (we know all about the latest Kardashian gossip, but little information about actual laws and policies), the Internet is seen as a democratic mechanism, reinvigorating public political debate. In fact, Habermas remains optimistic about the revival of the public sphere with a political community that transcends the nation-state. This new political community is based on equal rights and obligations of (global) citizens. Eleanor Roosevelt foresaw this as she was helping to author the Universal Declaration of Human Rights almost 65 years ago (1948).

The idea of public square—the public sphere—has been idealized even as access to it is controlled and limited by the state. [Participatory] democracy is messy. This messiness is an anathema to the state; the purpose of governmental states is to efficiently control its sovereign public. Yet, as Bhiku Parekh (2002) puts it: the role of the modern state is to reconcile the demands of (national) unity and diversity.

The modern state controls, via public policy, assimilation to and access to full citizenship. But in doing so, the state has created a caste system for citizens—the current education policy in the United States is such an example. It is with this access to the public sphere, to the public square that we see citizens and non-citizens responding to their own and to their multicultural needs. It is here where we see people become politically active. It is at this point when people join together and form social political movements to transform (or maintain) the polity.

The rise of the Internet has been both a hindrance and a boon to actual political activity. People read, gather information, and respond online and in blogs from the isolation of their rooms, or their favorite coffee shop. There are virtual communities and virtual actions. Though MoveOn and other groups have been able to motivate people out from the glow of the computer screen and into the streets. Politicians do not see much effort exerted by mass e-mailings and thus, give them short thrift. A modern-day version of the philosophical tree falling in the woods is how effective are protests when they are not reported out on? Or how effective are actions that do not require any sacrifice?

The point, though, is that people have to take responsibility for their society, and they cannot passively sit by and expect that the government will do no harm. With the "do no harm" dictum, harm can be read as maintaining the status quo, the hegemonic norm, as well as usurping power so that the liberal democracy ceases to exist.

Our founders noted that government was a necessary evil because men are not angels as per Madison in *The Federalist Paper* # 51, but that government needed to have checks and balances as Montesquieu had articulated in *The Spirit of the Laws*. Nietzsche's (1997) warning in *The Twilight of the Idols* that "liberal institutions immediately cease to be liberal as soon as they are attained: subsequently there is nothing more harmful to freedom than liberal institutions" (Chapter 10, # 38) needs to be heeded.

Politicians should lead promoting what is best for all their constituents and the country. But, in reality, partisanship coupled with the power of money in politics also means that politicians are beholden to their major contributors and to their political party. And, since most people do not pay attention to the actually day to day functioning of legislatures and agencies, the public is blind to what really gets enacted. If they are paying attention politicians easily pass these policies are using fear to persuade. Nietzsche continues by saying it is war that produces a permit for governments and for the governed and illiberal instincts to exist. We see this most vividly when we look at Germany's adoption of Nazism from Hitler's Enabling Act of 1933 forward. In contemporary US politics, we see it with the "war on terrorism" allowing the state to severely curtail the Constitutional rights of citizens and noncitizens alike. Stanley Milgram's (1962) experiments on obedience to authority show how easy it is for people to abdicate their responsibility to another in authority (or who appears to be in authority). Nietzsche had previously noted that, while people have will to power, they abdicate the responsibility for that power quickly. The key is to rekindle the idea of community, of being responsible for the state of the state. If citizens are not paying attention, because it does not affect them, then how easy is it then to normalize the entrenchment of others?

The next chapter examines the American Dream and the development of Democratic Calvinism in America. Before we can examine the markers of citizenship, and how public policy and societal norms control what keeps some people entrenched we need to question our myths. Unlike Nietzsche and Zizek, we should not be pessimistic about the role of either the citizens or the government in transforming the state into a true liberal democracy. In fact, change happens when people are working both inside the institutions of government and outside in society for the same goals.

Notes

1 The Jewish People were seen as not having an allegiance to a nation, as the nation-states were evolving in the seventeenth and eighteenth centuries, This was due in part to anti-Semitism, and to the Jewish people's religious nature coupled with anti-Semitic laws which isolated them. The French embraced Jews as citizens in 1791, since the practice of religion should not impinge on political rights of citizens.
2 The Nuremberg laws legalized and institutionalized the Nazis' race theories which removed Jewish (and other people not considered Aryans) citizens' civil and political rights, and ultimately dehumanized them.
3 See Benhabib (2011).
4 Social contract theory is that concept in liberal theory that we live in our polity understanding that we give up some rights/freedoms in order to co-exist peacefully, and have our rights and freedoms protected by the government. Some social contracts are explicit, the United States Constitution; some are implicit—the norms of society.
5 Rawls (1999, p. 87).
6 Locke (1952, p. 287).
7 This is reminiscent of the turn of the twentieth-century debate between nativist and assimilation lists over immigration—nativists stating that immigrants would taint Anglo-Saxon stock, and assimilation lists stating that everyone can become American. Horace Kallen stated that ethnic identity cannot be ignored or assimilated—their ties are to their ancestors—to be Americanized then was to be free of the stigma *foreigner*, America must allow difference, cultural pluralism.
8 Intersectionality is the critique of interrelated and interlocked oppressions (and privileges) and the institutions that maintain the oppression (or privilege), which may not be easily singled out. Sexism, racism, and classism are considered the dominant oppressive categories, and there are many others, including but not limited to ableism, ageism, religious, and transphobia.

References

Almond, Gabriel A. and Sidney Verba Parekh (1989) *The Civic Culture: Political Attitudes and Democracy in Five Nations.* Newberry Park, CA: Sage.
Anderson, Elizabeth (2019) *Private Government.* Princeton, NJ: Princeton University Press.
Arendt, Hannah (1958) *Human Condition.* Chicago, IL: Chicago University Press.
Aristotle and T. Sinclair (1981) *The Politics.* London, UK: Penguin Classics.
Benhabib, Seyla (2004) *The Rights of Others.* New York: Cambridge University Press.
Benhabib, Seyla (2011) *Dignity in Adversity.* Cambridge, UK: Polity Books.
Berman, Ari (2015) *Give Us the Ballot: The Modern Struggle for Voting Rights in America.* New York: Farrar, Straus and Giroux.
Brown, Wendy (2006) *Regulating Aversion: Tolerance in Age of Identity and Empire.* Princeton, NJ: Princeton University Press.

Carens, Joseph (2002) "Book Review." *International Migration Review* 36 (2): 597.
Cohen, Elizabeth (2009) *Semi-Citizenship in Democratic Politics.* New York: Cambridge University Press.
Dred Scott v. Sandford, 60 U.S. 393 (1857).
Foucault, Michel (1978) *The History of Sexuality: An Introduction.* New York: Vintage Books.
Habemas, Jurgen (1991) *The Structural Transformation of the Public Sphere: An Inquiry into a Category of Bourgeois Society.* Cambridge, MA: MIT Press.
Harris, Cheryl (1993) "Whiteness as Property." *Harvard Law Review* 106 (8): 1707–1791.
Heater, Derek (2005) *What Is Citizenship?* Cambridge, UK: Polity Press.
Hegel, G.W. and S. Houlgate (2008) *Outlines of the Philosophy of Right.* New York: Oxford University Press.
Isin, Engin (ed.). (2013) *Recasting the Social in Citizenship.* Toronto, Canada: University of Toronto Press.
Kallen, Horace (1924) *Culture and Democracy in the United States.* New York: Boni & Liveright.
Keyssar, Alexander (2009) *The Right to Vote.* New York: Basic Books.
Kymlicka, Will and Wayne Norman (2000) *Citizenship in Diverse Societies.* New York: Oxford University Press.
Locke, John (1952) *The Second Treatise of Government.* Thomas Peardon (ed.). New York: Liberal Arts Press, Bobbs-Merrill Inc.
Marcuse, Herbert (1964) *One Dimensional Man.* Boston, MA: Beacon Press.
Marshall, T.H. (1965) *Class, Citizenship and Social Development.* New York: Harper & Row.
Mayer, Milton (1955) *They Thought They Were Free: The Germans, 1933–45.* Chicago, IL: University of Chicago Press.
Mayer, Milton and Richard Evans (2017) *They Thought They Were Free: The Germans, 1933–45.* Chicago, IL: University of Chicago Press.
Milgram, Stanley (1962) *Obedience.* New Haven, CT: Yale University.
Montesquieu, Charles and Anne M. Coelher (1989) *The Spirit of the Laws.* Cambridge, UK: Cambridge University Press.
Myers, JoAnne and Joan Tronto (1998). "Truth and Advocacy: A Feminist Perspective." *PS: Political Science and Politics* 31 (4): 808–810.
Narayan, Uma (1997) *Dislocating Cultures.* New York: Routledge.
Nietzsche, Friedrich (1989) *Beyond Good and Evil.* New York: Vintage Books.
Nietzsche, Friedrich (1997) *Twilight of the Idols.* Richard Polt (trans). Indianapolis, IN: Hackett Pub.
Nussbaum, Martha (2010) *From Disgust to Humanity: Sexual Orientation and Constitutional Law.* New York: Oxford University Press.
Okin, Susan M. (1991) *The Justice, Gender and the Family.* New York: Basic Books.
Okin, Susan M. (1999) *Is Multiculturalism Bad for Women?* Joshua Cohen, Matthew Howard and Martha C. Nussbaum (eds). Princeton, NJ: Princeton University Press.
Parekh, Bhikhu (2002) *Rethinking Multiculturalism: Cultural Diversity and Political Theory.* Cambridge, MA: Harvard University Press.
Pateman, Carole (1988) *The Social Contract.* Palo Alto, CA: Stanford University Press.
Pateman, Carole (1989) *The Disorder of Women.* Palo Alto, CA: Stanford University Press.
Pateman, Carole and Charles Mills (2007) *Contract and Domination.* Cambridge, UK: Polity Press.
Phillips, Anne (1991) *Engendering Democracy.* University Park, PA: University of Pennsylvania Press.

Phillips, Anne (1998) *The Politics of Presence*. Oxford, UK: Clarendon Press.
Phillips, Anne (2007) *Multiculturalism without Culture*. Princeton, NJ: Princeton University Press.
Pogge, Thomas (2002) *World Poverty and Human Rights: Cosmopolitan Responsibilities and Reforms*. Malden, MA: Blackwell Press.
Rawls, John (1996) *Political Liberalism*, rev. ed. New York: Columbia University Press.
Rawls, John (1999) *A Theory of Justice*, rev. ed., Cambridge, MA: Harvard University Press.
Real ID Act of 2005. Pub.L. 109–13, 119 Stat. 302.
Rousseau, Jean Jacques ([1762] 2017) *The Social Contract*. Jonathan Bennett (trans). Accessed 2 January 2019, www.earlymoderntexts.com/assets/pdfs/rousseau1762.pdf.
San Antonio Independent School District v. Rodriguez, 9411 U.S. 1 (1973).
Sessions v. Morales, 137 S.Ct. 1678 (2017).
Smith, Adam (2015) *The Wealth of Nations*. New York: Simon and Brown.
Spinner, Jeff (1995) *The Boundaries of Citizenship: Race, Ethnicity and Nationality in the Liberal State*. Baltimore, MD: The Johns Hopkins University Press.
United Nations General Assembly (1948). The Universal Declaration of Human Rights.
Uniting and Strengthening America by Providing Appropriate Tools Required to Intercept and Obstruct Terrorism of 2001 (US Patriot Act). P.L. 107–56.
Verba, Sidney and Norman Nie (1987) *Participation in America: Political Democracy and Social Equality*. Chicago, IL: University of Chicago Press.
Young, Iris Marion (1990) *Justice and the Politics of Difference*. Princeton, NJ: Princeton University Press.
Zinn, Howard (2015) *The People's History of the United States*. New York: Harper Perennial Modern Classics.
Zizek, Slavoj (2007) *The Universal Exception*. New York: Continuum.
Zizek, Slavoj (2011) *Living in the End of Times*. New York: Verso Books.

3

MYTH AMERICA

Every nation has its stories. These stories are transmitted as part of our political socialization,[1] and our enculturation on why to be and how to be a good citizen of our hegemonic nation. Thomas Bender (2002) explained the need for this common story for all nations: "A history in common is fundamental to sustaining the affiliation that constitutes national subjects, [because] [n]ations are, among other things, a collective agreement, partly coerced, to affirm a common history as the basis for a shared future." The need for a common territory, language, religion, institution, holidays, and history all help tie a country's people to the nation itself. You might notice that the United States does not have a legal language, but we have a common language; we do not have a national religion, though we use the concept of Judeo-Christian norms to couch our nation's values and morality. Jill Lepore (2012, 2018) articulates that these histories—from those of our origins to the current framing of issues—are necessary myths that bind us together as citizens of a nation. "We hold these truths to be self-evident" in so much as we never question them. This chapter takes some of those truths, those myths, to task because they underpin our concepts of what it makes a good citizen, and thus, what supposedly makes a good nation. But first we also have to look at the values that we hold dear.

Values and Practice

The American values we see replicated in our founding documents and in the political rhetoric and policies are freedom, liberty, justice, and equality. Our politicians and policies tout these values, though the operating policies might violate them to allow for those with power to maintain that power. While that sounds a bit harsh and manipulative of the public, here is a prime example of how political rhetoric and policy around equality of pay in reality do not move us toward pay equality.

In 1961, President John F. Kennedy set up the Presidential Commission on the Status of Women. Former First Lady Eleanor Roosevelt presided over the committee with Esther Peterson. Peterson was a labor union advocate before she worked as a consumer advocate and in the Bureau of Labor on women's issues. Peterson stepped in when Mrs. Roosevelt could no longer chair. President Kennedy issued Executive Order 10980. This order was couched in the language of our American values: that women's basic rights were not respected due to customs and prejudices, thus we were not living up to our nation's values of freedom, human dignity, and democracy. He established the commission to not only help women in the workforce, but in turn strengthen the family, and thus, our national security.

One of the first rules of public policy making, while not making any real changes or impact, is to study an issue. Set up a select committee or commission to study a problem, until the people forget about that problem because they think the government is doing something about the problem or issue or opportunity. For Kennedy, whose base was the labor movement, this was an appropriate action—he appeared to be doing something about women's inequality, studying the issue, yet not taking definitive action. Most policy legislation about women in the workforce was of a paternalistic nature, protecting women from the harmful and rough workplace. Laws existed that limited women's working hours and conditions and even the types of jobs they might hold. Policies replicated the norms, and so did the labor laws including taxation policies and social security insurance that were (and still are) a proportion of their wages. The commission went on to document the discrimination that women faced in the workplace including the lack of paid maternity leave and affordable child care (issues that still impede women today).

While the commission could have, as some members wanted, proposed an Equal Rights Amendment, the October 1963 report that did get issued straddled both the acknowledgment of women's traditional gender roles and the inequalities women faced, legally and in the labor market. The most significant accomplishment that the Commission enabled was not only the formation of state Commissions on the Status of Women, but the enactment of the Equal Pay Act of 1963. In the early 1960s, women (white women, at that) were earning 63 cents to the male dollar.

The Equal Pay Act stated that all employees, without discrimination based on their sex, should be paid the same wages paid to those of the opposite sex for equal work, skills, and responsibilities under similar working conditions. Except there was an exclusionary clause:

> ... except where such payment is made pursuant to (i) a seniority system; (ii) a merit system; (iii) a system which measures earnings by quantity or quality of production; or (iv) a differential based on any other factor other than sex.

There were other issues—employers would implement the 25% pay reduction when offering a position to women, because women might go off and get married or have children. To date, in some fields, there are "mommy-tracks" that allow for more flexibility yet pay substantially lower than other positions in the same firm. Thus, women's pay has only been increased in the past fifty years to under 80.5 cents per male dollar on average, with women of color earning substantially lower. This impacts not only what a household may spend for necessities and what discretionary monies they have, but this also impacts women when they are eligible to retire since their social security (and other pensions) are keyed to their lower wages.

But, wait you say, there is the Lilly Ledbetter Fair Pay Act, which came about because Ledbetter took her employer Goodyear Tire (Ledbetter v. Goodyear Tire & Rubber Co [550 U.S. 618, 2007]) to court because she had found out they were paying her substantially less than her male colleagues. The Supreme Court decided that she should have taken the company to task at the beginning of her employment not the end. The Lilly Ledbetter Fair Pay Act was signed into being as President Obama's first action in January 2009. This law overturned the Supreme Court limitation on when someone needs to file an employment discrimination claim, and states that each subsequent act of discriminatory payment is a separate act, and retroactive.

Still, women are not receiving equal pay for equal work. And, while policy change is possible, it is incremental, if not glacial. This is partly because of how laws and policies get implemented, or not. Our norms are draped in those values that we all hold, but in actuality, the operative policies violate those values. Why, you may ask? We are taught that our salary is "private," and many companies prohibit the sharing of pay stubs.

The Power and the American Model

Power is the ability to influence and control, and in politics, this is seen as the distribution of goods and services, such as who gets what, where, when, and how. The common political model for power distribution is that of the Elite Power Model.

The Elite Power Model is an hierarchy; the people with power have common interests and goals, they are situated at the top with the laws, institutions, and norms below them, which are over the majority of the people. This is the traditional view of power in the United States, and power flows from the top to the bottom. It is the most common political model of government and claims adherents as different as Karl Marx and John Stuart Mill. There are political elites who are our leaders and our kingmakers (those behind the scenes that help leaders become leaders and then lead effectively—such as political parties and policy think tanks). There are economic elites who are heads of major corporations. There are social elites who help focus our cultural needs and norms. These elites provide funds and guidance along with influencing the public. The conflicts between these elites and their various and divergent interests, and how and by how much they influence our democracy gives us a pluralist model of the power elite; each sector vying for power. Robert Dahl ([1961] 2005) set forth perhaps the most famous of the pluralistic models of democracy, where unequal but competitive interest groups vie for power exerting their various resources to accomplish their goals. Charles Lindblom recognized that businesses as interest groups have far more influence (1977). The idea that what is good for business is good for America has its roots in nineteenth-century America when the government did not have monetary resources, but used land grants and its legislative powers to have private corporations undertake projects for the greater public good (canals, railroads, etc.).

Myths

Most of us pay little mind to, at best skim over, the first form of government that our founders enacted—our failed constitutional confederation. The Articles of Confederation were written in 1777 (and ratified in 1781) not only named the United States of America, but were in force until they were replaced in 1789 by the Constitution of the United States of America. The fact that we do not focus on our first failed government gives more force to our American Exceptionalism. Without self-reflection, we look down our noses at other countries failed attempts at democratization, such as what transpired after the Arab Spring.

Manifest Destiny, that notion that we were entitled to the land from sea to shining sea, has infused itself into how we look at property and personal space. We preference property ownership over renting. We spread our belongings to take up more space, even when we are in public—from manspreading to laying out belongings on a desk or table. We even like to have more space around us in a crowd. In other cultures, people will speak inches from another's face, Americans will take a step back to give themselves "space."

The myth of the rugged individualism is seen as declining help and taking responsibility for one's lot in life. This myth allows as to blame those who are poor for not pulling themselves up by their bootstraps to improve their life, or thinking that they must be lazy because they must not be working hard enough to earn enough to improve their conditions. This notion overlooks the realities that keep people in place and do not reflect on the benefits that those who are middle or upper class enjoy.

The key values—i.e. life, liberty, justice, equality—and what principles are held that impact these values, i.e. work hard and you will get ahead, are embedded in our hegemony. American hegemonic citizenship is articulated by the dominant social political and economic paradigm and ingrained in the American Dream of material consumption—the house with the white picket fence and all its suburban trappings including the stay-at-home wife/mother. It is the combined power of the hegemonic and dominant paradigm and the American Dream, which manifest in public policies such as those that push homeownership and in the hegemonic preferencing of property owners over non-property owners.

The power of hegemony is that it is unspoken, it is considered the norm, and it is the goal to which we must fully assimilate. We only identify the person who is othered—the non-white, the female, the homeless, the poor, the sexual minority, the non-Christian. It is this articulation of this othering that allows us to distinguish between citizens in a normative fashion that limits and entrenches citizenship. Based on citizenship theory, and public norms and policy as replicating and maintaining the norm, and thus, what one supposes is the public good. People who are negatively marked by any of these markers that are articulated in this book do not enjoy equality or all the rights a full citizen has; the restrictions are by public policy, societal norms the dominant social, political, and economic paradigm, and laws. But first we must understand what undergirds these structural norms that hold in place these norms.

Role of Government

Our founders, especially Thomas Jefferson, was taken with John Locke's *Second Treatise on Government*, which set forth a civil and political society that was based on equality, order in society, and protection of property. Jefferson borrowed Locke's "Reason, which is that Law teaches all Mankind, who would but consult it, that being all equal and independent, no one ought to harm another in his Life, Health, Liberty, or Possessions" and translated this to "life, liberty and the pursuit of happiness" in the Declaration of Independence. Happiness and property were conflated. (How much different would be our current debate on healthcare, if health was kept in?) Locke's reason for governments to exist was to protect these rights.

We find the role of our American government set forth quite clearly in the Preamble of our Constitution:

> We the people of the United States, in Order to form a more perfect Union, establish Justice, insure domestic Tranquility, provide for the common defence, promote the general Welfare, and secure the Blessings of Liberty to ourselves and our Posterity, do ordain and establish this Constitution for the United States of America.

To reiterate, the role of government is to adjudicate Justice, protect the people from conflict within and without our borders, to distribute and redistribute goods and services for the general welfare, and to promote liberty and prosperity.

How the government carries out these mandates is via federal legislation (laws) and public policies. While specific functions of governing are limited to the federal or national government—such as defense, treaties, coining money, and the post office, other functions are delegated to or shared with the states—from the police powers that govern our health and welfare, such as building codes, drinking, driving, and marriage ages, to the collection of taxes, adjudication of laws, and the punishment of transgressors. These federal laws and policies are tweaked by each state to fit their needs and circumstances. Finally, it is the 89,004 regional authorities and local municipalities[2] that actually deliver services to the people—plowing streets, providing police and fire protection, offering public health services, and providing elementary and secondary education, for example.

We also need to focus on that often overlooked clause: "more perfect" in the Preamble. The founders are not only reflecting on the failed government (and governments) that came before but are looking at this new one as aspirational. Note that the opening phrase is "We the people," not we the citizens.[3] Democracy is messy, it is a system of compromise on how we reach the public good. The underlying issue is who has the power to define the public good.

Questions that we need to think about throughout this book are: Are the various governments impartial, that is, who do they protect and serve? Who are "we the people"—are we only citizens, the propertied, or is it everyone on US territory? As James Madison wrote in *The Federalist Paper* # 51: "If men were angels, no government would be necessary. If angels were to govern men, neither external nor internal controls on government would be necessary."

The reason Rousseau wrote that republics were not good governments was that the people do not pay attention to what those elected representatives are actually doing, the elected officials are not being held accountable for doing what is in the best public interest. The electorate only pays attention at election time, and for many, they pay attention to only party affiliation and name recognition when they cast their votes. It does matter who in our republic are standing for election and who get to make the laws, as do their implementation and adjudication. Who has access to vote and influence—from campaign donations to lobbying to presenting full blown legislation[4]—is also critical.

The American Dream

The American Dream—that everyone has the opportunity based on their drive and ability to have a better life in America—was first conceptualized by the "City Upon a Hill" section of John Winthrop's (1630) "Model of Christian Charity" sermon delivered aboard the *Arabella* before the first group of Puritans disembarked in what became Massachusetts. "City upon a Hill" detailed a society in which everyone had the opportunity to prosper if they worked together and obeyed God's laws. By the time Thomas Jefferson penned the Declaration of Independence using John Locke's *Second Treatise of Government* as a template, this concept was articulated as "life, liberty and the pursuit of Happiness." Alexis de Tocqueville called this dream as "the charm of anticipated success" in his 1820s observation of this nation of individuals, *Democracy in America* (2000). Henry David Thoreau's *Walden* (1854) restates this: "If one advances confidently in the direction of his dreams, and endeavors to live the life he has imagined, he will meet with a success unexpected in common hours."

By the turn of the twentieth century, the American dream was a euphemism for upward economic mobility, à la the protagonists of Horatio Alger's rags to riches stories. James Truslow Adams' *The Epic of America* (1931) further popularized the "dream of a land in which life should be better and richer and fuller for everyone, with opportunity for each according to ability or achievement."

The American Dream is also translated into the suburban dream of living in a house with a white picket fence, family, and vehicles. Part of this dream comes from the idea that our founders thought if we owned property we would have a vested interest in ensuring the stability of the new country. Our founders also cherished the rural over the city life. At this point in our country's development, for all of us to have our own house would mean that some will be commuting from Nebraska because our statistical metropolitan areas (SMSA) are over developed and crowded. We also have policies that keep our neighborhoods separate (which will be discussed in Chapter 5, Propertied), and we have had policies that have enabled the purchase and financing of homes, which resulted in the 2007–8 real estate bubble, crisis, and recession.

Most people will identify themselves as middle class, whether they earn $25,000 a year or they earn over $175,000. Partly this is due to the misinterpretation of the idea that America is a classless society; what our founders meant by classless society was that we do not have a hierarchical noble class. A recent study from the London School of Economics by Jonathan Mijs of the International Inequalities Institute found that 95% of Americans firmly believe that America is a meritocracy, even though the country has become unjust and economically unequal (and, America is not alone in this—Mijs found that this was not limited to just the United States but in all the 23 Western countries studied). The US Census reported that the median income for a family of four was $59,035 as of September 2017.

Americans think of themselves as ordinary; their way of life is how everyone lives it. When there is a crack in the facade, and we see how the other side lives, we are aghast at the ignorance—how out of touch the very rich are to the everyday life from the high cost of bank fees and mortgages, to the lack of credit extended to many. The recent 2019 partial shutdown of the federal government, which resulted in 800,000 federal workers without pay even if they were working (and cascade of the contract workers from housekeepers to child care workers, consultants to restaurant workers out of jobs), unmasked the fact that, for over two years, 80% of Americans were living paycheck to paycheck. CareerBuilder Research had reported this out in 2017 that 78% of workers were living paycheck to paycheck, racking up addition debt, regardless of whether they earned $100,000 or held minimum wage jobs. The causes of this being attributed to the high cost of housing, food, and other necessities, coupled with "keeping up with the Jones," by measuring one's social and cultural status against what one thinks one's neighbors have. This leads to material overconsumption of goods and, coupled with perceived and planned obsolescence, leads people to purchase newer, supposedly better things.

We hold onto the myth of social mobility. Young girls dream of marrying their prince charming, but while Meghan Markle might have married into royalty, for most people marriages happen within their same milieu. Michael Hout reports that Americans' success (prestigious jobs and high-paying positions) depends on their parents' status; if they, especially the father, held a prestigious high-paying position, their children would likewise be successful. The myth that each generation would be more successful than the previous has actually given way to social stagnation and, in some cases, downward mobility.

As social and economic inequality deepens, as the rift grows wider, people tend not to socialize with people from different strata. Our neighborhoods are isolated from one another by infrastructure such as highways, or by gates that keep the other out and the same in. Schools—public and private, secular and nonsecular—tend to be segregated racially, socially, and economically, even almost 65 years post the landmark desegregation case Brown v. the Board of Education.

Part of the myth of social mobility is tied to the myth of meritocracy—that hard work, talent, and achievement will be rewarded. Research has found that it is who you know (connections), what resources you have (money and time, and what they can buy), and not what you know that privileges privilege. The myth of meritocracy is used to justify this privilege, one thinks one has hit a triple, when in fact, they were born on third base. For example, in New York City, where two-thirds of the public school eighth graders are children of color, less than 25% of the 5,000 accepted tested into the elite specialized high schools. Chris Hayes in his book *Twilight of the Elites* (2012) highlighted how this myth of meritocracy, further privileging resources and connections, exacerbates inequality and corruption. The spring 2019 elite college admissions scandal is just one example of the corruption around what Hayes labeled "the cult of smartness." Well-to-do parents paid tens of thousands of dollars to secure special testing circumstances, and, thus, for better test scores, or lied about their child's involvement in predominantly elite sports (sailing or tennis, for example). This scandal underscores how connections, not knowledge, are privileged.

Myth American

From the beginning of our country forward, we have held onto the illusion of the rural American farmer as living the virtuous life, the rugged cowboy or frontiersman as the epitome of the individual, and the myth that anyone from the backwoods born in a log cabin can become our greatest president. These myths are ingrained in our concept of who is the common American, the American ideal, as Walter Lippmann wrote, who is the "salt of the earth." Unspoken is that these images are of white males, what since the mid-twentieth century has been referred to as the White Anglo-Saxon Protestant (WASP) male norm we all need to assimilate toward. E. Digby Baltzell wrote *The Protestant Establishment: Aristocracy and Caste in America* (1987) that cemented the idea that the White Anglo-Saxon Protestant were the power elite in America—politically, financially, and socially.

In the early twentieth century, the Boy Scouts of America was founded to teach boys and young men to be leaders and good citizens and obey God, along with those outdoor skills to build their character and become productive workers in the industrialized corporate world. The Boys Scouts enjoy a special relationship with the US Military, the annual national jamboree is held at a military base. The Boy Scout Oath states: "On my honor I will do my best to do my duty to God and my country and to obey the Scout Law;[5] to help other people at all times; to keep myself physically strong, mentally awake, and morally straight." The Boys Scouts strove to help immigrant young men assimilate to the American ideal. While slowly they have been becoming more inclusive, allowing gay scouts (2013) and leaders (2015), and currently allowing young women and trans-youth to join; there has been a conservative backlash to these changes.

Furthermore, our acceptance of the Judeo-Christian societal norms—from what holidays we celebrate (Christmas), to our day of rest (Sunday)—blind us to the other Abrahamic religion (Islam) and other religions practiced in America.

Because of these images of the true American, people hold strongly to the myth of the American Dream—that America is a meritocracy. Hard work and talent is all anyone needs to (a) grow up to be the President of the United States, (b) to be rich, (c) to be famous, (d) whatever your dreams are made of.... This myth and its attending supports—the poor are lazy, the poor only have themselves to blame; the rich achieved their success on their own, mask structural inequalities and political realities that maintain the status quo.

We have individualized the problems and have undone the public supports. We have enveloped the Protestant Work Ethic—that one needs to work hard to get ahead, and success is measured by our hard work and discipline. Part of the Protestant Work Ethic, though we seem to have discarded it, is the emphasis on being thrifty and saving. Part this is due to the fact that 80% of Americans are living paycheck to paycheck, and 40% do not have savings of $400 in case of emergency. Another is that people who have to collect welfare are prohibited from saving money. At the same time, we also measure our success by our consumer culture—we are material creatures.

We believe that people cannot overcome the structures that keep them poor or criminal or apathetic, not because there are laws, policies, and cultural norms that entrench, but because they are meant to be poor, criminal, or apathetic. Americans have swallowed these myths about their fellow Americans, as if it were a form of Calvinistic Predestination—they are meant to be poor, criminal, or apathetic. If only they would work harder, for example, they will be blessed by being enabled to move to a better neighborhood with a better school district, so their children will be more successful than they are. But as Jonathan J.B. Mijs (2019) notes, as income inequality grows, so does the belief in meritocracy. The inequality gap is the United States, and in other Western countries, is both underestimated, which leads to a greater tolerance of inequality, and Mijs says this inequality is believed to be "the outcome of a fair, meritocratic, process where d=societal success simply reflects talent, ambition and hard work" (p. 2). Mijs' conclusion is that this is due, in part, to how the different classes are basically because each class does not really see how the other class lives—each group tends to remain in their own neighborhoods, schools, and marry within their social class. Without this visible awareness, they do not see the structural processes and institutions that reinforce the inequality (p. 23).

Our key ideals of free citizens and brave men are reinforced by the lines "The Land of the free and the Home of the brave," Francis Scott Key wrote this in 1814 in "The Star Spangled Banner"—the song that would become our national anthem, though most only know one of its four verses. The phrase "In God we Trust" our national motto adopted during the height of the Cold War (1956) is meant to distinguish the God-fearing, and blessed, America from the secular and godless Soviet Union. Though on our seal it is the phrase "*E Pluribus Unum*" (From Many, One), that our founders choose to underscore the federal nature of our government.

In today's neoliberal world we think of citizenship in principle as democratic and equal. It is the goal of liberal democracy operating with a liberal economic system to be a nation of good productive citizens. This principle implies that citizens are not only equal in status, but have the same access to opportunities and before a court of law. In reality, equality is aspirational, and for many just beyond their reach because norms, policies, and laws mark some citizens as other, as second-class citizens, and still others are failed citizens, and there are documented and undocumented noncitizens. The enfranchised and empowered people, our officials, and representatives tend to think, if thinking of the othered citizens at all, as deserving of their unequal status. Americans practice a form of democratic Calvinism predetermining the treatment of citizens. If they are considered virtuous citizens they have and are able to attain the markers of citizenship, they are property owners, productive, participatory, patriotic, and reproducing more citizens, they deserve all rights and privileges. If the citizen is has not or cannot attain one (or more) of the markers, they live in public housing, for example, they are seen as not deserving to be treated as full citizens and their rights are abridged.

Thus, if citizens are not seen as virtuous good citizens, we not only tolerate them, they are treated differently—they are controlled and regulated via social norms, policies, and laws. While there is the rhetoric of a recoverable and attainable equality, it is individualized to a fault i.e. if only they worked harder, they would have more access to material goods, they could live in a better neighborhood when in fact, it is a structural problem that is insurmountable. The status as second-class citizens is entrenched. From this entrenched position, could these citizens be regulated into non-citizenship? How do these invisible constraints and the web of laws and practices conspire to keep social political movements in place without the possibility of achieving their goals, thus allowing the venting of frustrations but maintaining the status quo.

The category Citizen is extremely contested and contextualized by cultural, political, historical, economic, situational, and place. In the United States, as elsewhere, good citizens own property, are productive, are patriots, have the right to autonomy/privacy (read as "control over mind, body and labor"), and have the right to practice (or not) their religion, among others things. In other words, the major markers of citizenship are property ownership, political participation, patriotism, procreative (reproductive), and productive. A good citizen achieves all of these ideals and goals without being marked.

Each subsequent chapter will articulate the ways in which law and norms, and biopower regulates and controls citizens marked by the markers.

The steadfast ideas about our democratic principles, which we repeated every morning of elementary school in the Pledge of Allegiance "with liberty and justice for all," are the ideas—freedom, justice, and equal political participation that we find in our founding documents. "All men are created equal" to "We the people" are ideals not reality. The reality is institutionalized in laws and social norms for reasons of security and stability or predictability (Cohen, 2009, p. 12), people are restricted by both policy and norms. In the chapter on Patriotism, the Pledge of Allegiance is explored in depth. Most of us do not even notice the restrictions, they are invisible to the naked eye unless we are affected or we are taught to the structural apparatus that constrains the other.

The myth of the gender (and race) neutral citizen covers up who the laws and policies consider privileged. Catherine MacKinnon in *Women's Lives, Men's Laws* (2005) lays forth how laws regarding rape, sexual harassment, and pornography continue to subordinate women, maintaining inequality. As Susan Bordo articulated in *The Unbearable Weight* ([1993] 2004), and as Senator Kamala Harris drove home in her questioning of the Supreme Justice candidate Brett Kavanaugh, "Can you think of any laws that give the government the power to make decisions about the male body?" (6 September 2018). There are no laws written on the white male body, while laws are freely written on the female, poor, or non-white body.

Gloria Steinem says patriarchy's goal is to be able to control reproduction (26 August 2016 on NPR's Fresh Air), but in reality, patriarchy has a further reach—it is one in which men hold the power—politically, socially, and economically. The myth is that patriarchy only impacts females, but in truth patriarchy impacts all—males need to measure up to standards of masculinity—to be the primary breadwinner, to be manly, and to make (or at least boast about) sexual conquests. These standards lead to what some call toxic masculinity and manifest as homophobia, aggressive sexual behavior, and bullying (see Michael Kimmel).

Another myth is that America is a Christian country; thus, Christian males are taught in their churches that males are superior to females, reinforcing patriarchy. In truth, even our first Senate unanimously signed the Treaty of Tripoli in 1796, which explicitly stated in Article 11: "*As the government of the United States of America is not in any sense founded on the Christian Religion,* as it has in itself no character of enmity against the laws, religion or tranquility of Musselmen…" (italics, mine).

The myth that we live in a meritocracy, that rewards come to those who work hard, overlook the laws that keep people in (their) place (as mentioned earlier equal pay laws, for example) or the societal norms that discount those who do not have the right connections or networks (the need to go to the right schools), manners, or dialect (demanding others code shift). This myth opens into the idea that rich people are more worthy than poorer people, for education, jobs, and benefits. This myth reinforces Calvinistic Predestination of who gets to be a good citizen, but in doing so it also overlooks those who inherit the good fortunes of their families, by assuming that success is always earned, not granted.

Closely connected to this is how justice and the rule of law plays out. Who makes the laws, and who enforces the law are also critical to understanding who is afforded justice, and who must abide the rule of law. Justice is one of those contested terms: Is it just, is it just for us (in the in group), and is it meant to protect the good citizens from the others? The most blatant examples of laws being written that disproportionately affect one group over another are drug laws. Crack, used by poor and minority populations, carries heavy sentence requirements, while Cocaine, used by wealthy white people, have light sentences, if the drug user is found guilty. Following Michael Brown's death in Ferguson, MO, in August 2014, and the ensuing civic unrest that followed that included the police bringing riot gear to a candlelight vigil, the Department of Justice, Civil Rights Division issued a report (4 March 2015) that concluded that both the policing and court practices in Ferguson negatively impacted African Americans disproportionately. African Americans accounted for most of the arrests and tickets, and the use of force was based on bias rather than African Americans committing more crimes than others (p. 64); and, only these persons were accused of resisting arrest. Tickets and court fees could result in extensive fines, where late, non- or partial payment might end up with the ticketed person doing time in jail (pp. 3–4). The report stated that Ferguson's enforcement practices were shaped by revenue needs rather than public safety concerns (p. 2). Furthermore, these practices infringed on First and Fourth Amendment violations of African Americans (pp. 16–28) including the use of excessive force.

Laws and Justice

While we have become slowly more inclusive, the current obvious scapegoating of immigrants, people who are transgender, women, and people of color unfortunately makes the unseen discrimination and misogyny almost benign because it is seen as the law or it is the norm. It is anything but benign. It has a cost of maintaining the status quo, and as we may see now, as the Germans experienced in the 1930s (see both Mayer (2016) and Jaraush (2015)). In a chapter entitled "But Then It Was Too Late," Mayer quotes a colleague: "To Live in this process is absolutely not to be able to notice it.... Each step was so small, so inconsequential, so well explained, or on occasion, 'regretted'... developing from day to day than a farmer in his field sees the corning growing. One day it is over his head" (p. 167, philologist in Mayer). These norms and policies are seemingly naked to most of our eyes because they do not directly affect us, allowing us to carry on our daily lives thinking we are (all) free and equal, as we mark our place or even descend from aspirational liberal democracy. Laws are not always just, ethical, or moral.

Most of us do not even notice the restrictions; they are invisible to the naked eye unless we are affected, or we are taught to see. Since hindsight is 20/20, and it's always easier to critique another. An example of how people are entrenched will be by using how German Jews became noncitizens in the 1930s. Building on the preexisting anti-Semitic attitudes, the first law was an anti-kosher butchering law couched as an animal rights law. Since this law only affected the Jewish population that kept kosher, other citizens did not take notice. Only in hindsight do we now see clearly this slippery slide into noncitizen. The lens will then be turned back onto the United States.

Let us look at one of the starkest examples of the grossest legitimization of intolerance that occurred in Germany under Nazi rule, culminating in the Holocaust. It should be noted that anti-Semitism existed in Europe prior to the twentieth century—Jewish people were seen as outsiders and separate from many of the Europeans because of their religious practices and their strong cultural practices. When Jewish people were extended legal rights and citizenship during the eighteenth and nineteenth centuries, Jews began to assimilate, casting aside some of their own cultural practices to belong to the citizenry. While some of the laws were masked by other motivations, such as the prevention of cruelty to animals, others were blatantly anti-Semitic.

Germans who were Jewish were being legislated out of their citizenship by draconian laws. Jewish students were restricted from attending public schools and universities with the passage of the "Law Against Overcrowding in German Schools and Universities" on 25 April 1933. This law restricted the number of Jewish students to not exceed 1.5 of the total number of students in that school or university. Jewish students were put on vacation. After *Kristallnacht*, on 15 November 1938, Jewish students (and Gypsies) were prohibited from attending German schools.

The Nuremberg Laws on Citizenship and Race were adopted on 15 September 1935, and two months later, a supplemental decree was issued that explicitly deprived German Jews of their German Citizenship:

> ARTICLE 4. (1) A Jew cannot be a citizen of the Reich. He cannot exercise the right to vote; he cannot hold public office.

1937 and 1938 saw laws restricting Jewish people from certain occupations and economic activity. The first of such laws banned Jews from many professional occupations, from accountant to dentist to teachers of German citizens. In April 1938, Jews had to register their property and wealth, and in June, this registration was expanded to their businesses. They were further prohibited from providing or trading specific commercial services that July, including practicing medicine. By September, this prohibition was expanded to include all legal practices. That July, Jews over the age of 15 were required to carry police issued identification cards. By mid-August, Jewish women had to add the name Sarah, and Jewish men the name Israel to all their legal documents including their passports, which as of 5 October were required to bear a red "J" for *Juden*.

On 9–10 November 1938, the "Night of the Broken Glass," or Kristallnacht occurred. "Spontaneous" mobs attacked Jewish people in their homes, places of work (7,500 business destroyed), places of worship (1,000 synagogues were burned), and on the streets. Just fewer than 100 Jews were killed, and many more injured; 30,000 Jews were arrested and sent to concentration camps.

This attack was carried out by paramilitary personnel and civilians. The German police forces did not intervene to protect the Jewish people or their property. The ultimate blaming the victims occurred when, on 12 November, the Nazi government fined Jews one billion marks to pay for the damages related to *Kristallnacht*.

Because Jewish people were no longer citizens, they had no voice, they were legitimately intolerated, and there was no escape civilly or socially. So in 1939, when Jews lose the right to tenancy and are moved to Jewish houses and are prohibited from holding government positions or from being out of doors after 8 p.m., in the winter, or 9 p.m., in the summer, they are no longer seen by the populace as anything but the Jewish question/problem.

Once a government and the dominant culture legitimize intolerance, no one seems to notice, it is hegemonic. Intolerance becomes invisible, and the others become entrenched as second class, not fully able to access their rights or be heard. Hegemony, as Ewick and Silbey (1998) had stated, is the unthinkable. But, this is not all that unthinkable here in the United States. August 11-12 2017, the alt-right and white nationalists convened the Unite the Right march in Charlottesville, Virgina. The police stood by idly while torch and gun bearing men marched and chanted anti-semitic slogans through the college town. The following day one of the participants drove his vehicle into counter protesters killing Heather Hyer and injuring 19 others. The president's comments on August 15 days after the violence were seen as supportive of the white nationalists when he stated there was hatred, bigotry and violence on many sides...with very fine people on both sides."

The stories, histories, and myths that we tell ourselves about who is the good citizen, and thus, on the flip side, who does not deserve all the privileges, rights, and benefits afforded to all allows us to discount, to overlook, and to blame those who are undeserving. We then believe that we are all potentially equal. When we have structural and systemic conditions that entrench our fellow systems, we just do not see them because those structures and systems do not affect all of us.

Summary

Every person is politically socialized about what it means to be a good citizen in their country, what the country values and holds as their values. It is part of the history that is taught in our schools, it is also what is not taught and how this colors our perspectives. These myths and stories, the national holidays, and loyalty pledges ties us together. What we do not see, what we are not taught, is that these myths are unrealistic renditions of what we all may attain, but they underpin our policies and norms. Manifest destiny underpin property rights. Individual initiative allows us to look down on the poor without seeing the structures such as that keep people poor, yet give others privilege. Good citizens assimilate to the hegemonic ideal, unfortunately, not all citizens can achieve these ideals. The non-achievers are kept in place by polices, regulations, and norms that those who are not affected do not see.

Notes

1 The sources of political socialization are families, religions, education, media, and colleagues. Each tells us stories on what is the hegemonic norm, how to be in community, how to make decisions, how to assimilate, and what is expected of the citizen.
2 Per The US Census Bureau 2012 Census of Governments. This number is actually decreased from 2007 Census, which had 89,476 governments. The governments that the Census of Government measures are the counties, municipalities, townships, special districts—fire, water, waste disposal, etc., and independent school districts.
3 More on this in Chapter 6.
4 See Jane Mayer's book *Dark Money* on the influence of ALEC.
5 The Scout law: A Scout is trustworthy, loyal, helpful, friendly, courteous, kind, obedient, cheerful, thrifty, brave, clean, and reverent.

References

Adams, James Truslow ([1931] 2001) *The Epic of America*. New York: Simons Publications.
Alexander, Michelle (2012) *The New Jim Crow: Mass Incarceration in the Age of Colorblindness*. New York: The New Press.
Alger, Horatio (2010) *The Horatio Alger Treasury*. M. Keeney (Compiler). Booklocker.com, Inc.
Articles of Confederation ([1777] 2015) in Erin Ackerman and Benjamin Ginsberg (eds), *A Guide to the United States Constitution*, 3rd ed. New York: W.W. Norton.
Baltzell, E. Digby (1987) *The Protestant Establishment: Aristocracy and Caste in America*. New Haven, CT: Yale University Press.
Bender, Thomas (2002) *Rethinking American History in a Global Age*. Berkeley, CA: University of California Press.
Benhabib, Seyla (2004) *The Rights of Others*. New York: Cambridge University Press.
Benhabib, Seyla (2011) *Dignity in Adversity*. Cambridge, UK: Polity Books.
Bordo, Susan (2004) *Unbearable Weight: Feminism, Western Culture and the Body*, 10th Aniv. ed. Berkeley, CA: University of California Press.
Careerbuilder Research (2017) "Living Paycheck to Paycheck Is a Way of Life for Majority of U.S. Workers, According to New CareerBuilder Survey." Accessed 25 January 2019, http://press.careerbuilder.com/2017-08-24-Living-Paycheck-to-Paycheck-is-a-Way-of-Life-for-Majority-of-U-S-Workers-According-to-New-CareerBuilder-Survey.
Carens, Joseph H. (2000) *Culture, Citizenship and Community: A Contextual Exploration of Justice as Evenhandedness*. Cambridge, UK: Oxford University Press.
Child Citizen Act of 2000. Pub.L. 106–395.
Cohen, Elizabeth (2009) *Semi-Citizenship in Democratic Politics*. New York: Cambridge University Press.
Constitution of the United States of America ([1789] 2015) in Erin Ackerman and Benjamin Ginsberg (eds), *A Guide to the United States Constitution*, 3rd ed. New York: W.W. Norton.

Dahl, Robert ([1961] 2005) *Who Governs: Democracy and Power in an American City.* New Haven, CT: Yale University Press.

Department of Justice, Civil Rights Division (4 March 2015) "Investigation of the Ferguson Police Department." Washington, DC. Accessed 26 April 2019, www.justice.gov/sites/default/files/opa/press-releases/attachments/2015/03/04/ferguson_police_department_report.pdf.

Ewick, Patricia and Susan Silbey (1998) *The Common Place of Law: Stories from Everyday Life.* Chicago, IL: University of Chicago Press.

Feder, Shira (2019) "All the European Countries Where Kosher and Halal Meat Production Are Now Forbidden." Accessed 10 March 2019, Forward.com/food/416983/all-the-european-countries-where-kosher-and-halal-meat-production-are-now/.

Hayes, Chris (2012) *Twilight of the Elites.* New York: Crown Publishing.

Jaraush, Konrad (2015) *Out of Ashes: A New History of Europe in the Twentieth Century.* Princeton, NJ: Princeton University Press.

Jones, Kathleen (1993) *Compassionate Authority: Democracy and the Representation of Women.* New York: Routledge.

Kennedy, John F. (1961) "Executive Order 10980 Establishing the President's Commission on the Status of Women." Accessed 30 January 2019, catalog.archives.gov/id/300011 or presidency.ucsb.edu/documents/executive-order-10980-establishing-the-presidents-commission-the-status-women#axzz1UU8oizn3.

Key, Francis Scott (1814) *Star Spangled Banner.*

Kurz, Sebastian (2018) in Liam Hoare "Chancellor Sebastian Kurz on Kristallnacht: 'For Too Long, We Looked Away from the Horrors'." Accessed 1 December 2018, www.thejc.com/news/news-features/austria-chancellor-sebastian-kurz-on-kristallnacht-for-too-long-we-looked-away-from-the-horrors-1.472162.

Kymlicka, Will and Wayne Norman (1994) *Citizenship in Diverse Societies.* New York: Oxford University Press.

Ledbetter v. Goodyear Tire & Rubber Co., 550 U.S. 618 (2007).

Lepore, Jill (2012) *The Story of America.* Princeton, NJ: Princeton University Press.

Lepore, Jill (2018) *These Truths: A History of the United States.* New York: W.W. Norton.

Lilly Ledbetter Fair Pay Act of 2009 (Pub.L. 111–2, S. 181).

Lindblom, Charles E. (1977) *Politics and Markets: The World's Political Economic System.* New York: Basic Books.

Locke, John (1952) *The Second Treatise of Government.* Thomas Peardon (ed.). New York: Liberal Arts Press, Bobbs-Merrill Inc.

Loewen, James W. (2008) *Lies My Teacher Told Me: Everything your American History Textbook Got Wrong.* New York: The New Press.

Mackinnon, Catherine (2005) *Women's Lives, Men's Laws.* Cambridge, MA: Belknap Press.

Madison, James (2015) "Federalist Paper #51 (1778–9)." In Erin Ackerman and Benjamin Ginsberg (eds), *A Guide to the United States Constitution*, 3rd ed. New York: W.W. Norton.

Marshall, T.H. (1964) *Class, Citizenship and Social Development.* Garden City, NY: Doubleday.

Marx, Karl and Friedrich Engels ([1848] 2010) *The Communist Manifesto.* Public Domain Books.

Mayer, Jane (2016) *Dark Money: The Hidden History of Billionaires Beyond the Rise of the Radical Right.* New York: Anchor Books.

Mayer, Milton and Richard Evans (2017) *They Thought They Were Free: The Germans, 1933–45.* Chicago, IL: University of Chicago Press.

Mijs, Jonathan (2019) "The Paradox of Inequality: Income Inequality and Belief in Meritocracy Go Hand in Hand." *Socio-Economic Review* 1–29. doi:10.1093/ser/mwy051.

Mill, John Stuart (2010) *On Liberty.* Accessed 30 January 2019, www.gutenberg.org/files/34901/34901-h/34901-h.htm.

Myers, JoAnne and Joan Tronto (1998) "'Truth' and Advocacy: A Feminist Perspective." *PS: Political Science & Politics* 31 (4): 808–810.

Okin, Susan Moeller (1986) *Is Multiculturalism Bad for Women?* Princeton, NJ: Princeton University Press.

Pateman, Carole (1988) *The Social Contract.* Palo Alto, CA: Stanford University Press.

Phillips, Anne (1991) *Engendering Democracy.* University Park, PA: University of Pennsylvania Press.

Pogge, Thomas (2002) *World Poverty and Human Rights: Cosmopolitan Responsibilities and Reforms.* Malden, MA: Blackwell Press.

Rousseau, Jean Jacques ([1762] 2017) *The Social Contract.* Jonathan Bennett (trans). Accessed 2 January 2019, www.earlymoderntexts.com/assets/pdfs/rousseau1762.pdf.

Scott, Joan Wallach (2010) *The Politics of the Veil.* Princeton, NJ: Princeton University Press.

Sessions V Morales, 137 S. Ct 1678 (2017).

Thoreau, Henry David ([1854] 2017) *Walden.* N.P.: Chump Change Press.

Tocqueville, Alexis de (2000) *Democracy in America.* Henry Reeve (trans). New York: Bantam Classics.

United States Census Bureau, Census of Governments (2017) Accessed 29 January 2019, www.census.gov/econ/overview/go0100.html.

Universal Declaration of Human Rights (1948) Accessed 15 November 2019, http://www.un.org/en/universal-declaration-human-rights/.

Winthrop, John (1630) "Model of Christian Charity." Collections of the Massachusetts Historical Society (Boston, 1838), 3rd series 7: 31–48. Accessed 10 March 2019, history.hanover.edu/texts/winthmod.html.

Young, Iris Marion (1990) *Justice and the Politics of Difference.* Princeton, NJ: Princeton University Press.

Zinn, Howard (2015) *The People's History of America.* New York: Harper's Perennial Modern Classics.

4 PATRIOTISM

How do we perform citizenship? The current "taking a knee" protest by the National Football League (NFL) athletes is, depending on your perspective, an attack on patriotism or a patriotic act meant to highlight a grave injustice. Patriotism is defined as military service, loyalty to country, and obedience to the government. Patriotism also extends to who may or may not dissent, and how those acts are perceived by law enforcement and the general public. This chapter looks at each of these subcategories, and how the virtue and act of patriotism mark citizens. Who may be so marked, thus, operationalizing Alistair MacIntyre's (1995) theory that patriotism is a virtue and an expression of loyalty, prestige, and gratitude of one's country. Though as MacIntyre wrote, justification for such loyalty relies on morality, and at certain intersections, patriotism is not neutral and may be a vice. Patriotism does rely on some form of reciprocity—what we gain from our allegiance. But, if we do not gain something, or feel we are left out of the national project, in the case of America—liberty and justice—do we become lesser citizens as we make this critique? (Beiner, 1995, p. 209). Michelle Obama, the former first lady, was called "un-American" when, from the campaign stage on 18 February 2008 in Wisconsin, she stated that for the first time in her adult life she was "proud of my country"; a critique of the racism that still infuses the country. Her fist bump with the then president-elect on election eve (4 November 2008) was painted not as a gesture of success, but that of terrorist's signal.

Colin Kaepernick, the former quarterback of the San Francisco 49ers, knelt (took a knee) during the playing of the National Anthem before the 2016 preseason and regular season games to protest police brutality of African American men (women are also victims of police violence) and other forms of social injustice. Soon, other athletes and performers were also taking the knee. White players stood with their hands on their friends' shoulders in solidarity. While veterans' groups applauded this action—stating this is why they served; to allow for first amendment rights to be practiced on—the Trump administration took umbrage and used these protests to denigrate the players' patriotism. On 25 September 2017 at a rally, Trump called on the NFL owners to fire any "son of a bitch" who protested. Soon after, he retracted other championship teams' invitations to visit the White House such as that of the basketball team the Golden State Warriors.

To claim that a loyal citizen must turn a blind eye to actions of the government, or as Theodore Roosevelt (1914) wrote, "To announce that there must be no criticism of the President, or that we are to stand by the President, right or wrong, is not only unpatriotic and servile, but is morally treasonable to the American public." Most Americans claim to be patriots, whether or not they support the particular government currently in power and its policies. *Patriot* is what William Connolly (1993) might refer to as a "contested term." We all know what we mean when we say we are, or that someone is, a patriot, but we never really define it. Patriotism is not the just blind loyalty of the "my country right or wrong" genre. It is a willingness to defend the country or to make it better—to dissent if necessary if one believes the policies, laws, or norms are not living up to the ideals set forth. As Conover et al. (2004) note the concept of citizenship is deeply rooted and the idea of citizenship as a "desirable activity" and "the powerful underlying motivations of citizens who want a 'nativistic' and culturally defined national civic identity" (p. 1063).

George Orwell, in the essay "Notes on Nationalism" (1945), wrote:

> By "nationalism" I mean first of all the habit of assuming that human beings can be classified like insects and that who blocks of millions or tens of millions of people can be confidently labelled "good" or "bad". But secondly—and this is much more important—I mean the habit of identifying oneself with a single nation or other unit, placing it beyond good and evil and recognising no other duty than that of advancing its interests. Nationalism is not to be confused with patriotism. By "patriotism" I mean devotion to a particular place and a particular way of life, which one believes to be the best in the world but has not wish to force on other people. Patriotism is of its nature defensive, both militarily and culturally. Nationalism, on the other hand, is inseparable from the desire for power. The abiding purpose of every nationalist is to secure more power and more prestige, not for himself but for the nation or other unit in which he has chosen to sink his own individuality.

Patriotism

Today, nationalism and patriotism are being conflated. Patriotism is, in short, the affection for one's country and values and the responsibility one has toward those values—being able to see shortcomings and areas in need of improvement. Nationalism is the more militaristic of the two concepts, with the nationalist believing politically in their country, right or wrong, and that their country is superior to all others and should dominate all. Nationalism was, pre-World War II, associated with the development of the nation-state, and it was not until after World War II that nationalism became a seemingly an identity wrapped in irrational doctrine of great emotionality—"my country right or wrong"—intertwined with manipulative militaristic power and aggression (Breuilly, 2008).

Patriotism is, then, the exact opposite of nationalism. Nationalism is a betrayal of patriotism. By putting our own interests first, with no regard for others, we erase the very thing that a nation holds dearest, and the thing that keeps it alive: its moral values.

The exception to being marked by patriotism negatively seems to be men of means—these men have been allowed to skip drafts and military service, yet are not marked by not serving. These men, most noticeably in the political arena, announce their patriotism by wearing the flag on their lapel. Rousseau, in the opening paragraph of Chapter 15 of the third book of *The Social Contract*, warns of what happens when money can be used to buy citizens' way out of public sacrifice and service:

> As soon as public service ceases to be the chief business of the citizens, and they would rather serve with their money than with their persons, the State is not far from its fall. When it is necessary to march out to war, they pay troops and stay at home: when it is necessary to meet in council, they name deputies and stay at home. By reason of idleness and money, they end by having soldiers to enslave their country and representatives to sell it.

You are either with us or against us. Patriotism plays out today—from military service to supporting wars to who are "heroes" to "birthers" and to immigration issues. While gay men and lesbians are now allowed to openly serve in our military, there are still other Americans who have not been able serve, either because of their religion or are discriminated against in such service by their gender (women could not serve in combat positions until 2016) or what is currently being played out in the courts: the tweeted whim of President Trump declaring a ban on transgender persons from serving in the military. This ban, if enacted will cost the military a lot of years of training and expertise, a similar situation happened in 2002 when the military discharged openly homosexual soldiers who were Arabic speakers at the start of the "War on Terrorism." Yet, at the same time, foreign nationals and those with criminal records may serve. There is, also, the issue of the draft versus a volunteer army. Who do we draft? Who can evade the draft? The other issue around patriotism is seen in our rushes to war by politicians and citizens alike.

The second definition of patriotism is loyalty to country. Can one be loyal to the country and dissent, or is it the blind faith and allegiance of "Love it or Leave it"; "You are either with us or against us"; "My country right or wrong"? This section will explore who has the right to dissent.

The last definition of patriotism is a variation of loyalty, must one follow the rule of law blindly without questioning? Is the answer to this blind obedience dependent on the person's status as patriot? Does everyone have the right to dissent? Is the answer to this blind obedience dependent on the person's status as a patriot or not? Or is it who is in authority, and thus, we abdicate our responsibility to the authority figure?[1]

The Loyalty Oath

Every morning in elementary school since the 1930s, American school children rise to repeat the Pledge of Allegiance as part of their political socialization. As adults, we repeat the Pledge at the start of public governmental meetings. This loyalty oath, written in 1892, couples our form of government (a republic, a representational democracy with a president as a head of state) and our key values—liberty and justice for all, as we pledge to the flag, the political symbol of our country, never again to be divided.

The history of the Pledge of Allegiance, though, is firmly rooted in this nation's white nationalist roots. Francis Bellamy, a socialist and former pastor at Boston's Bethany Baptist Church, wrote this patriotic tribute for the weekly magazine, *Companion,* the largest circulation weekly of its time, to celebrate Christopher Columbus' discovery of America. Columbus' discovery of America is yet another myth, until recently that elementary students have been taught as one of the United States of America's origin stories, but why? It might be to underscore the European heritage of the nation.

Today, we know that Christopher Columbus did not discover America. First, because there were already peoples living in what became the United States. And, second, because there is evidence that other explorers found (north) America: the Norse explorer Leif Ericson landed in what would become Newfoundland in the year 1000, and seventy years before Columbus' voyage the Chinese explorer Zheng He not only circumnavigated the world, but also mapped both North and South Americas. Christopher Columbus never set foot on North America, he and the three ships he commanded first reached land in what is now the Bahamas and, in subsequent voyages, explored Central and South American coasts.

America might have been a nation of immigrants, when Bellamy wrote the Pledge, it was written as a nativist oath. The Pledge was a short poem that was meant to help unite and assimilate Anglo-Saxon citizens against the waves of new immigrants coming from southern and Eastern Europe (Italians, Slavs, and Jewish persons) countries, which he thought of as having "institutions [which were] entirely at variance with our own." As Bellamy and others saw the newcomers as unsavory and even dull-witted: he wrote "we cannot be the dumping ground of Europe and bloom like a flower garden."[2] In a speech to the people of Malden Massachusetts, Bellamy exclaimed: "while we honor the man Columbus, [we are here to] celebrate America today." The America "to which the world is bowing, was built purely of Anglo-Saxon stuff. Those mighty men of the Lord that settled Massachusetts, the sturdy Dutchmen of New York, the clean Quakers of Pennsylvania, the cavalier stock that established itself on the James—these were the true makers of America."

The phrase "One Nation Under God" was inserted into the Pledge in 1954 during the Cold War, the House of Representative's House Un-American Activities Committee hearings and the Senate's Army-McCarthy Senate hearings to distinguish Americans from the godless, un-god-fearing Communists. We are able to root out the third grader commies who would not repeat this phrase—though Jehovah Witnesses, among other religious sects, who do not idolize (graven) images, also do not say the pledge.

The presentation of the Flag and singing of the National Anthem start most sporting events, though "play ball" is not the last refrain of the anthem. A military flyover starts many an NFL game (and other sporting events). In the stands, active and veteran military members are cheering spectators shown on the jumbotron. These displays of patriotism act to unite the fans and as a recruiting tool for the military.

The Pledge of Allegiance is nothing more than an early articulation of our national conceit of American Exceptionalism. Americans, regardless of political affiliation, believe that the United States is the chosen democracy, and our values and policies of liberty and justice the best. Thus, the United States is morally, economically, and militarily superior to all other countries. The United States is the leader of the free world. We export our democracy—to other countries via treaties and policies at the end of wars, for example. Japan's post-World War II constitution, written by General Douglas MacArthur and his staff in 1946, is based on our own.

Seymour Martin Lipset (1997) noted that Alexis de Tocqueville wrote the term American Exceptionalism in his multi-volume *Democracy in America*, which compared the success of the American democracy to that of the French and Russian projects. America was the manifestation of its liberal ideology: a nation of individuals who came together as equals to successfully solve public problems. Lipset studied how the nation became the model for the modern world—a meritorious, capitalistic, rights-based ideology grounded in individualism and religion.[3]

Rising to repeat the Pledge of Allegiance was challenged by the Jehovah's Witnesses, whose beliefs include not saluting any image or symbol, the flag represents a government. Jehovah's Witnesses believe the Laws of G*d, and the Kingdom of Heaven is their true government, thus superseding those of any worldly government. The West Virginia Board of Education passed a resolution compelling the recitation of the Pledge in 1942. Young students who refused to stand and recite the Pledge, including the two Barnette girls, following their religious teachings and those of their father, were expelled from their elementary public schools for insubordination, and their parent were subjected to fines and jail. West Virginia State Board of Education v. Barnette, 319 U.S. (1943) was decided, though not on the basis of the free exercise of religion, but on freedom of speech. The school district could not compel the recitation, for as Justice Robert Jackson wrote for the majority: "If there is any fixed star in our constitutional constellation, it is that no official, high or petty, can prescribe what shall be orthodox in politics, nationalism, religion, or other matters of opinion or force citizens to confess by word or act their faith therein."

The import of the recitation of the Pledge mirrored the rise of investigations into anti-American behavior by the House Un-American Activities Committee (HUAC), which came to be in 1938. The purpose of this committee was to investigate subversive and disloyal behavior on the part of American citizens and organizations with ties to the Communist Party. During the height of the Cold War, the anti-Communist hysteria was at a feverish pitch. The most famous case was that of Alger Hiss, a Department of State official, who helped organize the United Nations. Hiss was accused of being a spy by Whittaker Chambers, who had previously testified that Hiss was a known Communist in the 1930s and 1940s and who had passed him state department papers. Hiss was accused and found guilty of perjury in 1950 because he had known Chambers, though by another name. Though Hiss continued to claim his innocence until his death, Chambers' testimony and book *Witness* (1952), along with other soviet era cables that implicated Hiss as a Soviet agent, impacted many Americans. The future president, then a congressman, Richard M. Nixon was nominated vice presidential candidate in 1952 because of this case. This case also gave way to Senator Joseph McCarthy's (Wisc-R) claim that the State Department and other government agencies were infested with Communists. The Senator aggressively interrogated witness and what we now term "McCarthyism," unfounded public attacks on political opponents, began what history calls the divisive "witch hunts" for Communists in America. As chair of the Senate Permanent Subcommittee on Investigations McCarthy waged a war against Communism; in 1954, he accused the US Army of being infiltrated by Communists because of lax security. Senator McCarthy used a combination of anti-intellectualism and the homosexual panic coupled with the intense Red Scare but with vague real Communist ties. During three months of televised hearings, known as the Army-McCarthy Hearings, the proceedings finally came to a halt when the lawyer hired by Army, stood up to the badgering by the Senator with the phrase "Senator...Have you no sense of decency?" By this time, many Republican colleagues had begun to step away from the unorthodox methods and attacks. It should be noted that Roy Cohen, was McCarthy's chief investigator, and the anti-intellectualism of McCarthyism is still vibrant.

Today we find ourselves with a different challenge to our loyalty. The question of whether or not the sitting president, Donald Trump, attained office with the help of the former head of the Soviet era KGB, Vladimir Putin, and whether or not our sitting president trusts Putin over US intelligence. This is far beyond the scope of this book; the president uses the same language of witch hunts and loyalty oaths to make his case.

Military Service

At the Constitutional Convention in Philadelphia, there was talk about extending enfranchisement to those who served in the militia during the Revolutionary War. The moral argument was simple: a country cannot ask people to risk their lives as they did for the fight for independence and not grant them the rights and obligations of citizenship (Keyssar, 2000, p. 9).

In the recent past, African Americans and homosexuals were not fully integrated into our armed forces. Unfortunately, women are still marked in the military—while now able to serve in "combat" positions in all the forces, their bodies are compared to men's bodies in uniform as the norm for promotion through the ranks, and they are also victims of sexual assault. Currently, as this chapter is being written, transgender persons are also marked, and their service to our country is being denigrated.

Military service is considered to be the penultimate marker of citizenship; it is the ultimate form of patriotism, putting your life on the line for your country. From the earliest Greek democracies, through Machiavelli's distrust of the mercenary soldiers—the idea is that of the citizen-soldier being the ultimate loyal protectors of the state. Rousseau echoed this sentiment "Every Citizen must be a soldier as a duty and none may be so by profession" (Heater, 1999, pp. 64–65).

Mercenaries did fight in our Revolution and aliens may serve, today and, depending on the administration, receive credit toward earning American citizenship if that is their goal. According to the Selective Service System, all males, citizens or not, born after 31 December 1959 need to register for selective service within 30 days of their eighteenth birthday per Proclamation 4771 signed by President Carter in 1980, which reactivated Selective Service. This registration would enable military inscription should a draft be instituted. For males, registering also enables them to be eligible for federal funding for higher education loans, and Pell grants, job training programs and federal employment; and if noncitizens, naturalization. Since the Vietnam Conflict (1963–1975), though, the military has relied on voluntary enlistment, a professional military, instead of an involuntary military filled via a draft conscription.

Involuntary conscription started with men drafted into their state militias during the Revolutionary War. A federal draft to fight the War of 1812 was defeated on the floor of Congress. Federal conscription, as well as by the Confederacy, was conducted during the Civil War. Men, though the conscripted, could send a substitute in their place or pay a current soldier to extend their service. The 1863 Enrollment Act was the first federal conscription, which led to the New York City Draft Riots (13–16 July 1863) as working class men became enraged at being drafted into a war against slavery.

Frederick Douglass saw military service as a pathway to citizenship for black men. "Once let the black man get upon his person the brass letter, U.S., let him get an eagle on his button, and a musket on his shoulder and bullets in his pocket, there is no power on earth that can deny he has earned the right to citizenship." Congress passed the First Confiscation Act and Second Confiscation Act, which stated that all enslaved persons fighting for (or working for) the Confederate Army to be "forever free." The catch was that they had to be on Union soil to be freed persons. After President Lincoln signed the Emancipation Proclamation in 1863, black men were recruited into the Union Army as part of the United States Colored Troops, who were led by white officers and paid less for their services than their white counterparts.[4]

It should also be noted that Jehovah's Witnesses who besides not saluting political images, also do not serve in the military, or in any adjunct position that might support the military. During the Civil War, when faced with the draft, many Jehovah Witnesses were jailed.

Quakers, another pacifist religious sect, when called to service during the Civil War did heed the call[5] to serve, but subsequently Quakers became conscientious objectors and worked to promote peace.

World War I again saw a need for conscription into the United States military due to a strong isolationist and anti-war movement. The 1917 Selective Service Act allowed for exemptions for men with dependents, essential occupations, and anti-war religious beliefs such as those held by Quakers. The poor and minority men were conscripted first since they did not have essential skills and occupations.

The only peacetime draft occurred prior to the United States entry into World War II. While many Americans supported the war effort, and thus the draft, three groups were notable for opposing conscription and ended up evading the draft and being imprisoned—members of the Nation of Islam, the Japanese Americans who were relocated into internment camps because there was fear that they would be allied with the Japanese Army (there were Japanese American troops who did serve), and Communist sympathizers. There were also conscientious objectors who either worked in non-combatant military positions or in civilian camps, among these were Jehovah's Witness,[6] the Amish, Quakers, and other religious sects that were non-violent. Today, many of the religious sects allow their adherents to decide for themselves whether or not to serve.

Uniform restrictions, though, made service difficult for many. Until 1988, wearing religious clothing and items such as Yarmulkes (Jewish head ware that indicated respect for G*d above) inside buildings in uniform was not allowed. In Goldman v. Weinberger, 475 U.S. 503 (1986), the Supreme Court found that the Free Exercise clause had a looser interpretation in the military, because the military had to enforce obedience, commitment, and *esprit de corps*. Wearing of religious apparel even though it did not interfere with military duty was prohibited. Congress subsequently revised the military code in 1988, which now allows for religious items to be worn. In 2014, the Department of Defense allowed Sikh men to wear their hair long under their turbans, as long as they can have the tight fit necessary to enable the wearing of a gasmask.

Gender and the Military

Women, until recently, were not allowed to serve in combat positions, though they served on the frontlines as nurses and supply convoy operators. Women have served openly or secretly in our military or in support of military operations. From the Revolutionary War forward, women have been instrumental. Women not only worked as nurses or cooks, some disguised themselves as men and served in combat. Deborah Sampson Gannett was one of these women who cross-dressed to serve as Robert Shurtliff, partially because she could earn more as a soldier. She served, was wounded, and found out, but in the end, she was recognized as the first female soldier, granted an honorary discharge, and awarded a pension, and in 1983, the Massachusetts legislature declared 23 May as Deborah Samson day.[7]

Over 400 women cross-dressed to serve during the Civil War in the Union and Confederate armies. Dr. Mary E. Walker was awarded the Medal of Honor for her service at the Battle of Bull Run. By the Spanish American War, women's service as nurses were recognized, and the Army Corp of Nurses was established. Over 35,000 women served as nurses, secretaries, and operators during the World War I. They also took over the what were considered to be the men's entry positions into white-collar jobs as secretaries while the men were serving. When the men returned, they no longer valued those jobs since the women could handle the office machinery, the typewriter, and being a secretary became a dead-end pink-collar position without a career ladder.

Similarly, during World War II, the federal government encouraged women to do their patriotic duty on the home front and take positions in shipyards and munitions plants. Propaganda such as Rosie the Riveter encouraged women to enter what was considered the male workforce to make up the labor shortfall caused by men going off to war. Over 6.6 million women entered the industrial and factory forces to turn out military supplies and arms. These jobs paid living wages, above what the women had earned prior to the war, so that at the end of the war, women had to be forced to vacate those jobs and resume gendered and lesser-paid work as positions such as teachers or secretaries. Congress passed a law in 1949, firing these women in order to allow men to take back their jobs, at the same time, there was a social push to encourage women back into the home, and to produce children.

Throughout the rest of the twentieth and beginning of the twenty-first centuries, women heeded the patriotic call to join the military service. Until 2013, women were not allowed to serve in combat, per se, though they regularly came under fire as they drove supply trucks (any student of war learns that attacking the supply lines shortens the war[8]) or worked as medics in the field. Not being able to serve in combat positions also had the effect of not allowing women to be promoted to the highest ranks, since combat service was a prerequisite (as was filling out a uniform as a male's body did).

Homosexuals

Until 2010, gays and lesbians could not openly serve in the US military, though they have served while closeted since the Revolutionary War. While the military did not have an anti-homosexual policy prior, acts of sodomy were grounds for dishonorable discharges. Homosexuals were seen as a potential security risk. During World War I, the Navy, in what became known as the Newport Sex Scandal (1919), purged homosexual men. During World War II, an order to purge lesbians in service lead to Eisenhower's Sergeant Johnnie Phelps to tell him, her name would be on the top of any list of lesbians to be purged. In 1975, while serving in the US Air Force, Leonard Matlovich revealed his homosexuality. He was discharged, and when a Court of Appeals ordered his reinstatement, the Air Force offered him money to not return, which he took. In 1982, the Department of Defense issued a statement that "Homosexuality is incompatible with military service." When President Bill Clinton tried to integrate the military, the policy that emerged was one of "Don't Ask, Don't Tell." This policy leads to more women proportionally being dishonorably discharged from the military than their actual numbers. This was because women would be approached by men for dates, and if they turned the men down, they would be accused of being lesbians. This put women in a bind—they could either go out with the men or be accused of being lesbian. "Don't Ask Don't Tell" was repealed in 2013.[9]

Transgender Military Personnel

As previously noted, there have been women who have (cross) dressed as men to serve in the United States military from the American Revolution on. Cross-dressing, though, is not the same as being transgender. In 1963, people with what is now considered to be gender dysphoria have been excluded from military service as per the US Army regulation 40–501. Under President Obama, transgender military personnel were allowed to serve openly in the US Military as of 30 June 2016. Newly enlisting members who were transgendered could openly identify as such as of 1 January 2018. Under President Donald Trump, the ban against trans-military personnel is being reinstated, though at this writing, it is being contested in courts since one's sexual expression and genitalia has nothing to do with military service and defense positions.

Veterans

Today, we not only see veterans overlooked in their post-service lives (from the lack of sufficient care, to housing and employment issues), but we are seeing alien veterans deported.

That states have given preference to patriots, which is seen by state and federal civil service laws which give veterans either extra credit on civil service exams, or preferring veterans over those who have not served in the military. This preferential practice was held as constitutional in Personnel Administrator of Massachusetts et al. v. Feeney, 422 U.S. 256 (1979). The practice was placing veterans on civil service hiring lists before non-veterans (in some states veterans receive a bonus 10 points added to their civil service exam scores). The decision was reached based on the assumption of gender neutrality—that males were the predominant class of veterans as of 1979. (In Massachusetts, only 2% of veterans were females.) Thus, the law's formula, as Justice Thurgood Marshall pointed out in his dissent, is the practical result of a gender-based hierarchy; males were hired in the higher grade, more responsible and remunerative civil service positions and females in the lower status civil service jobs (clerks and secretaries).

Who Gets to Protest?

The history of dissent is wrapped up in our American history, and myths—the nation was formed out of revolution, after all. The right to dissent is enshrined in the First Amendment of our Constitution's Bill of Rights, yet many see this right as counter to our democracy since it challenges the status quo. Others see the right to dissent as a way to make the democracy live up to its aspirational and moral goals. But from almost the very first, dissent—written and other—against the nation was seen as anti-American, and the government put in place controls, the earliest were the Alien and Sedition Acts of 1798.

In the twentieth century, the Federal Bureau of Investigation surveilled and infiltrated many groups seen as anti-American from (and not limited to) the Civil Rights movement to the anti-war movements, the environmental movement to religious groups from Branch Davidians to Muslims, and today, the current Black Lives Matter movement. The US Patriot Act was signed into being a month after the terrorist attacks on the World Trade Center and Pentagon on 11 September 2001 (actually it had been sitting on Attorney General Ashcroft's desk the summer before). The act, which most read gave the various police agencies and the Justice Department more power to surveil and imprison potential terrorists, was meant to give police more power over criminals that they had lost to the liberal Supreme Court under Chief Justice Earl Warren (wiretapping, etc.).

From the decades long black civil rights movements to the more strategically specific taking over Senate offices to be heard before major votes such as those before the (failed) votes to repeal what is now called Obamacare, protesting or dissenting is one of the legitimate sources of power that citizens hold. Most Americans think of social protests as happening on the political fringe by political outsiders. Most think this because the media does not report on protests, or they give equal time to be "fair" to counter protests, even when the counter protest is dwarfed by the main protest or march. (The March for Women's Lives, 25 April 2004 in Washington, DC, had over 1.5 million participants, but the *New York Times* gave equal space to the few hundred counter protesters spread along the march route praying for the women and fetuses.) Those people who are part of the power elite—politicians, economic elites, media pundits—also work to discredit protestors by framing the movement (or protest) as violent, especially if it results in property damage, and un-American. The days after Michael Brown was killed by a police officer in Ferguson, Missouri (August 2014), the protestors marching in silent vigil were met by a militarized police force in heavy riot gear. The Charlottesville, Virginia, Unite the Right march over a weekend in August 2017, in which far-right extremists and white supremacist brandished torches and guns and resulted in the deaths of counter protesters, was met with little police presence. The aftermath had the president normalizing the extremists with his comment that there were good people on both sides.

Politicians have been normalizing gun violence with offerings of their "thoughts and prayers," while children in schools, people in houses of worship, or at concerts, bars, Walmarts, and theaters are gunned down instead of putting forth legislation for gun control. We are witnessing the young people of Parkland, Florida's Marjory Stoneham Douglas High School organize marches and voter registration campaigns to vote out those politicians. The majority of politicians continue to deflect the focus on guns by focusing on the mental health of the shooters, not the guns and ammunition used. The National Rifle Association promoted arming all, including teachers, because a good guy with a gun will be able to take out the bad guy. The police might not be able to distinguish a good guy with a gun especially if that good guy is a person of color. The young protestors were being painted as the radical other and harassed with death threats—for demanding legislative action on gun control measures.

While some protest by taking the knee, others take to the streets to protest the unequal justice of black men and women, and children losing their lives to summary judgments by police for driving while black (Sandra Bland and Philandro Castile, for example) to minor crimes such as selling loose cigarettes (Eric Garner), brandishing a toy (Tamir Rice), or reaching for his wallet (Amadou Diallo). White-alleged killers are captured alive to face the judgment of a jury of their peers, such as Dylann Roof (Charleston, SC, mass shooting in the historically black Emanuel African Methodist Episcopal Church in 2015), James Holmes who opened fire in the Aurora, Colorado, movie theater in 2012, or Nikolas Cruz, the gunman in the Parkland, Florida, high school shootings. Proportionally as well as historically, white men commit more acts of mass shootings (and domestic violence). While we want the government to ensure citizen safety, we do not want them to curtail our constitutional rights to protest.

Summary

Declaring one's loyalty and military service are one of the key ways one enacts their citizenship. If you get marked as not being a patriot, for your actions or inactions—protesting or for something as simple as not wearing a flag lapel pin—your loyalty to the country may be contested. Labeling someone as un-American means that they are suspect, they are not in tune with American customs and traditions, they are not to be trusted, and they are to be feared or hated. But as Noam Chomsky has pointed out, calling someone un-American is the most common form of social control—pointing out, ridiculing someone who is not in harmony with our America, and who is not working toward a similar goal. But challenging the status quo, protesting, dissenting is, on the other hand, as American as can be.

The term may be hurled from both sides. The government's action such as the immigration bans and calls for walls at the southern border is being called un-American since we are a nation of immigrants, and those who, in the name of national security, call those who oppose the walls and the immigration control un-American for not wanting to protect the country and its citizens. If it is their act of protesting that is being labeled unpatriotic, it is not only their actions, but what they are protesting about that may be called into question.

It is somewhat hypocritical that loyalty to country might be contested by someone who did not answer the call to service, who avoided the draft because of their education, marital status, or infirmity. It is also necessary to point out that what we call un-American might actually be the most American thing of all. The editors of *The St. Louis Post-Dispatch* stated, "the things we hurry to denounce as un-American" are often "peculiarly and distinctly American .... A better and broader view." They concluded, "Seems to be that these problems are of our own creation, and are to be solved only by ourselves" (Gage, 2017). And, of course, we all know what is "American."

Notes

1 See Stanley Milgram's (1961) Yale University Obedience experiments.
2 https://oregonhumanities.org/rll/magazine/encore-fall-winter-2011/under-god/
3 https://www.hoover.org/research/still-exceptional-nation
4 www.militarytimes.com/military-honor/black-military-history/2018/02/12/black-union-soldiers-fought-a-costly-battle-for-equal-pay/
5 http://ramwebs.wcupa.edu/jones/his480/reports/civilwar.htm
6 scholarship.law.marquette.edu/cgi/viewcontent.cgi?referer=https://www.google.com/&httpsredir=1&article=3549&context=mulr
7 *See* Alex Myers' *Revolutionary.*
8 *See* Sun Tzu aka The Sun King's *Art of War.*
9 Berube (1990).

References

Beard, Rick (12 February 2018) "Black Union Soldiers fought a Costly Battle for Equal Pay." *Military Times*. Accessed 16 January 2019, www.militarytimes.com/military-honor/black-military-history/2018/02/12/black-union-soldiers-fought-a-costly-battle-for-equal-pay/.

Beiner, Ronald (1995) *Theorizing Citizenship*. Albany, NY: State University Press.

Berube, Allan (1990) *Coming Out Under Fire*. Detroit, MI: Free Press.

Breuilly, John (2008) "Introduction, John Breuilly." In Ernest Gellner (ed.), *Nations and Nationalism*, 2nd ed. Ithaca, NY: Cornell University Press.

Chambers, Whittaker (1952) *Witness*. New York: Random House.

Connolly, William (1993) *The Terms of Political Discourse*. Princeton, NJ: Princeton University Press.

Conover, Pamela Johnston, Donald Searing and Ivor Crewe (2004) "The Elusive Ideal of Equal Citizenship: Political Theory and Political Psychology in the United States and Great Britain." *The Journal of Politics* 66 (4): 1036–1068.

Ellis, Richard J. (15 November 2011) "Under God." Accessed 10 January 2019, oreganhumanities.org/rll/magazine/encore-fall-winter-2011/under-god.

Gage, Beverly (21 March 2017) "How Un-American Became the Political Insult of the Moment." *The New York Times Magazine*. Accessed 15 February 2019, www.nytimes.com/2017/03/21/magazine/how-un-american-became-the-political-insult-of-the-moment.html.

Heater, Derek (1999) *What Is Citizenship?* Cambridge, UK: Polity Press.

Keyssar, Alexander (2000) *The Right to Vote: The Contested History of Democracy in America*. New York: Basic Books.

Lipset, Seymour Martin (1997) *American Exceptionalism: A Double-Edged Sword*. New York: W.W. Norton.

Luck, Merriam (1943) "War-Exemption from Military Service." *Marquette Law Review* 27 (4): 10.

MacIntyre, Alasdair (1995) *Theorizing Citizenship*. Ronald Beiner (ed.). Albany, NY: State University Press, pp. 209–228.

Milgram, Stanley (1961) *Obedience*. New Haven, CT: Yale University.

Myers, Alex (2014) *Revolutionary*. New York: Simon and Schuster.

Orwell, George (1945) "Notes on Nationalism." Accessed 15 January 2019, http://www.orwell.ru/library/essays/nationalism/english/e_nat.

Personnel Administrator of Massachusetts et al. v. Feeney, 422 U.S. 256 (1979).
Roosevelt, Theodore (7 May 1914) "Kansas City Star." Accessed 29 December 2019, www.loc.gov/item/21021610/.
Rousseau, Jean Jacques ([1762] 2017) *The Social Contract*. Jonathan Bennett (trans). Accessed 2 January 2019, www.earlymoderntexts.com/assets/pdfs/rousseau1762.pdf.
Schmidt, Mark A. (18 April 2004) "Patriotism and Paradox: Quaker Military Service in the American Civil War." http://ramwebs.wcupa.edu/jones/his480/reports/civilwar.htm.
Tocqueville, Alexis de (2000) *Democracy in America*. Henry Reeve (trans). New York: Bantam Classics.
Tzu, Sun (2015) *The Art of War*. North Charleston, SC: CreateSpace.
West Virginia State Board of Education v. Barnette, 319 U.S. 624 (1943).

5

PROPERTIED

In 1963 Malcolm X spoke of the origins and purpose of three major revolutions—the American, French, and Russian revolutions—and what they all had in common was that they were over land (property):

> Look at the American Revolution in 1776. That revolution was for what? For Land. Independence. How was it carried out? Bloodshed. Number one, it was based on land, the basis of independence...The French Revolution—what was it based on? The landless against the landlord. What was it for? Land...The Russian Revolution—what was it based on? Land. The landless against the landlord...
>
> So I cite these various revolutions, brothers and sisters, to show you—you don't have a peaceful revolution. You don't have a turn-the-other-cheek revolution. There's no such *thing* as a nonviolent revolution. [The] only kind of revolution that's nonviolent is the Negro revolution. The only revolution based on loving your enemy is the Negro revolution. The only revolution in which the goal is a desegregated lunch counter, a desegregated theater, a desegregated park, and a desegregated public toilet; you can sit down next to white folks on the toilet. That's no revolution. *Revolution is based on land. Land is the basis of all independence. Land is the basis of freedom, justice, and equality.* (italics, mine)

In short, Malcolm X claimed that the landless, property-less Negro had nothing to bring about a revolution for. In subsequent speeches, Malcolm X continued to underscore that the American black population had nothing to fight for since they do not own property; thus, they will not achieve equality, because "land is basis of all independence. Land is the basis of freedom, justice, and equality."

On 26 February 2016, Trayvon Martin was returning from a trip to the store for candy and iced tea to the gated community of The Retreat at Twin Lakes in Sanford, Florida, where he was visiting his father at his father's fiancée's townhouse. The neighborhood watch patrol, George Zimmerman, recognized the hoodied teen as not belonging in the mixed ethnicity community. After contacting the police, Zimmerman confronted the young man, which resulted in a scuffle and Martin being shot. Zimmerman's defense was the Florida's 2005 "Stand Your Ground Law," a variation of the Castle Doctrine. The justification for Trayvon Martin's murder was because he was an unknown in a gated community, again speaks to the power of property. The number of gated communities have increased since the 1960s, and the security (and privacy) afforded by the gated community is an indication of society's problems supposedly being left at the gates. The gated community becomes a marker of xenophobia as it allows for homogeneity within its borders, shrinking the civil community until it is nonexistent except for the likeminded residents who also think they are removed from civic responsibility (Blakely, 1997; Benjamin, 2009). Research has found that America is spatially segregated not only residentially, but educationally and socially today, by class as much as by race, whether or not one is living in a protected gated community or not. The impact of this cloistering of America is that people get marked as not full citizens depending on where they are spatially.

Property ownership was once a primary consideration for citizenship. It is still considered to be a marker for both social and political capital, and it is also necessary to be considered a full citizen. Thomas Jefferson changed John Locke's concept of property to the pursuit of happiness when he cribbed, "Life, liberty and the pursuit of happiness" for our Declaration of Independence from John Locke's *Second Treatise on Government* (our founders were the first yuppies). At the Constitutional Convention of 1787, James Madison suggested that property was a marker of not only citizen but would allow for that vested interest necessary to legitimize and sustain the republic; suffrage was linked to property ownership, not only for voting but also for qualifications for elected office. This idea was sent to a committee to fix specific property qualifications. The idea was dropped because the committee could not agree on what the specific property qualifications would be, so it became a matter for the states to set voting requirements or enfranchisement. Today, while you do not have to own property to vote, property ownership still is very much a marker for citizenship. If one is marked by not having property, or the right type of property, one is limited in how they might live, in their access to their constitutional rights, and the programs that might lift themselves from poverty. Property rights from possession to inheritance not only incentivize over-accumulation but allow for the privileges that entrenched inequality (Stevens, 1999, p. 105). The Constitution protects property rights through the Fifth and Fourteenth Amendments' Due Process Clauses and the Fifth Amendment's Takings Clause: "nor shall private property be taken for public use without just compensation."

Hannah Arendt stressed that one of the preconditions for political participation, what we would now label as social and political capital—the ability to work toward the community functioning effectively for all—is the ability to establish a private household. In short, the private household as property allows for personal and political agency. This agency is echoed by the intertwining of the properties of property—what values (economic, social, and political) and legal rights ownership interest bestows on the property owner. Our founders also considered the family to be the building blocks of the nation.

Property from Locke to our founders is seen as real, tangible items, or as James Madison stated property "embraces everything to which a man might attach value and have a [legal] right." Raiz Haider (2018) explored the meaning of property from a philosophical perspective from David Hume's idea that property, and the possession thereof, was an artificial construct based upon settled (social) rules that allow for civil stability, without conflict (as opposed to prior to these settled rules/laws possession was based on brutal strength, force and/or chance). Jeremy Bentham furthers this idea of a social construct, an "established expectation" of how property and its ownership is as one that exists because of laws. Bentham did not believe in property rights as a natural right (p. 13). Cheryl Harris (1993) further postulates that American law recognizes a property is an entitlement of the rights of people with respect to tangible things, yet she also puts forth that the interest in whiteness itself is a property and this, too, is an entitlement and a right to exclude those without (pp. 1713–1714).

Our founders were not the last to equate citizenship with property, even though during the Jacksonian era, property ownership was no longer a stated qualification for voting. Our founders had thought that having property gave citizens a vested interest in ensuring the stability of the nation. Property ownership has been preferenced throughout our history as key to building a strong nation.

Home ownership reached its height in 2004 at 69%; it is only slightly lower today, 64%, over 10 years after the 2008 housing crisis. The preference for home ownership remains today, and it can be found in the mission statement of Housing and Urban Development (HUD). HUD's mission is to ensure Americans have access to fair, affordable housing and opportunities *to achieve self-sufficiency, thereby strengthening our communities and nation* (italics, mine). It can also be found in the "American Dream" of a (single-family) house, with a picket fence, and so on—even though, at this point for all to have a single family home, we would have to commute in from South Dakota for our jobs on either coast.

In the United States, property ownership—specifically, home ownership—has been glorified as the best way to accumulate wealth, to begin to eliminate (or at least begin to mitigate) economic inequality, and enter the middle class, yet there have been barriers to do so from governmental regulations, such as zoning, and not extending governmental privileges such as the GI bill to all who served and from societal impressed norms such as redlining and real estate covenants. Thus, the impetus for President George W. Bush signing into being the American Dream Downpayment Act on 16 December 2003 was to give access to those who were racially redlined out of homeownership. His administration thought that by lowering down payments (initial equity) to purchase homes, racial and class discrimination could be eliminated as home ownership was seen as per the President's statement as he signed the law into being "good for America, it is good for our families, it is good for our economy… [to help minority and low-income buyers]…to achieve an important part of the American Dream." Little did President Bush, members of his administration, or many economists realize what was in the future. The mortgage industry took advantage of these and other banking loopholes and deregulation that helped to precipitate the 2007 housing (real estate) bubble burst and subsequent recession, which resulted in 10 million people losing their homes. Prior to 2008, there was an housing surplus; now, 10 plus years past the recession, there is a new housing crisis—a shortage of affordable housing. Gentrification, stricter mortgage regulations, and millennials' sadled with higher-education debt is changing many into perpetual renters.

If property ownership is not seen as the means to attain the economic stability and mobility inherent in the American Dream, what is the effect? What happens when you do not have access to the American Dream, when you are not a property owner, are you less a citizen, do you have less rights? This chapter will look specifically at two instances where not owning property affects citizenship—homelessness and living in public housing—and how property taxes, redlining and zoning regulations also affect citizenship.

The right to property seems to trump other rights. Property rights, especially private property rights, are said to protect individual liberties and thus are seen as human rights. Property rights protect only the individual liberties of those with property; those without property or with undervalued property have limited to no individual rights. Thus, property rights are NOT human rights. Property rights, as practiced in our liberal democracy, have given way to a dual-classed citizenship. The right to property supersedes other rights in our liberal democracy from the right to privacy to the right to assemble, and it affects other basic human rights and most importantly, as Arendt noted, the right to political voice.

For civic republicanism to work—that is for citizens to be conscientious and active members of the community—they need to be both economically and socially independent in order to have the luxury of time to participate and to be objective. Real property ownership is seen, thus, as a marker of the good citizen. Since property owners pay taxes, they are also seen as worthy of the state's protection and the entitlement to rights. Mayor Rudolph Giuliani (NYC) articulated this when he started to ban licensed street vendors from midtown

Manhattan in the mid-to-late 1990s because they were unfairly competing with store owners and restaurants that paid rent and, therefore, taxes. While it is understood that the city needed to ensure the public's health and safety, and do so by regulating street vendors, under the Giuliani, and other administrations, street vendors were harassed by:

> endless arrests and exorbitant fines, delaying their ability to work, destroying their products, denying them a fair hearing, driving them from areas where they have vended for years at the whims of giant corporations, passing regulations governing their livelihood without any notification, failing to acknowledge the contribution they make to our city, disrespecting them when they attempt to voice their grievances, and in many other ways impeding their right to vend on the streets of New York City.[1]

The basic argument is that property ownership gives the citizen the most important vested interest: the stability and maintenance of the state.

Some people were property, themselves, and did not have the right to own property. Slaves were property of their owners. Female slaves were valued more than male slaves because they could produce more slaves (either by sexual congress with a male of their own choosing, by live animal husbandry, a male slave that the master selected, or by her master himself). State of Missouri v. Celia in 1855 was found that as property, Celia, as a female slave, could not defend herself from being raped by her owner.

Women were not seen as full citizens because they were not (save for a few) property owners in their own right, and mostly because of the lack of inheritance rights. The mid-nineteenth century's Married Women's Property Rights Act (NY 1848) began to end coverture—the common law concept that a woman, when she married, was basically not a singular legal being, and her civil existence was subsumed by her husband's; or, as Justice Blackstone had written, she became civilly dead. Thus, married women could not own property, enter into contracts, own her wages, or otherwise act without their husband's authority or permission. The NY state law became the model for other states as they adopted laws to end coverture, but it was not universal. During the Vietnam Conflict a woman tried to enroll in the State University as an in-state resident, but at that time, her husband was stationed out of state. The state declared her permanent residence where her husband was living. Until 1979, a married woman in Florida could sell material property (things such as sofa) she brought into a marriage only with her husband's permission.

Home ownership is related to positive social change. The founders discussion of property as a marker having a stake in the polity, being vested in the survival and progression of the new country was key to the republican model. The founders based their thinking on not only on Locke's articulation of property rights as a natural right, but on Blackstone's Common Law commentaries that echoed the rationality of Montesquieu, which stated that only men with real property had such a stake in ensuring that the community persevered, they were the ones directly affected by laws, and by virtue of property ownership independent to participate in public decision making (voting) (Keyssar, 2000, pp. 8–9). The poor, in this case, also the property-less, were seen as potentially threatening "the interests of property" by acting on their own best interests and revolting (John Adams, in Keyssar, p. 9). We are, thus, able to trace the entrenchment of (real) property as a marker of citizenship. While there were those who advocated for a more egalitarian, though still male, suffrage, this idea did not have traction except on the local levels.

Zoning

The government on all levels federal, state, and local used laws, policies, and programs controls property by limiting home ownership, to segregating neighborhoods by both race and social class, and maintaining class and racial composition of neighborhoods. Zoning regulations, for instance, started as part of the state and local governments' police powers to regulate public health and safety and subsequently as a way to ensure homeowners' investment in their largest financial asset as Fischel (2001) explains how zoning became exclusionary.

Studies also find that segregation of neighborhoods due to zoning regulations, governmental policies, and financial lending practices, coupled with white flight, have allowed the segregation of races and the development and maintenance of racial stereotypes. The neighborhood racial composition became markers of poverty and crime, and dilapidated housing stock. Quillian and Pager (2001) found that, in their study, the higher the percentage of young black men in a neighborhood led white resident respondents in integrated neighborhoods to perceive the neighborhood to be crime ridden, overestimating the relationship of crime and race, regardless of the actual crime statistics. This perception can be translated into a fear of crime, which perpetuates the negative prejudicial stereotypes, not only encouraging racial profiling, but equating blacks with poverty and thus, inferiority (p. 750).

What we now know as zoning regulations had their start with nuisance laws in San Francisco in 1885. San Francisco banned laundries from certain areas that in effect banned Chinese immigrants from these neighborhoods, and the Supreme Court overturned this ban in 1886. Over on the East Coast, Boston and New York City were adopting building codes, especially aimed at tenements (i.e. requiring air shafts for proper ventilation) in 1885. Boston had building height restrictions—90 feet for Copley Square, for instance (which the Supreme Court deemed legal). In 1909, Los Angeles banned heavy industry and commerce from certain neighborhoods. New York City set forth its first comprehensive zoning in 1916. This comprehensive zoning plan regulated building design and purpose along with delineating separate residential and commercial zones and some mixed-used areas. That zoning could be used to exclude certain members of society was highlighted in 1921 by President Herbert Hoover's Commerce Secretary's Advisory Committee on Zoning, the mission of which was how the use of zoning may "maintain the nation and the race."

Zoning and Property Values

The first landmark constitutional challenge to zoning regulation was Village of Euclid v. Ambler Realty Co., 272 U.S. 365 (1926) in which the village had adopted zoning ordinances to prevent the spread of industrialization from the City of Cleveland from encroaching on the village. The Realty company claimed that the zoning ordinances basically had reduced the property value of the land it owned by limiting its future use and sued the village on due process claims. The Supreme Court found in favor of the village, ruling that zoning regulations are justified by the use of police power (to protect the health and welfare of its citizens) and are necessary for the public welfare as determined by circumstances, conditions and the locality.

The concept of zoning regulations limiting future use and, thus, property value was challenged in Lucas v. South Carolina Coastal Zoning Commission, 505 U.S. 1003 (1992). In this case, Lucas had purchased two beachfront lots on a barrier island in 1986 with plans to build two homes, one to sell and the other for him, and was thwarted when South Carolina adopted the Beachfront Management Act put forward by the South Carolina Coastal Zoning Commission. This act was meant to limit and/or prohibit construction on the barrier islands, to protect them from erosion, and in turn to protect the coast of South Carolina from storm damage. Lucas claimed that this act was an uncompensated total taking (Fifth Amendment concept of eminent domain) of his property's value. Justice Antonin Scalia writing for the majority (though there were three concurring majority opinions) basically stated that depriving a property owner from all economic beneficial use (and thus, the property's value) because there is a public need is depriving the owner of the property itself. Thus, for the first time, we have the right to increased property value that the government cannot under the guise of public need deprive us from.

In 2005, another Supreme Court case extended the concept of public use under the Fifth Amendment's Takings Clause. In Kelo v. City of New London (CT), 545 U.S. 469 (2005), which involved the use of eminent domain in the transfer of property from one private owner to another for economic development and growth, the Court ruled that eminent domain is justified because it (economic growth) benefits the entire community.

The effect of zoning regulations dictated land use, separating incompatible land uses—residential from industrial, for example—to protect the character, property values and encourage appropriate and uniform development of communities. These laws were upheld by the Supreme Court as being part of the government's police powers to protect the health and welfare of its citizens.

The first planned community built as part of the New Deal was Arthurdale in West Virginia. In Secretary of the Interior Howard Ickes' public housing project, Arthurdale was built in 1933 under the Public Works Administration and was one of First Lady Eleanor Roosevelt's priority projects. It relocated residents of Scott's Creek to Arthurdale, which had homes with three acre plots to encourage subsistence farming, a progressive school, a community center, and a co-op. When Mrs. Roosevelt asked for the housing to have indoor plumbing, Secretary Ickes replied, "Then how would we tell the poor from the rich?" The residents were selected by a local community vetting process to live in Arthurdale, and though they were impoverished, they were predominantly white and married with families, in short to ensure its success. [Mrs. Roosevelt was astutely aware of the racial and anti-Semitic discrimination.]

Arthurdale and the 98 other homestead projects were deemed economic failures due to their construction costs, the dependence on government relief because three acres were insufficient to grow enough food, and there was no stable industry. Arthurdale is still an active community, the children of the original residents grew up to be doctors and teachers, the school is still operating, and the current community continues to flourish. The idea of giving impoverished people the tools and dignity to improve their lives was successful.

Redlining

The 1934 National Housing Act under the New Deal set up the Federal Housing Authority (FHA). The goal was to insure mortgages to increase home building and ownership. Coupled with the Federal National Mortgage Association (Fannie Mae), established in 1938, and the Servicemen's Readjustment Act of 1944 (aka the GI Bill), American home ownership increased. But these mortgage lending programs not only focused on single-family housing, the programs reflected societal prejudices and were available for middle-class white families assuming that they would be the most stable.

The FHA drew neighborhood boundaries around the riskiest—non-white regardless of class—neighborhoods, a practice known as redlining. Minorities were prevented from acquiring homes in white neighborhoods, while homes in white neighborhoods received beneficial appraisals. Homes in the redlined districts were valued significantly less than those in white neighborhoods; this valuation has resulted in homes in these districts being worth less than half of similar homes in white neighborhoods today.

To maintain the character of these neighborhoods, private deeds contained restrictive covenants prohibiting the sale of homes to minority racial, religious, and ethnic groups, including Blacks, Asians, and persons of the Jewish faith, depending on the area of the country (Southern California might exclude

Mexicans and Northern California might exclude Asians, for example). In 1950, FHA announced they would not underwrite homes with restrictive covenants, but this practice did not stop. Restrictive covenants still exist to insure that certain neighborhoods maintain their aesthetic—prohibition against painting homes other than the neighborhood approved palette or having a pickup truck parked overnight in their driveway. In 2010, a neighborhood in Charlotte, North Carolina, posted a copy of an historic deed that states: "This lot shall be owned and occupied by people of the Caucasian race only." While the homeowners association claimed that they posted this restrictive covenant to remind the homeowners about other prohibitions, such as fencing, the City and the National Association for the Advancement of Colored People (NAACP) recognized the psychological discrimination, freezing out those who saw this racial restriction from wanting to live there, and, thus, violating the Fair Housing Act (Rose, 2010).

The Supreme Court had ruled against private restrictive covenants in Shelley v. Kraemer, 334 U.S. 1 (1948), saying that they were not enforceable in court under the Equal Protection clause of the Fourteenth Amendment. In 1916, the court had ruled against governmentally mandated racial discrimination via a Louisville, Kentucky, civil ordinance that prohibited the sale of real property in white neighborhoods to black people (and the inverse) in Buchanan v. Warley, 245 U.S. 60 (1916). The Fair Housing Act of 1968 was put in place to prohibit discriminatory lending and rental practices including prohibiting racial, ethnic, and religious restrictive covenants.

Real Estate Steering

According to Glantz and Martinez (2018), there are still 61 metropolitan areas in which modern-day redlining still exists. Redlining exists, in a modified form, from denial of mortgages to people of color at a rate of 2.7 times that of white applicants to charging them higher interest. Redlining along with lower property valuations in minority neighborhoods results in what is called wealth asset gap.

The home value gap from the redlining and property valuation continues over generations. Not only does it cause property asset gaps, but when there is no longer valuable property to develop, developers and those in search of affordable housing turn to these undervalued neighborhoods, thus, gentrification, begins.

Economic Development and Gentrification

The federal government has long been involved in promoting economic development through the use of land grants—from the land grants that established the canal system in the early nineteenth century to the railroads to build the transcontinental railroad in the 1860s. To encourage settlements (and passengers), the federal government passed the Homestead Act (1862). Under this act, which started land rushes, US citizens could get 160 acres of unoccupied land west of the Mississippi River and east of the Rocky Mountains for an application fee of $18. Settlers then needed to live and make improvements on the land for five years.

While zoning regulations may be considered a form of gentrification because it separates residential space from initially industrial space, perhaps the most insidious form of gentrification by government was undertaken by using highways to reroute populations. Urban planners such as Robert Moses, the builder of parks, used parkways to move people out of congested urban areas. Moses also was infamous for developing public housing projects to clean up congested tenements. Planning and developing highways and their exits as a form of urban rebirth became easier with federal funding under the 1944 Federal Highway Act and the 1956 Highways Act, which gave us the interstate system.

The automobile had overtaken public transportation as a mode of transport to and from work in the cities to, what would soon be called, the bedroom communities that ringed the cities. Not everyone was welcomed in those bedroom communities. Some because of poverty, race, or ethnicity could not move to the suburbs and were left to live in the cities. So while some planners built public housing projects to move and contain populations, others allowed for highway exits to doom some areas to economic oblivion or used the highways themselves to divide the town into good and bad housing sectors. Still others used the highways to clear out slums or tenement areas from the center of cities and towns. When residents of these neighborhoods marked for clearing moved to other neighborhoods within that city or town, the domino of white flight to the suburbs was exacerbated and urban area sprawl began.

In the 1960s, urban renewal was another government funded project that decimated neighborhoods deemed poor and congested, with out-of-date housing stock. These projects demolished vibrant communities, relocating residents either to public housing projects or other neighborhoods. Urban renewal happened in cities large and small. The film *Lost Rondout: A Story of Urban Renewal* captures the destruction under the rubric of modernization and urban renewal of a vibrant historical working class waterfront neighborhood of an Upstate New York small city. The urban renewal project there demolished over 500 buildings, both residential and those with small business—grocery stores, shoe and clothing stores, and restaurants—replacing the residential with bland but more modern housing for the middle class and relocating many to housing projects.

While today urban planners, politicians, and citizens look back at the lost historic neighborhoods with some nostalgia, urban renewal, now called community and economic development, takes place by the siting of stadiums and other public projects. These projects raze poorer neighborhoods and allow for gentrification and the influx of wealthier residents. Both urban renewal and economic development rely on the fact that the existing residents of the neighborhoods about to be demolished do not have the social and political capital necessary to fight these drastic changes.

In 2019, there is a movement back into urban areas by the affluent because of the appearance of safety viewed by the lower number of quality-of-life crimes, along with lower violent crime rates, even though affluent residents are seen as potential crime victims because of their affluence. While new white residents might stand out in previously predominant minority neighborhoods, not all the gentrifiers are white, there are also minority artists and professionals.

Another factor is that the areas being gentrified has housing stock that is more affordable, and those moving in can afford to renovate. Gentrification is seen as both an attribute, allowing the current residents to also access the goods and services that gentrification brings if they remain in the neighborhood themselves, or if they had owned their property, profit from the sale thereof. The residents that are negatively impacted are those who are forced to move because they can no longer afford the rent increases, and/or there is less affordable rental housing in the area on the market. Some municipalities enact rent stabilization controls to protect residents from price gouging.

Natural Disaster Relief and Inequality

Smiley et al. (2018, 2019) have found that natural disasters and federal relief programs favor property owners over renters. Property owners, especially white households and people with more education, tend to gain wealth after natural disasters such as hurricane flooding. These households tend to be able to take advantage of more programs including property buyouts because they own the house and the land. Minority households, especially renters, tend to lose ground and suffer greater income inequality. This is due to the minority households and renters not being able to take advantage of all emergency funding opportunities due to their lack of credit and the higher cost to rent another residence immediately after a disaster because the number of units available have shrunk, causing an increase in market rents. They also have other costs such as replacing transportation and household goods, which might not be covered. The authors of both studies looked at the Federal Emergency Management Agency (FEMA) responses to natural disasters over a 14-year period. White households studied in the same county as minority households, gained \$126,000 after FEMA pay-outs, while minority household only gained \$27,000 to \$29,000. Their conclusions were that the recovery programs are built around private property owners' need to restore or replace their private property. The programs are not designed to realistically help renters reclaim or replace their residences, increasing poverty levels and income inequality.

Property Taxation and Education

Another prominent right of property is connected to our public-school system: where you live and the school your attend. It is the 65th anniversary of Brown v. the Board of Education (347 U.S. 483, 1954), which set in notion desegregation in the South. In the North you attended school based on neighborhood. Neighborhood segregation was based on housing costs and zoning. This was challenged by Paul B. Zuber when he won a federal court decision (affirmed later by the Supreme Court) in Taylor v. New Rochelle Board of Education (1961) that had allowed for a segregated black school, Lincoln Elementary. Zuber fought de facto segregation. In the south segregation was overt, in the north he said bigots wear suits and ties, not sheets (referring to the Klan).

In the landmark Brown v. Board of Education of Topeka, 347 U.S. 483 (1954) the Supreme Court unanimously declared that establishing black or white only public schools was discriminatory under the Equal Protection clause, thus, throwing out the "Separate but Equal" doctrine established in Plessy v. Ferguson, 163 U.S. 537 (1896). Chief Justice Earl Warren wrote: "In the field of public education the doctrine of 'separate but equal' has no place," as segregated schools are "inherently unequal." In the Brown case, Linda Brown was denied schooling at the nearby public school since that was a white-only school; she had to travel across town to the inferior black school. Northern states did not think that this decision applied to them since most public elementary schools were neighborhood centric—and these neighborhoods were segregated by "social" criteria not government fiat. Fifty years later, in the case Parents Involved in Community Schools v. Seattle School District No. 1, 551 U.S. 701 (2007), the court's decision was that Seattle and Louisville respective voluntary integration programs were unconstitutional under the Equal Protection clause of the Fourteenth Amendment because they used racial balancing in a mechanistic way to determine what public schools students would attend. The upshot was that neighborhood segregation was *de facto* based on private choices, not *de jure* or caused by the state, thus, according to Chief Justice John Roberts opinion, segregation was "a product not of state action but of private choices" and not for the state to fix. But as Richard Rothstein (2017) writes, the state is very much involved in the "racially explicit policies of federal, state and local governments… [which] segregated every metropolitan area in the United States." Programs such as community development, public housing, and urban renewal (see Atlanta, GA, or Kingston, NY's *The Forgotten Rondout*); highway construction that separated and isolated neighborhoods (Albany, NY); zoning, law enforcement, and federal mortgages (Levittown, Long Island) all built on and exacerbating the social norms and choices. These segregated neighborhoods remain even though the racially motivated housing programs that entrenched them might be forgotten; housing is now supposedly available based on affordability—i.e. if you can afford to live in an affluent neighborhood.

In the end, though, public schooling still relies on its predominant supplemental funding from property (school) taxes. In San Antonio Independent School District v. Rodriguez, 411 U.S. 1 (1973), the court found that this public financing schema (which exists throughout the country) did not violate the Fourteenth Amendment equal protection rights of poorer students because there is *no right to education* in the Constitution.

Using the shock doctrine or disaster capitalism set forth in Naomi Klein's 2007 book, post-Katrina New Orleans saw the implementation of the all-charter school system—the Recovery School District. This has been declared a failure on many levels; 40,000 students now attend 70 charter schools (9 students in 10).

All 7,000 teachers pre-Katrina were fired. The racial makeup of the teachers went from 72% black in 2003–2004, to 49% black 10 plus years later; teacher turnover has doubled because of reliance on Teach For America (TFA), short-term commitments and charter schools, which do not allow for unionization. Students are now bused over 1.8 miles, further on average, to the school of their choice, but the Education Research Alliance for New Orleans was told by one-third of the principals that they cherry-picked and recruited the best students, thus not insuring the most equitable system for disadvantaged students. In 2014, community groups filed a federal civil rights complaint stating that the charter school reform was devastating, calling the closing of the public schools as part of the charter reform the second storm.

New York University education professor and Network for Public Education (NPE) founder Diane Ravitch (2013), who once raved about charter school models, said of the New Orleans model,

> That model requires firing all the teachers, no matter their performance, allowing them to reapply for a job, and replacing many of them with inexperienced TFA recruits. That model requires wiping out public schools and replacing them with privately managed schools that set their own standards for admission, discipline, expulsion, and are financially opaque. These heavy-handed tactics require a suspension of democracy that would not be tolerated in a white suburb, but can be done to powerless urban districts where the children are black and Hispanic (Kimmett, 2015).

That many students from the Lower Ninth Ward did not return is also at issue, and may give rise to the improved test scores and graduation rate (as of 2014, New Orleans population had shrunk by 29%). While the test scores and graduation rates have risen, the question remains, do test scores reflect teaching future political participants to think critically or to conform?

Charter schools, once hailed as a way around inadequate schools and funding, are also problematic. Charter schools do not have to hire unionized teachers nor follow state curriculums. One only has to look at one of the aftermaths of Hurricane Katrina, which was for the City of New Orleans the redesigning of the worst performing public school system in Louisiana (67th out of 68 school districts in the state) into the 80% charter school district "Recovery School District" (110 charter schools, 17 public schools). This redesign meant the firing of all the unionized and experienced teachers and the reliance on Teach for America for teachers. Students are subjected to testing and a strict disciplinary code. Students unable to perform academically or who do not meet the conduct code are relegated to the remaining public schools (either before they enter or during the academic year). The result of this is that the charter schools might be performing well, but they are failing the students.

The perfect storm wreckage of the devalued property is found in property tax assessment, which provides 50% of the funding stream for local public education in most districts, and the state and the federal governments provide the rest. The schools and their budget is the most local form of government and meant to produce productive young citizens to maintain the local community. Educating young people includes giving them the skills to work in the community. This why you find high school classes on agriculture and animal husbandry in farming communities and criminal justice in communities where prisons are the major employer. Education is seen as a public good that will serve the local community and economy. The downside of this is that in poorer communities they too educate to keep their future community members trapped within their community—because they do not have the extra funds to help give the students the skills they need to improve their lives or community.

With the property tax revolt, which was started in California with Proposition 13 (1978) under then-Governor Ronald Reagan, monies for education decreased substantially. Prop 13 limited the annual real estate tax to 1% (which may only increase a maximum 2% until the property changes ownership) of the property's assessed value, and when that property was sold, the assessment would increase. The effect of this has been to drain the public education system in California including at the collegiate level. Many states followed this path. The side effect of this is that older people who might have saved tens of thousands over their residency, now in downsizing, they feel the costs of the new assessment on their new homes.

Public Housing and Renters

If you are a renter, you not only have to be worried about paying your rent on time, you also need to not have the police called to your home for any reason. Many towns are putting into place nuisance laws, also known as disorderly house or crime-free house ordinances. The municipalities adopt these laws because repeated visits by the police—for any reason, drug activity, domestic violence—detracts from the neighbors right to peaceful and quiet enjoyment of their property and neighborhood. These local ordinances punish renters by forcing landlords to evict them, not renew their lease, or order them to not contact the police if the property has been cited for any level of criminal activity happening on the property, or perceived criminal activity in which the police are called, including calls for help during a domestic violence incident. Domestic Violence is one of the leading causes for women to become homeless, and these laws exacerbate the situation (Mead and Pappas, 2017). There is a negative effect on tenants' health and welfare since these laws discriminate against tenants, who might have the law used against them to force them to move and, in some cases, become homeless, or the law might keep the tenant from reaching out to the police when in need, for fear of being evicted (Moran-McCabe et al., 2018).

These ordinances are being adopted across the country. The first use of these laws was in 1987 in Portland, Oregon, to regulate drug activity. Over the past forty years, these laws are a way for municipalities to pass the responsibility of controlling and mitigating problem residents to landlords. In many municipalities, if the police are called over three times to a residence, regardless of the reason, the tenant—who may be the victim or the perpetrator—is at fault. Tenants can be evicted even for issues that were not prosecuted or if the tenant is found not guilty.

In some towns, landlords are also setting up blacklists of tenants that they will not rent to because of these issues. In other cases, there are apartment complexes that will not let tenants have visitors who have criminal records visit.

Some municipalities have ordinances that require that landlords to have permission or a license to rent their property, and in order to have such a license, it requires the property to be available to be inspected without a warrant (contrary to the Fourth Amendment) at any point in time. Thus, rental properties have forfeited the tenants' right to illegal searches and seizures. The inspectors can look for issues of public health—i.e. sanitary conditions—or public safety such as the availability and viability of smoke detectors, or for any other reason.

These types of no-knock inspections are familiar to people who are living in public housing. During the mid-1980s, many public housing authorities adopted and put clauses in leases that allowed inspection of the residence without a warrant or probable cause. These clauses were put into the leases to be able to rid the public housing of criminal behavior, such as using or dealing drugs, weapons possession, or prostitution. Many housing authorities felt these measures were warranted because of the gangs, drug violence, and other criminal activities that were the scourge of these housing developments. These clauses were legal because the tenants willingly consented to them when they were the first holders of such a lease. Subsequent lease holders might not have willingly consented, and one might say that a person/family that needs affordable public housing might not have the wherewithal to object or even have really read the lease.[2] But, you might say, they are benefitting from government-subsidized housing that makes it affordable, so what if they give up their right to privacy and their right against illegal searches?

People living in public housing also do not have the right to assemble with whomever they want. They may face eviction if their grandchild, who has a criminal record, visits because that is one of the lease conditions. In 2010, a young man was arrested for selling drugs, and his address came up as his aunt's, who lived in New Orleans public housing for 30 years, though he did not live with her, nor have her permission to use her address. While she appealed this eviction, many people do get evicted because of actions of others. Many of the housing authorities do have a "one strike and you are out" rule. Under federal laws, public housing authorities may evict families if there is alcohol abuse, any involvement in criminal behavior, or criminal drug-related activity on or off the public housing property by any member of the household including a guest.

Homelessness

Since the Civil War, the homeless population was documented as living on the Bowery (NYC), which had a proliferation of dive bars, cheap lodgings, prostitutes, and crime. This homeless population was made up of draft dodgers to alcoholics to ne'er do wells and "bums." Today, while the Bowery is now home to multimillion-dollar condos and galleries, homelessness has not disappeared; there or anywhere. In fact, the homeless population has grown and is not at all homogenous in demographics[3] or origin. The homeless populations range from families who have been evicted or burnt out, to teenage runaways, LGBTQ youth, to victims of domestic violence, to people living in overcrowded situations like those bed-sharing, to the deinstitutionalized, to those who have served prison time, to veterans from the Vietnam Conflict, and the current conflicts, to those who just cannot afford the cost of housing, to the jobless, and to the substance abusers—the homeless population and their needs are varied.

There is a crisis of homelessness exacerbated by the housing crisis of 2007, the increased number of formerly incarcerated who are less likely to receive public benefits and housing, and gentrification. What has been changing, though, is how governments and society view and treat these homeless; no longer are there just bans on panhandling and laws that prohibit vagrancy and loitering. And, instead of providing affordable housing, many communities over the past 10 years are criminalizing the homeless. Laws have been made that prohibit sleeping in vehicles and sleeping in public, camping in public parks, and even feeding the homeless. Public and private architecture is being erected using hostile architectural elements that includes spikes on flat surfaces and wavy pavement that make sitting or camping impossible, to restrict vagrancy in order to move the homeless along. According to the National Law Center on

Homelessness and Poverty, criminalization of homelessness is not only costly, but further entrenches the homeless because, once they have a criminal record, it is harder for them to secure a job or housing (Bauman, 2016, p. 2).

Summary

Homeownership is still viewed as a way into the American dream of wealth accumulation and social mobility, but it may not be possible for all. Housing availability is still controlled by zoning and other restrictions (Rothstein, 2017; Goodman and Mayer, 2018). People who are renters, in public housing or in private housing, are also subjected to losing their housing because they have lost access to their constitutional rights, just because they are not property owners.

Notes

1 Food Vendors Union Local 169v and The Urban Justice Center, Street Vendors Unite! Accessed 4 June 2019, http://nyf.issuelab.org/resources/14908/14908.pdf.

2 In 2016, a federal court did invalidate the East Chicago Housing Authority's ability to conduct warrantless searches of apartments and even the use of drug sniffing K9 unit dogs in the hallways.

3 African Americans make up an estimated 45% of the homeless population despite only being 12% of the national population. Seventeen LGBTQ youth are 40% of the homeless youth population (only 7% of general youth), 18 persons with disabilities are 40% of those who are homeless (16% of general population) (Bauman, 2016).

References

Bauman, Tristia (primary author). (2016) *No Safe Place: The Criminalization of Homelessness in U.S. Cities.* Washington, DC: National Law Center on Homelessness and Poverty.

Bauman, Tristia (primary author). (2016) *Housing Not Handcuffs.* Washington, DC: National Law Center on Homelessness and Poverty.

Benjamin, Rich (2009) *Searching for Whitopia: An Improbable Journey to the Heart of White America.* New York: Hachette Book Group.

Blakely, Edward (1997) *Fortress America: Gated Communities in the United States.* Washington, DC: Brookings Institute Press.

Blauweiss, Stephen and Lynn Woods (2016) *Lost Rondout: A Story of Urban Renewal.* Woodstock, NY: Woodstock Arts Studios.

Buras, Kristen and Raynard Sanders (2018) "History Re-written Masking the Failure of the Recovery School District." Accessed 26 January 2019, theneworleanstribune.com/main/history-rewritten-masking-the-failure-of-the-recovery-school-district/. See also theneworleansimperative.org/research-and-reports/.

Bush, George W. (16 December 2003) "President Bush Signs American Dream Downpayment Act of 2003." https://georgewbush-whitehouse.archives.gov/news/releases/2003/12/20031216-9.html.

Caro, Robert A. (2012) *The Power Broker: Robert Moses and the Fall of New York*. New York: Alfred A. Knopf.

Cook, Blanche W. (1999) *Eleanor Roosevelt Vol 2 1932–1938*. New York: Viking Press, pp. 136–152.

Fischel, William A. (2001) "An Economic History of Zoning and a Cure for Its Exclusionary Effects." *Florida State University Critical Issues Symposium*, 8–9 November 2009.

Food Vendors Union Local 169v and The Urban Justice Center, Street Vendors Unite! Accessed 4 June 2019, http://nyf.issuelab.org/resources/14908/14908.pdf.

Glantz, Aaron and Emmanuel Martinez (15 February 2018) "For People of Color, Banks Are Shutting the Door to Home Ownership." www.revealnews.org/article/for-people-of-color-banks-are-shutting-the-door-to-homeownership.

Goodman, Laurie and Christopher Mayer (2018) "Homeownership and the American Dream." *Journal of Economic Perspectives* 32 (1): 31–58.

Haider, Rais (2018) "The Phenomenological Origins of Property." *UWSpace*. https://uwspace.uwaterloo.ca/handle/10012/13937.

Harris, Cheryl (1993) "Whiteness as Property." *Harvard Law Review* 106 (8): 1707–1791.

Howell, Julia and James R. Elliott (2019) "As Disaster Costs Rise, So Does Inequality." *Socius: Sociological Research for a Dynamic World* 4: 1–2. doi:10.1177/2378023118816795.

Keyssar, Alexander (2000) *The Right to Vote*. New York: Basic Books.

Kimmett, Colleen (2015) "10 Years after Katrina, New Orleans' All-Charter School System has Proven a Failure." Accessed 28 January 2019, inthesetimes.com/article/18352/10-years-after-katrina-new-orleans-all-charter-district-has-proven-a-failur.

Klein, Naomi (2007) *The Shock Doctrine: The Rise of Disaster Capitalism*. New York: Henry Holt.

Locke, John (1690) *The Second Treatise of Civil Government*. www.constitution.org/jl/2ndtreat.htm.

Madison, James (1906) *The Writings of James Madison 101*. Gaillard Hundt (ed.). NY; G.P. Putnam and Sons. p. 174.

Malcolm X (1963) "On Property and Revolution." www.africanholocaust.net/news_ah/malcolm_revolution.html.

Married Women's Property Rights Act. Accessed 15 November 2018, memory.loc.gov/ammem/awhhtml/awlaw3/property_law.html.

McCabe, Brian J. (2013) "Georgetown University 2013 Study: Are Homeowners Better Citizens? Homeownership and Community Participation in the United States." *Social Forces* 91 (3): 929–954.

Mead, Joseph and Marissa Pappas (9 November 2017) "When Calling 911 Makes You a 'Nuisance' and Gets you Evicted." *The New York Times*. Accessed 25 January 2019, www.nytimes.com/2017/11/09/opinion/nuisance-ordinances-eviction-violence.html.

Moore, Stephen (30 July 1998) "Proposition 13 Then, Now and Forever." The Cato Institute. Accessed 15 January 2019, www.cato.org/publications/commentary/proposition-13-then-now-forever.

Moran-McCabe, Katie, Abraham Gutman and Scott Burris (2018) "Public Health Implications of Nuisance Laws." *Public Health Reports* 133 (5): 606–609.

Quillian, l and Pager, D. (2001) "Black Neighbors, Higher Crime? The Role of Racial Stereotypes in Evaluations of Neighbourhood Crime." *American Journal of Sociology,* 107 (3), 717–767.

Ravitch, Diane (2013) "Charter Schools Are a Colossal Mistake, Here's Why." Accessed 20 November 2018, www.alternet.org/2013/10/diane-ravitch-charter-schools-are-colossal-mistake-heres-why/.

Rose, Julie (6 February 2010) "Hidden in Old Homes, a Segregationist Past." Accessed 20 January 2019, www.npr.org/templates/story/story.php?storyId=122484215.

Rothstein, Richard (2017) *The Color of Law.* New York: Liveright Publishing.

Semuel, Alana (18 March 2016) "The Role of Highways in American Poverty." *The Atlantic.* Accessed 15 January 2019, www.theatlantic.com/business/archive/2016/03/role-of-highways-in-american-poverty/474282/.

Shapiro, Thomas M. (2006) "Race, Homeownership and Wealth." *Washington University Journal of Law & Policy* 20: 53–74.

Shapiro, Thomas M. and Heather B. Johnson (2003) "Good Neighborhoods, Good Schools: Race and the Good Choices of White Families." In Ashley Doan and Eduardo Bonilla-Silva (eds), *White Out: The Continuing Significance of Racism.* New York: Routledge.

Smiley, Kevin T., Junia Howell, and James R. Elliott (2018) "Disasters, Local Organizations and Poverty in the United States, 1998 to 2015." *Population and Environment* 40 (2): 115–135. doi:10.1007/s11111-018-0304-8.

State of Missouri v. Celia, a Slave (1855) Records from Callaway County Circuit Court Celia File No. 4496 in State of Missouri vs. Celia, A Slave: Index to the Record of Proceedings. Accessed 12 April 2018. http://law2.umkc.edu/faculty/projects/ftrails/celialins.html.

Stevens, Jacqueline (1999) *Reproducing the State.* Princeton, NJ: Princeton University Press.

Thaler, Jason S. (1995) "Public Housing Consent Clauses: Unconstitutional Condition or Constitutional Necessity?" *Fordham Law Review* 63 (5): 1777–1807.

Violations of the Human Rights of Persons Experiencing Homelessness in the United States A Report to the Special Rapporteur on Extreme Poverty & Human Rights October 16, 2017. Washington, DC: National Law Center on Homelessness and Poverty.

Walker, Blair (1 September 2010) "Eviction Threat, for No Reason." *AARP Bulletin.*

6
POLITICAL PARTICIPATION

Good citizenship is more than obedience to the laws; everyone, *all* citizens and noncitizens, aspirational citizens, and failed citizens have to obey the laws. Good citizenship is then much more; it is acting upon such citizenship to make public decisions; it is having the political agency to participate in the public sphere. Good citizenship is participating in public decision-making on all levels, local, regional (county), state, and federal levels—and at a bare minimum, that is voting. But good citizenship is more than just voting. According to Hannah Arendt, good citizenship is democratic self-determination—the need to have efficacy and to critically think and make decisions—and to be able to collectively deliberate on all matters affecting the public—civil and political—community.

In essence, this active citizenship is civic republicanism. It is being fully engaged and not just making informed choices once a year at the polling place and letting the elected officials govern without input. This is the fear that Rousseau had about republics; that citizens would abdicate their responsibility to those elected to represent them without real accountability. Active citizenship means to be involved in the life of the community, from working on political campaigns, to attending neighborhood/local town/city meetings, contacting government officials (elected and appointed), serving and deliberating on juries and commissions, being involved in civic organizations and, in some cases, being a social justice advocate and protesting, being a dissident to achieve positive change, for example, Martin Luther King Jr.

But to be that active citizen, to be civically engaged, a person needs the ability, the time, and the (public) space to successfully deliberate, share, examine issues from different perspectives, and if necessary, confront other community members in order the develop the commonalities that will result in policies and programs that work for the community. This political agency, who actually gets to participate in this type of public deliberation and decision-making, is one of those human conditions of free action among equals, according to Arendt. What happens then if only those who have the luxury to participate do so, or if access to the most common denominator of political participation, the voting booth, is blocked?

This chapter looks at how political participation—political agency—is a marker of citizenship, and how that political agency gets extended or limited, to whom and why, and what effect has on public policy and decisions. Is voting a right, a duty, or a privilege, or something only the right people should do? What about other types of public participation—public meetings or on a jury, for instance? If only one segment of the population is affecting public policy, what is that impact on the public good? This chapter looks at those issues that impact the goal of civic republicanism: citizen participation, from lack of access to the voting booth; from the federal Voting Rights Act, to state laws that actually govern how, when, and whether citizens may vote, even in federal elections (Voter ID legislation and gerrymandering), to the lack of free time and ability to engage in public ideas. While voting is seen as the epitome of political citizenship, voting is a right not an obligation. This coupled with the increased policy of voter suppression and intimidation and, on the federal level, the politics of the electoral college and Senate representation make it increasingly difficult to have an impact with one's vote through the polls.

While this chapter will touch on how citizens are disenfranchised (it is more difficult to register and vote than it is to purchase a gun), voting is not the only means of political participation especially when one looks at actual voter turnout numbers, which are much lower than those who are registered to vote—in some local elections, only 13% of the registered voters may vote. Local school board elections and budgets, which are seen as the most local form of local government impact citizens and making future citizens, have the lowest voter turnout.

Citizenship as a Desirable Activity

If only one segment of the population is affecting public policy, what is that impact on the public good? This chapter looks at those issues that impact the goal of civic republicanism: citizen participation, from lack of access to the voting booth (from reneging on the Voting Rights Act and allowing voter suppression to voter ID legislation and gerrymandering), to lack of free time and ability to engage in public ideas. While the voting is seen as the epitome of political citizenship, voting is a right not an obligation. This coupled with the increased policy of voter suppression and intimidation and, on the federal level, the politics of the electoral college and Senate representation make it increasingly difficult to have an impact with one's vote through the polls.

The most articulated form of political participation is voting, even though voter turnout is depressingly dismal; in presidential election years, if voter turnout is 60% of the registered voters, we get excited—but only 80% of the eligible population is registered to vote, so that is basically only 40% of the population who vote. Voting is seen by most as *the* marker of citizen participation, yet voting, while a right, is one that you have to exercise, and we know how much people want to exercise. The state with the easiest voter registration and voting access, as of 2018, is Oregon followed by Colorado and California; New York is just at number 26, and Texas, Indiana, Tennessee, Virginia, and Mississippi make up the states where voting access is the most problematic. Yet, our political rhetoric is hinged on voter participation. Thus, this chapter will look at voter purges, voter suppression, and disenfranchisement, along with who has the luxury to participate in other forms of political discourse—attending meetings and hearings to protesting. In short, this chapter will explore who gets a seat and a voice at the political table—this is probably the most concrete aspect of citizenship.

Voting

While one of our myths of "one man/person, one vote" might hold true in local, state, and some federal elections, it does not mean that there is equal representation. Each state has only two senators, which means that states with less population have equal voting power in the upper house of the Congress than states with many residents. The House of Representatives is based on population. Recently, Chris Hayes tweeted: "Queens has more people than *SIXTEEN* states, fyi."[1] (Queens is one of the five boroughs that make up New York City.) It also matters who actually votes.

Sidney Verba and Norman Nie set forward the classic, though narrow, definition of participation as "acts that aim at influencing the government, either by affecting the choice of government personnel or by affecting the choices made by government personnel" (p. 2). This definition includes voting, contacting elected representatives, and participating in campaigns but exclude other acts such as protesting, marching in parades, and other expressive acts of support and or dissent, information sharing, affiliation with voluntary civic organizations, and all acts of civic engagement and efficacy.

Their findings reflect that *who* participates matters. Verba and Nie found that those persons with high-economic social status tend to participate more and agree with government policies that tend to be conservative, reflect the status quo, are highly individualistic (i.e. blame individuals for their poverty), and relieve government of the duties set forth in the Preamble to the Constitution. This actually holds true to the classic 1954 study entitled *Voting* by Berelson, Lazarsfeld, and McPhee who did a deep dive into the 1948 presidential elections surveying the people of Elmira, New York. Their work describes the how and why people vote, their perceptions of politics and issues, and the impact of class, colleagues, and religion. The upshot of their study is that people vote as they are socially and economically.

From Verba and Nie's original study of voting in 1972 to the Pew Charitable Trust's studies on participation in 2014, research has found that the percentage of citizens eligible to vote (18 years old and over, citizens and non-felons or not unincarcerated) but not even registered to vote has remained constant, roughly 20% (21.4% in 2014). According to a 2016 Per Charitable Trust study, the unregistered lack political efficacy, they do not think that their vote matters. This group also dislikes politics or thinks that government does not affect them.

Can you think of anything that you did today that government at any level was not involved in? If you said your woke up in bed: there are those pesky "Do Not Remove Under Penalty of the Law" tags on pillows and mattresses to protect public health. Or, maybe you went to the bathroom, where you relieve yourself and how that gets processed is a governmental concern from sewage processing plant to leach field, plus there *are* public health laws against public urination. The air we breathe is regulated, as is the water we drink or we fish from. Some level of government is involved in most everything we do, except thinking. The purpose of government is laid forth in the Preamble to the Constitution, in short to protect people, adjudicate fairness, and to distribute and redistribute goods, resources, and services.

Of the people who *do* vote but do so sporadically according to the Pew Charitable Trust (2017) study, they do not feel politically informed enough to make a decision. Sixty-two percent have never been approached by a candidate (or their representative), the government, or by a non-governmental agency to register to vote. But the other impact of these non-voters and sporadic voters is their lack of political agency and social capital to affect their communities. They are not likely to attend community meetings (only 5% do so) or donate to political organizations (less than 1% do). Though, 15% have engaged in unpaid and volunteer work, many are engaged in their church, temple, or mosque community activities.

Voting Rights

Voting or giving consent by the governed to the government is referenced in the Declaration of Independence. Voting rights are seen as a negative right—the freedom from, in this case, from being denied or abridged because of race, color, or former servitude (the Fifteenth Amendment), sex (in the Nineteenth Amendment), or the failure to pay poll taxes (Twenty-fourth Amendment), and the age is set at 18 (in the Twenty-sixth Amendment). Each Amendment has made suffrage more inclusive.

Policies and practices related to the most basic form of participation—voting—scaffold this form of structural and institutional maintenance of the status quo—the protection of those in the elite. A brief history of voting rights exposes the unnamed assumptions that gird the status quo.

The United States Constitution, as signed in 1787, did not explicitly grant citizenship nor voting rights, but left the states to develop their own suffrage laws. This basically allowed the states to determine who the people—the citizens—were. Of the 13 original states, all except Connecticut, Delaware, New Jersey, and Rhode Island expressly mentioned the male gender as a requirement along with either property—either land or a specific value of estate and/or taxpaying requirement (except for Vermont) along with a specific length of residency. Connecticut, New Hampshire and Rhode Island were the states without residency requirements. Only three states—Georgia, South Carolina, and Virginia—specifically mention being a member of the white race as a requirement to vote. Only in New Jersey were women permitted to vote, until 1807 (Keyssar, 2000). As you can see, property was a marker for voting; thus, the beginning of the structural underpinnings of voting as a marker of full citizenship only geared to those of higher social status. As statehood was extended to other states, property requirements were slowly dropped from suffrage eligibility, yet a link between financial status—tax paying or paying a poll tax—remained part of the qualification.

Many states had suffrage requirements as per the Floridian Supreme Court case, Lamar v. Dillon (1893), that concluded "where the Constitution does not explicitly fix the right of suffrage or prescribe the qualifications of voters, it is competent for the legislature… to do so" (Keyssar, 2000, p. 135). Florida restricted the right to vote on state public expenditures to property owners or taxpayers, thus allowing some women to vote in school board elections.

Fast forward, on the Federal level enfranchisement has been extended via amendments to the Constitution to include freed male slaves (Fifteenth Amendment, 1869), women (Nineteenth Amendment, 1920), and those 18–21 years of age (Twenty-sixth Amendment, 1971). A prohibition against poll taxes (a way Southern and some Northern states had found to circumvent the Fifteenth Amendment) and the failure to pay any other tax to limit who may vote was ratified in 1964 as the Twenty-fourth Amendment. Though, the specifics for voting registration and elections were still left up to the states. The Voting Rights Act of 1965 was put into place to remove other state and local barriers to voting participation in seven southern states (Alabama, Georgia, Louisiana, Mississippi, North Carolina, South Carolina, and Virginia), providing criminal penalties for voting interference and putting federally appointed election registrars in those counties where there were significant obstacles to black people registering to vote. Further federal legislation in 1975 amended the Voting Rights Act to not only outlaw literacy tests specifically, but mandated bilingual ballots, and/or oral assistance. Both the 1965 Voting Rights Act and the 1975 amendment noticeably increased voter registration among eligible black people. But black voters were still facing discrimination at the election booth from voter purges to being refused a ballot at the polls, so the Voting Rights Act was renewed in 2006 for another 25 years.

Shelby v. Holder, 570 U.S. 529 (2013) was the Supreme Court case that resulted in the rollback of the Voting Rights Act until Congress enacts a more current formula for declaring which counties should be covered by Section 5 of the Voting Rights Act. Shelby County Alabama filed a federal suit asking that Section 5 of the Voting Rights Act be declared unconstitutional. Section 5 required those jurisdictions with a track record of election discrimination to submit proposed changes to voting procedures to either the federal district court in District of Columbia or to the US Department of Justice, a form known as preclearance, before they go into effect. This oversight would prevent minority voters from any potential harm from the changes. Shelby County filed with the US District Court for D.C. in 2010, and this court and the US Court of Appeals for the District of Columbia circuit (2011) both upheld the constitutionality of Section 5. Shelby County appealed to the Supreme Court. On 25 June 2013, the Supreme Court ruled that the coverage formula was 40 years out of date, and thus, section 5 was inoperable until Congress develops a new formula. Chief Justice John Roberts wrote the opinion of the court, he restates Shelby County's claims that "in the covered jurisdictions, '[v]oter turnout and registration rates now approach parity. Blatantly discriminatory evasions of federal decrees are rare. And minority candidates hold office at unprecedented levels.'" Justice Ruth Bader Ginsburg writing in dissent said, "[T]hrowing out preclearance when it has worked and is continuing to work to stop discriminatory changes is like throwing away your umbrella in a rainstorm because you are not getting wet."

The result of this decision was that five states immediately reintroduced their voter identification laws and began restricting voter registration.

Voter Identification (ID) Laws

While Arizona's requirement that potential voters produce proof of United States citizenship was struck down by the Supreme Court (2013), and five states' voter identification laws were either modified or struck down in 2016 (Kansas, North Carolina, North Dakota, Texas, and Wisconsin), voter identification laws are proliferating supposedly to alleviate voter fraud at the polls.

Thirty-four states, as of 2018, require a valid ID in order to vote, though the Help America Vote Act of 2002 does not require such. Indiana was the first state to require a valid (Federal or State) photo id to vote in 2006, which the US Supreme Court upheld in 2008 in Crawford v. Marion County Election Board 9553 U.S. 181. Justice Stevens wrote:

> The relevant burdens here are those imposed on eligible voters who lack photo identification cards that comply with SEA 483. Because Indiana's cards are free, the inconvenience of going to the Bureau of Motor Vehicles, gathering required documents, and posing for a photograph does not qualify as a substantial burden on most voters' right to vote, or represent a significant increase over the usual burdens of voting. The severity of the somewhat heavier burden that may be placed on a limited number of persons—e.g., elderly persons born out-of-state, who may have difficulty obtaining a birth certificate—is mitigated by the fact that eligible voters without photo identification may cast provisional ballots that will be counted if they execute the required affidavit at the circuit court clerk's office. Even assuming that the burden may not be justified as to a few voters, that conclusion is by no means sufficient to establish petitioners' right to the relief they seek.

The idea behind voter ID laws is the fear of voter fraud. Voter fraud—impersonation of a registered voter, duplicate voting, or fraudulent registration and or voting (including absentee voting)—that would be prevented by voter ids is extremely rare. Since 2015 (through November 2018), there have been a total of 75 convictions by individuals in the 50 states and the District of Columbia: 38 convictions for fraudulent registration or voting; 7 impersonations; and 30 duplicate voting convictions. There have been 38 ineligible votes cast either by felons or non-citizens, less than half were by noncitizens (15), which a valid id might have stopped from voting. The majority of voter fraud is conducted by invalid ballot petitions, altering vote counts, buying votes, or illegal assistance at the polls, which voter ids would not stop. There were roughly 130 million votes cast for the 2016 presidential election; 113 million votes cast for mid-term elections 2018. So, that is less than .00003% of the votes cast for those two elections (Heritage Foundation, 2019).

Since 2010, 25 states have made it harder to voter. Fifteen states have enacted strict photo ids requirements. Eleven states have laws that make it harder to register to vote, six states have shortened early voting days and hours, and three made it harder to restore voting rights for former felons (Brater et al., 2018).

Valid voter identification cards are supposedly to eliminate voter fraud, yet the number of persons committing voter fraud annually may be counted on one hand each. However, identification cards do not eliminate election fraud, such as the recent 2018 North Carolina House Congressional District 9 election, which had such ballot tampering that the vote was never certified, and the State Board of Elections in February 2019 called for a new election to be held. This then begs the question: Why the big push to have voter identification laws? Who does not have a valid Id? What are the impediments to get one?

In North Dakota, Native Americans who live on reservations, which normally do not have street addresses, had to get new voter identification cards that listed street address for the November 2018 general election since the Supreme Court did not overturn the North Dakota election law that required street addresses instead of post office boxes. Many saw this law as silencing the Native American vote, though its effect actually lead to a slight increase in Native American voters because tribal leaders worked hard to get identification with street addresses to voters.

Voter registration laws are decentralized, and thus vary from state to state, as per the Constitution. In the United States, citizens have to exercise their right to vote, and for some, that exercise starts 30 days prior to the actual election date when they have to formally register at the County Board of Elections. While some states now allow same-day election voter registration, most have prior registration requirements. The reasoning for prior registration is that it limits the possibility of voter fraud and political corruption, but in reality, this extra step is an obstacle to working people's ability to register, especially since most Boards of Elections are only open during business hours and are located in County Seats.

While Motor Voter—the National Voter Registration Act of 1993—made registration a bit easier, it is based on the assumption that most people have driver's licenses. As of 2014, only 69% of teenagers have their driver's licenses by the end of their teens—thus skewing the age of drivers upwards (Beck, 2016).

Voter registration in general is geared to the more educated and affluent citizen. Voter participation rates for all types of elections prove this out—voters tend to be better educated, affluent, whiter, and older than the general population. In order to boost voter turnout, there are proposals for universal suffrage, which is controversial and partisan; Democrats tend to favor this more than Republicans. Some states are implementing same-day registration, and others are adopting laws that automatically register voters. Early voting and voting by mail also increases voter participation.

College-age potential voters might not think government affects them and are not registered to vote; by the time they do get interested in an election, it may be too late to vote. Even with on-campus voting registration drives, college students might have problems. In Texas, students can use a gun permit to register to vote but not their student identification card. In Dutchess County, New York, students from three local colleges had to enlist the help of the New York State American Civil Liberties Union (ACLU) and file suit because the County Board of Elections denied their registrations because they did not list their dormitory rooms on their registrations only their college addresses. The students had looked up senior citizen residence registrations and discovered that the senior citizens did not list their apartment numbers on their registrations. (Pitcher v. Dutchess County Board of Elections, [S.D.N.Y.,

Case No. 12 CV 8017 (direct) 2012]). The county did not want the (transient) students to vote in the local races, in which they might have a greater impact; even though local laws affect students.

Other states have moved polling places off campuses to make the act of voting harder for students. When a proposal was made at the beginning of the 2019 Congress to make Election Day a federal holiday, Senator Mitch McConnell (R-Ky), Senate Majority Leader, called the proposed bill a "power grab" by the Democrats. In short, making voting easier would change the voting dynamics of those who keep the current Republican and Democrat politicians in office. The assumption is that new voters would be younger, poorer, and people of color, those who do not have the transportation or the free time to stand in lines to vote.

Voter Suppression

Voter Purges

The standard for cleaning up voter rolls comes from the 1993 National Voter Registration Act (aka Motor Voter Act). Yet, in the past five years (2013–2018), four states have conducted improper purges—Florida, New York, North Carolina, and Virginia. Voter roll purges take place under the seemingly good intention to clean up voter registration rolls from names of persons who have moved or are ineligible to vote. In 2000, the State of Florida Secretary of State Katherine Harris (R) removed the names of people who had names similar to those of felons, since former felons until the November 2019 ballot initiative passed, were disenfranchised. The scrubbed rolls removed over 57,000 names of which many were false positives (not the same person by way of birthdate, or other identifying traits); some election commissioners ignored the list, but in the end, over 1,000, 88%, persons of color were purged who should not have been (Greg Palast). Another purge took place when unforwardable postcards were mailed to addresses of military personnel stationed abroad.

Such purges do not only happen in Southern states. New York City rolls were cleaned up for the 2016 presidential elections. This process resulted in 200,000 names improperly being removed from the rolls, leaving people in Brooklyn unable to cast their votes according to the New York Attorney General (Brater et al., 2018).

Voter Challenging and Caging

Voter suppression can be as subtle as a poll inspector upon not finding one's name on the poll list to just shrug their shoulders and say you cannot vote today. They are legally supposed to hand you a paper ballot (also known as a provisional ballot) so you could vote, and then before the vote is certified, your eligibility to vote has been affirmed by the Board of Elections. This subtle voter suppression was documented in democratic heavy Ulster County New York, the republican Elections commissioner condoned this according to the Democratic Elections Commissioner (Dittus, 2018).

Voter suppression in more contested and uncontested parts of the country ranged from closing or moving polling places. For example, in 2018, Dodge City, Kansas, temporarily relocated its polling place outside of the city limits and to a location that was one mile from public transportation stops. In Upstate New York, one ward, with working- and lower-class residents, has had its polling place relocated to a location not accessible by public transportation. In North Carolina, in 2014, one-third of the early polling places were relocated, impacting black voters (Roth, 2015). In 2018, North Carolina also closed 20% of its early polling locations.

Another method of limiting voters is by not allowing voters to have absentee ballots without providing a justification or to reject absentee ballots. In North Carolina, absentee ballots have been illegally collected by a third party for the past two-year election cycles, and investigations into election fraud are ongoing since a number of absentee ballots were never returned to the Board of Elections. In Florida, there are reports of mail-in ballots not being received in time to mail them back, or as was the reported case of military personnel, not having their votes counted because they were returned too late and held at the post office distribution centers; this might just be attributed to incompetence, but in close races, absentee ballots might make the difference.

How ballots are actually designed are also a subject for misleading voters to cast votes erroneously or to miss voting for some candidates or propositions. Palm Beach County, Florida, was the home of the infamous hanging chad in 2000, which lead some Jewish voters to vote accidently for the candidate known for his anti-Semitism. In New York State, voters need to remember to turn over their ballots for some votes. Other ballots are designed such as the ones used in Broward County Florida in 2018, which lead 30,000 people voting in the gubernatorial race to overlook the senatorial race because that race was beneath a block of instructions in the middle of the ballot.

In some cases, there is also voter intimidation at the polling place, or incorrect or misleading information sent to voters regarding voting access. Voter intimidation ranges from challenges by poll workers regarding names and addresses on registration information (from New York to Hawaii) to flyers announcing Immigration and Customs Enforcement (ICE) Officers will be at polling stations in Milwaukee, Wisconsin (ICE does not patrol polling places). Incorrect polling information was sent to Allegheny, Pennsylvania voters by their Board of Elections, and while the information was subsequently corrected, other voters in other states were misinformed about deadlines for absentee ballots by political parties and candidates (Missouri, Montana, and New York).

Kansas Secretary of State Kris Kobach, known for his voter disenfranchisement practices, enforced a proof-of-citizenship law, which had been previously found unconstitutional. This resulted in 35,000 potential voters not registering, and thus, not voting (Ayala, 2018).

The ability to vote—to have the luxury of time to register to vote and to go to the polls (and stand in line, if necessary)—is important. Some states have been limiting the hours polls are open (Iowa, for example) or eliminating early voting; while other states, such as New York, are passing legislation to allow early voting. When legislation was proposed in early 2019 to make Election Day a federal holiday, Senate Majority Leader Mitch McConnell (R-Kentucky) called that a power grab by Democrats since it would encourage more Democrats to vote; this from the Senator from Kentucky where one out of four citizens are currently disenfranchised. Sandusky, Ohio, recently took the step to swap out Columbus Day as a paid holiday with Election Day, to encourage more voter turnout.

Felons

The right to vote is important as is who gets to vote. People with felony convictions are one group who have lost their right to vote, sometimes for life. With the increased rates of mass incarceration and to maintain private prison populations and other contracts (see Angela Davis' work, there is fear some states can criminalize and incarcerate as they deem necessary). Only two states allow incarcerated felons to vote—Maine and Vermont. In 21 states, persons with felonies who are currently incarcerated or on probation or parole are prohibited from voting. In 13 states, those convicted of felonies are permanently disenfranchised. Felon disenfranchisement disproportionally affects the black and Latino populations since these groups make up roughly 30% of the total American population, they also represent almost 60% of the prison population. Recently in the 2018 election, Floridian voters voted for Amendment Four, which reinstates voting rights to those formerly convicted of felonies (except for those convicted of sex crimes or violent crimes). Implementation of Amendment Four is being slow walked as the Republican officials do not have clear guidelines, and may fear that these 1.4 million, soon to be re-enfranchised voters, might vote as Democrats. New Mexico is also considering allowing felons to vote.

Other State Legislative Tactics

Closed v. Open Primaries

Another hurdle to voter participation is the difference between open (all registered voters may participate) and closed primaries. A closed primary only allows for those registered as members of that political party in which candidates are being primaried. With the trend toward registering to vote and not declaring a political party affiliation, closed primaries disenfranchise those not enrolled in a political party.

Redistricting and Gerrymandering

The Constitution requires a census every 10 years so that the state legislatures may be able to apportion congressional districts appropriately. The founders settled upon the Great Compromise—where representation was to be based on population. To appease the Southern states, who had a smaller population size than the Northern states, the population was counted by "adding the number of free Persons, including those bound for Service for a Term of Years, and excluding Indians not taxed, three fifths of all other Persons" (Article One Section 2). This formula in the Three-Fifths Compromise counted slaves as three-fifths a person, but it became moot in 1868 when the Thirteenth Amendment ended slavery.

The remnants of this counting to determine representation remains, though, when people in prison are counted as living in the district in which the prison is located and not in their home districts. Counting prisoners as residents of where they are imprisoned means that the people of that usually rural district get more representation and inflates their political influence; while the prisoner's preincarceration home district loses political influence. One also needs to be cognizant of the fact that prisoners do not remain in one facility for long stretches of time—they are moved around based on prison safety, crowding, and other circumstances. While this might not matter if the prisoner has a life sentence, due to the effects of mass incarceration (see Michelle Alexander's book *The New Jim Crow*, for example), this can be translated into a lack of political influence that affects funding and other policies—schools, infrastructure, job training—that might impact recidivism in their home districts. A few states, California, Delaware, New York, and Maryland, have passed laws that require prisoners to be counted in their home districts in the case of redrawing legislative districts.

When people are away for school or business, for instance, they are counted for the Census as if they were home, what the Census Bureau considers as their "usual residence" of where they live and sleep (which may not be the same as their voting residence or their legal residence). It should be noted that persons at boarding school or traveling on business tend to be of higher social and economic status than prisoners.

A similar group that has been miscounted previously are members of the armed forces. As of 2020, troops will be counted as being residents of wherever their home base is for the 2020 census, regardless of where they are deployed. This is different from the 2010 census, which counted the armed forces member's residence as where they first enlisted from, not where they were stationed. Districts around military bases will, thus, see an uptick in population count, and the political ramifications.

The Department of Commerce is the federal agency that oversees the Census. For the 2020 census, the agency wanted to add a citizenship question to the form, supposedly to address voter registration issues, yet voter registration is handled on the state level. The intent of adding this question was seen by many to be a way to intimate those residents, who are not citizens including undocumented aliens from participating, in the Census. Nonparticipation would result not only in an undercounting of people residing in the United States, but also would impact funding and public service delivery. The Department of Commerce v. New York (Docket 18-966, 2019) deemed that, while agencies may have both stated and unstated reasons for their decisions including policy preferences that are in line with their administration's policies, the reason stated for adding this question appear contrived, arbitrary, and capricious, but at the same time, the court ruled that adding such a question is permissible.

It is the state legislatures that take the information from the Census and draws congressional and state districts, counting the number of residents so that each district has approximately 711,000 persons per representative. In 1913, Congress set the number of representatives to 435 (each state has two senators). Gerrymandering is reapportionment of voters to give an unfair advantage to a particular political party or racial or ethnic group. The lawmakers in the state legislatures, who draw the districts, also benefit themselves, so they have little incentive, especially if their party holds the power in the statehouse, to change. Partisan gerrymandering is counter to a democratic republic in so much as the power to draw districts gives politicians the ability to choose their voters, instead of the voters choosing them.

The Supreme Court in 2017 sidestepped two partisan gerrymandering cases—Wisconsin (Republican) and Maryland (Democrat). Justice Kagan has pointed out that with mapping technology improving, partisan gerrymandering will get worse. Extreme partisan gerrymandering might be seen as punishment for voters' past political allegiances, if so, this would violate the First Amendment. North Carolina is home to one of the most gerrymandered districts. The Republican-controlled State House of Representatives redrew their district map in 2011 so that the Republicans held 10 out of the 13 congressional districts. One of the map drawers said it was only 10, because they could not figure out a way to advantage the Republicans in 11 districts. North Carolina's 12th congressional district holds the title for the most gerrymandered. Gerrymandering can dilute a voter's impact because it may keep all one party's voters in check. The two gerrymandering cases that the Supreme Court decided in June 2019 actually state that the Constitution does not bar partisan gerrymandering that favor one party over another, and that it is beyond the reach of federal courts to decide partisan election maps (Rucho v.

Common Cause, Docket No. 18-422; Lamone v. Benisek, 585 U.S. ___ [2019] and Benisek v. Lamone, 588 U.S. ____ [2019]). These decisions are counter to the decision in Bethune-Hill v. Virginia Board of Elections, 580 U.S. _____ (2019), which found that it was impermissible to use race to create state legislative districts.

Civic Republicanism

Attending neighborhood and local public meetings and hearings are important forms of civic engagement. The public needs access to information about these meetings, and if the notification means are still public notices published in print newspapers, we have a big problem This was a problem 40 years ago when people still subscribed to newspapers, and still did not read the public and legal notices usually printed in small type fonts at the back of the paper. Most municipalities still require the publication of public notices (usually twice over a period of days prior to the hearing), plus the posting of such notice in a public building (the bulletin board in town hall) (Myers, 1980; Einstein et al., 2018). It is more of a problem today with newspaper circulation dwindling. Besides knowing about the upcoming meetings, this form of engagement requires both the free time and the ability to engage. Public meetings and hearings are usually scheduled for evenings, which limit attendance. People who work evenings, people with children, people with long commutes, and those unable to drive in the evenings have limited participation. Another limiting factor is the ability to participate, to fully understand the implications, and/or the technological and complicated plans and processes.

It should come as no surprise that the poor and working-class people, women, and people of color tend to participate less in public affairs, including public decision-making, and therefore do not have their needs and interests represented (Mansbridge, 1980). Amy Gutmann (1980) found that participatory democracy silences disadvantage groups as it preferences white middle-class men's authority. Her work looks at how there was an increase in school segregation because white affluent voices were heard over those of the minority groups. In short, existing oppressions get reproduced and reinforced. Almost 40 years later, a study of public participation in public hearings around zoning and housing development in the Boston area found that the people who attended and spoke at the meetings and hearings still did not represent the community. Most of the participants tended to be male, older voters, long-time residents, and homeowners. While women were 51% of the community, at the meetings, they only spoke 43% of the time (Einstein et al., 2018). The people who attend and engage at public hearings not only are unrepresentative of the community, but were more likely to be socioeconomically advantaged as per the updated work of Sidney Verba (Scholtzman et al., 2012). Einstein et al. (2018) also noted that these participants were likely to attend multiple meetings, to be informed, and to engage the expertise of lawyers and engineers to converse with politicians on an even playing field.

Jury Duty

In *Democracy in America* (1835), Alexis de Tocqueville wrote that serving on a jury and deliberating was a civic duty and a means of civic education, for it was the "most efficacious means for the education of the people which society can employ" (p. 337). The Supreme Court decision in Powers v. Ohio, 499 U.S. 400 (1991) reiterated the right and Tocqueville's main reason for citizens to serve on juries: civic education and responsibility. Besides voting, serving on a jury is one of the only other rights and responsibilities reserved to only citizens. Yet many citizens begrudge this civic responsibility, viewing it as a tedious obligation. While we are guaranteed a jury of our peers, who gets to serve on a jury is a process where the jury pool is selected from community members. Jury lists are compiled using public records: driver licenses or voter registration. From these lists, the jury pool is randomly selected to complete a qualification form. To further qualify, you must be 18 years or older, a citizen, have resided in the judicial district for at least one year, be adequately proficient in English to complete the juror qualification form, have no disqualifying mental or physical impairments, not be currently subject to felony charges that are punishable by a year or more in prison, and never have been convicted of a felony (the exception is if your rights have been legally restored). While other groups have been exempted previously, (teachers, women) currently there are only three groups exempt from jury duty: active military, fire and police officers, and local, state, and federal public officials. Some states such as Massachusetts will also excuse primary caregivers to a permanently disabled person because that person would be at risk if the caregiver were out of the home for jury duty. And, from that pool, lawyers from both sides of a case can through *voir dire* challenge the fitness of a potential jury member either for cause or using their peremptory challenge without stating a reason.

Until 1979, less than 15% of juries included women. The Supreme Court case Duren v. Missouri, 439 U.S. 357 (1979) found unconstitutional laws and judicial practices that exempted women from jury duty based solely on their sex. The Court found excluding women from jury pools violated the "fair cross section" of the community, a jury of one's peers, requirement of the Sixth Amendment.

Is the Systemic Underrepresentation of Minorities Unconstitutional?

In the case of State of Iowa v. Peter Veal 2018, the Iowa Supreme Court, while conditionally upholding his conviction for first-degree murder and attempted murder, has remanded his case to the district court since he claims a Sixth Amendment violation, saying there were not enough persons of color in his jury; thus, he was not tried by a jury of his peers. The jury pool numbers of the two panels combined were four African Americans out of the 157 members of the jury pool (Trial Transcript Vol. 2, pp. 12–13). The defense objected to this new jury pool on the same grounds as the first jury pool, but the trial court found that the deviation of percentage of African Americans in the jury pool from the percentage of African Americans in the Webster County population was acceptable. The Sixth Amendment is the right to an impartial jury and it entitles the criminally accused to a jury drawn from a fair cross section of the community. In this case, the jury pool was pulled from both the voter registration list and drivers licenses issued in Webster County, Iowa. African Americans only make up 5.5% of Webster County's population, due to felony convictions, 32% of the voter list and 27% of the driver's license list were excluded from serving on the jury. The jury pool, even after a second empanelment, was only 1% African American. Veal's claim is that his Sixth Amendment rights were violated by this low number of potential jurors.

In the Supreme Court case of Flowers v. Mississippi, 588 U.S. ____ decided 21 June (2019) in which a white prosecutor had intentionally kept black people off of a black man's (six!) trials for murdering four persons, in a 7–2 decision, Justice Kavanaugh wrote for the majority stating that the prosecutor had ignored one of the Constitution's basic guidelines: "Equal justice under the law requires a criminal trial free of racial discrimination in the jury selection process."

Protests

Another form of political participation is via lobbying legislators and protesting. Both have inherent costs and risks. One needs the time to lobby, the money to travel if one is lobbying a state legislator or a federal one, and depending on the issue, the social and political risk of outing one's self as a undocumented immigrant, poor, a domestic worker, anti-war, or (fill-in-the-blank). Lobbying may take the form of some form of contact with a government official or legislator to make your needs and position known, before they make a decision, or proscribe a policy or law. It may be as simple as a postcard, e-mail, or phone call; it may be as personal as having a face-to-face meeting or speaking up at a public hearing. Protests are a more intense form of lobbying—the protest might be silent symbolic gestures and signs or taking over legislative offices to make a point. The most recent 2017–2018 proposed Congressional votes to repeal and replace the Affordable Care Act (also known as Obamacare) had persons with preexisting conditions actively advocating and protesting at district legislative offices and in the halls of the Capitol. For these lobbyists and these protesters, their access to affordable and adequate health care made them effective and sympathetic one issue protestors. The evening news showed pictures of persons in wheelchairs being forcibly removed from hearing rooms and offices, even as they were being called a mob by the opposing side in order to discredit them.

Social and political movements have become a slow, but staple tool for redressing institutional and political wrongs, gaining a foothold in conventional politics, and to affect change—or maintain the status quo, In short, political movements have become a form of political participation for those who are enfranchised and the disenfranchised. As Barrington Moore noted, some people "put up with being victims of their societies and…at other times they become very angry and try with passion and forcefulness to do something about their situation" (1978). From the Black Civil Rights movement to the Black Lives Matter movement, from Woman's Suffrage to the "Me Too" movement, from the labor movements to Occupy Wall Street (and beyond), there have been many movements by those who have felt that they were not full citizens, who were and are subjugated by the political and power elites.

Just looking at how society, the media, and the governmental institutions react or in the silence, the social and political movements allow us to see how people might be marked as less than other citizens who are part of the status quo. In the 1950s and early 1960s, fire hoses and dogs were turned on Civil Rights protestors seeking the right to the ballot box and the end to segregation. Martin Luther King Jr.'s (1963) Letter from a Birmingham Jail addressed to his fellow clergy who called his protests "unwise and untimely" were themselves overlooking the injustices which brought about the protests. The protestors were called un-American, unruly mobs, and/or were thrown in jail, even though dissent is constitutional. Even after they have seemingly seen political success—such as the Civil Rights movement achieving both the Voting Rights Act and the Civil Rights Act—there is still societal and political institutional oppression. In this case, what Michelle Alexander calls the New Jim Crow, which is the prison industrial complex (Angela Davis) that maintains itself via the war on drugs that target black men.

The politics of the bureaucracy just to hold a parade or protest is daunting to those who are politically savvy, and for those who are not, navigating the permits and costs are prohibitive. The Occupy Wall Street movement started in a private park that did not have a curfew, yet they could not get permits for port-o-johns or sound equipment.

As this is being written, over 20 states are writing anti-protest legislation—from making it a form of "economic terrorism" to block traffic to eliminating liability for deaths or injuries caused by police or others trying to disperse protestors. Eight pieces of anti-protest legislation passed in North Carolina, North Dakota, South Dakota, Oklahoma, and Tennessee from heightened penalties to charges of criminal trespass if near "critical infrastructure" to prohibitions from covering any part of one's face while protesting. The language in these pieces of legislation, some proposed by American Legislative Exchange Council (ALEC),[2] are chilling—from the use of variations of the term terrorism to weaponizing free speech on campus.[3] The effect these laws have on the First Amendment rights from free speech, to the right to assembly, to the right to dissent, especially when the protests are peaceful, are chilling. One of our myths is that we were founded as a country in protest; the Boston Tea Party was an action against taxation without representation. One only has to think of the candlelight vigil in Ferguson, Missouri, after Michael Brown's death, and these peaceful marchers being met by police in full riot gear to realize the lack of privilege that some groups have.

The Flip Side

The other side of this is to see who does have access to influence elections and legislation. The abundance of monies in campaigns courtesy of the lack of campaign finance reform, coupled with the Citizens United v. Federal Election Commission, 558 U.S. 310 (2010) that equated campaign contributions as a form of protected political speech under of First Amendment, allow for candidates to reach more potential voters, impact voter turnout, and influence candidate's campaigns. Equating money as a form of political speech comparable to the free speech or even the individual contributions to campaigns by individual voters is seen as disingenuous by many. What Citizens United did was extinguish the difference between express advocacy and electioneering. Prior to the Supreme Court decision, corporations were limited by the Internal Revenue code that said 527 organizations were for social welfare purposes and, as such, could not spend their money advocating for one candidate over another, nor could they use a candidate's name within 60 days of an election in a sponsored advertisement. Corporations were already considered persons as per the Santa Clara County v. Southern Pacific Railroad Company, 118 U.S. 394 (1886) decision's headnote (written by the court reporter), which succinctly stated that corporations as "persons" are entitled to the same equal protection rights as individuals. Citizens United extended political speech as falling within this concept of corporate personhood. Corporations can also hold moral and religious opinions. The Hobby Lobby decision—Burwell v. Hobby Lobby, 573 U.S. ___ (2014)—gave closely held for-profit and not-for-profit corporations religious and moral exemptions from legislation they objected to, in this case, extending birth control to their employees under their health insurance policies.

The use of Political Action Committees (PAC) as a major source of campaign funding, enabling some candidates to build up campaign war chests that, literally, can drown out their opponents' messages. The new use of social media by all political actors also helps to focus potential voters on issues and candidates.

Once a candidate is in office, not only does name recognition help keep them in office, but they are lobbied by groups that point to their memberships as a source of potential votes. The American Medical Association, National Rifle Association, and American Israeli Public Affairs Committee are just three of the top PACS that use their clout to impact legislators and legislation. ALEC works to promote corporate legislative interests to legislatures on the state and federal level. ALEC, in short, presents model bills to legislators that promote the interests of corporations over that of workers and the public interest.

It should be noted that this is not really new—the federal government had used private corporations to provide for the public interest when the federal government did not have the funds to, for instance, build the canal system or railroads. The federal government gave land to the corporations to undertake these endeavors, and also used their legislative powers to help make the canals and railroads profitable.

Summary

The upshot is that the opinions of those who have the time and ability to participate perpetuate the inequality and submerge the needs of those who might also want to participate but, for circumstances from work to family to life, do not have the ability to do so. Women, people of color, and the poor are impacted by the costs of obtaining identification to vote, along with the unseen costs of voting—transportation to the polls, the time in lines, and the time missing from work. While some people may say this is just the cost of being able to participate in democracy, these costs are unfairly burdening those who are not privileged. Simply put, the least amount of voting restrictions yields higher voter turnout and thus the voices of all.

A plank from the 2012 platform of the Republican Party of Texas which, reads as follows:

> We oppose the teaching of Higher Order Thinking Skills (HOTS) (values clarification), critical-thinking skills and similar programs that are simply a relabeling of Outcome-Based Education (OBE) (mastery learning), which focus on behavior modification and have the purpose of challenging the student's fixed beliefs and undermining parental authority.

Education also affects future employment, and if one does not have the luxury of time to engage in the public sharing of ideas, what is that impact?

Who gets to impact the political decision-making process is important, and who has full political agency is a mark of who we consider to be worthy citizens. Who gets to act in the public sphere to cast a vote, have their voices heard at a public hearing, deliberate as a jury, or even protest is part of the privilege of being acknowledged as a full citizen.

While, it might be welcomed by those in power to have a docile and obedient citizenry, democracy is not stagnant, it is messy and it is aspirational. As John Mills advocated in *On Liberty* (1869), silencing and suppressing opinions is counter to progress, hearing all opinions allows truth to be understood, without all voices heard what is left is "the dogma becoming a mere formal profession, inefficacious for good" (Ch. 2, par 44).

Notes

1 Hayes, Chris (25 June 2019) Twitter @chrislhayes, 11:21 p.m.
2 www.alec.org/model-policy/critical-infrastructure-protection-act/
3 drive.google.com/file/d/1wUs1BV7EVS4rbG-3UBFxsm5ZSlRIFa36/view

References

Alexander, Michelle (2012) *The New Jim Crow*. New York: The New Press.

Arendt, Hannah and Margaret Canovon (1999) *The Human Condition*, 2nd ed. Chicago, IL: University of Chicago Press.

Ayala, Rebecca (5 November 2018) "Voting Problems-2018." Accessed 5 November 2018, www.brennancenter.org/blog/voting-problems-2018.

Beck, Julie (22 January 2016) "The Decline of the Drivers License." *The Atlantic*. www.theatlantic.com/technology/archive/2016/01/the-decline-of-the-drivers-license/425169/.

Bee, Vanessa A. and Oren Nimni (17 June 2018) "There Is No Right to Vote." *Current Affairs*. Accessed 2 January 2019, www.currentaffairs.org/2018/06/there-is-no-right-to-vote/.

Berelson, Bernard R., Paul F. Lazarsfeld and William N. McPhee (1954) *Voting*. Chicago, IL: University of Chicago Press.

Berry, Jeffery M., Kent E. Portney and Ken Thomson (1993) *The Rebirth of American Democracy*. Washington, DC: Brookings Institute Press.

Brater, Jonathan, Kevin Morris, Myrna Perez and Christopher Delucio (2018) "Purges: A Growing Threat to the Right to Vote." New York: Brennan Center for Justice New York University School of Law. Accessed 2 January 2019, https://www.brennancenter.org/publication/purges-growing-threat-right-vote#Embed.

Burwell v. Hobby Lobby, 573 U.S. ___ (2014).

Constitution of the United States (1787) Accessed 2 January 2019, www.archives.gov/founding-docs/constitution.

Crawford v. Marion County Election Board, 9553 U.S. 181 (2008).

Dahl, Robert (1961) *Who Governs? Power in an American City*. New Haven, CT: Yale University Press.

Davis, Angela (2000) *The Prison Industrial Complex*. Oakland, CA: AK Press.

Dittus, Ashely, Commissioner of Elections, Ulster County NY in conversation 20 November 2018.

Einstein, Catherine L., Maxwell Palmer and David Glick (2018) "Who Participates in Local Government, Evidence from Meeting Minutes." *Perspectives on Politics* 17 (1): 28–96. Accessed 15 December 2018, www.cambridge.org/core/journals/perspectives-on-politics/article/who-participates-in-local-government-evidence-from-meeting-minutes/C6505940E607B6392C4A8F53A9363DB1.

Ferguson, Andrew G. (3 May 2013) "The Joy of Jury Duty." *The Atlantic*. Accessed 2 January 2019, www.theatlantic.com/national/archive/2013/05/the-joy-of-jury-duty/275444/.

Flowers v. Mississippi, 588 U.S. _____ (2019).

Gilens, Martin and Benjamin I. Page (2014) "Testing Theories of American Politics: Elites, Interest Groups and Average Citizens." *Perspectives in Politics* 12 (3): 564–581.

Gutmann, Amy (1980) *Liberal Equality*. New York: Cambridge University Press.

Gutmann, Amy and Dennis Thompson (2004). *Why Deliberative Democracy?* Princeton, NJ: Princeton University.

Heritage Foundation (2019) "Voter Fraud Map Page." Accessed 2 January 2019, https://www.heritage.org/voterfraud.

Howitz, Sally (23 March 2016) "Getting a Photo ID to Vote Is Easy: Unless You're Poor, Black Latino or Elderly." *The Washington Post*, Accessed 23 March 2016, https://www.washingtonpost.com/politics/courts_law/getting-a-photo-id-so-you-can-vote-is-easy-unless-youre-poor-black-latino-or-elderly/2016/05/23/8d5474ec-20f0-11e6-8690-f14ca9de2972_story.html?utm_term=.3a3dafe84d7e.

Ingraham, Christopher (22 October 2018) "Low Voter Turnout Is No Accident, According to a Ranking of the Ease of Voting in All 50 States." *The Washington Post*. www.washingtonpost.com/business/2018/10/22/low-voter-turnout-is-no-accident-according-ranking-ease-voting-all-states/?utm_term=.09430b829a19.

Keyssar, Alexander (2000) *The Right to Vote: The Contested History of Democracy in the United States.* New York: Basic Books.

Kimmett, Colleen (28 August 2015) "10 Years After Katrina, New Orleans' All-Charter School System Has Proven a Failure." *In These Times*.

King, Martin Luther (Jr.) (16 April 1963) "Letter from a Birmingham Jail." Accessed 2 January 2019, www.africa.upenn.edu/Articles_Gen/Letter_Birmingham.html.

Mansbridge, Jane (1980) *Beyond Adversary.* New York: Basic Books.

Mill, John Stuart (1869) *On Liberty*. Accessed 5 May 2019, www.utilitarianism.com/ol/two.html.

Moore, Barrington (1978) *Injustice: The Social Bases of Obedience and Revolt.* London, UK: Palgrave Macmillan.

Myers, JoAnne (1980) *Public Policy Communication*. Troy, NY: Rensselaer Polytechnic Institute.

The New York Times (2018) "Mid-Term Election Voter Turnout and Photo Ids." Accessed 2 January 2019, www.nytimes.com/interactive/2018/10/05/opinion/midterm-election-voter-turnout-photo-id.htm.

Palast, Greg (January 18, 2001) "Florida's Disappeared Voters: August Disenfranchised by the GOP." Accessed 20 August 2019, www.thenation.org/article/floridas-disappeared-voters-disengranched-GOP/.

Pew Charitable Trust (2017) *Why Are Millions of Citizens Not Registered to Vote?* Philadelphia, PA: A Chartbook from Pew Charitable Trusts.

Pitcher v. Dutchess County Board of Elections [S.D.N.Y., Case No. 12 CV 8017 (direct) 2012].

Republican Party of Texas (2012) "2012 Republican Party of Texas Report of Platform Committee and Rules Committee." Accessed 2 January 2019, www.empowertexans.com/wp-content/uploads/2012/07/2012-GOP-Platform-Final.pdf.

Roth, Jonathan (23 November 2015) "Study: North Carolina Polling Site Changes Hurts Blacks." Accessed 2 January 2019, http://www.msnbc.com/msnbc/study-north-carolina-polling-site-changes-hurt-blacks.

Santa Clara County v. Southern Pacific Railroad Company, 118 U.S. 394 (1886).

Scholtzman, Kay, Sidney Verba and Henry Brady (2012) *The Unheavenly Chorus: Unequal Political Voice and the Broken Promise of American Democracy.* Princeton, NJ: Princeton University Press.

Shelby v. Holder, 570 U.S. 529 (2013).

Tocqueville, de Alexis ([1835] 2004) *Democracy in America.* Arthur Goldhammer (trans). New York: Library of America.

Tomasky, Michael (8 November 2018) "Fighting to Vote." *The New York Review of Books*. Accessed 8 November 2018, https://www.nybooks.com/articles/2018/11/08/fighting-to-vote/#fnr-1.

Verba, Sidney and Norman Nie (1972) *Participation in America*. New York: Harper and Row.

Voting Rights Act, 79 Stat. 437, 1965.

7

THE PRODUCTIVE CITIZEN

Liberal economic theory, known as Capitalism in the vernacular, and citizenship are seemingly interdependent: individual initiative and individual rights allows for a supposed malleable, mobile socio-economic class structure and, thus, the equality of opportunity for citizens.

Reality strips away the assumptions that we all have equal economic rights and the social mobility that assumes. Capitalism trumps equality. But as Thucydides said, we can and do punish the poor and the weak for being poor and weak. We favor the wealthy, as being strong and authority figures. Or, as Martin Luther King, Jr. (1964) put it: "We all too often have socialism for the rich and rugged free market capitalism for the poor." As Justice Louis Brandeis supposedly said, as per Ralph Nader (2000),[1] "We can have a democracy or we can have great wealth in the hands of a comparative few, but we cannot have both." The critical thinkers of capitalism, from Marx to Max Weber (1930) to Habermas (1973) and beyond, all explore the tensions between capitalism and democracy. Weber questioned: "How can democracy and freedom be maintained in the long run under the dominance of advanced capitalism?" Habermas, in his analysis of advanced capitalism, noted the concentration of wealth in just a few industries (which today we can expand to a concentration of wealth in just a few persons), the use of the state to both stabilize the economic swings and legitimized economic activities, along with nominal wage increases to placate the dissatisfied workers. We can see the manifestation of this with both the government's bailout of the banks, which were deemed too big to fail, in the financial and mortgage crisis of 2008 and the 2011 Occupy Wall Street Movement (OWS), which popularized the phrase "We are the 99%," encouraging many fast-food workers and other minimum-wage workers to organize, slowly given rise to minimum wage increases.

Democracy is seen as the engine of the neoliberal free market, and the demos as civil society working only to serve its neoliberal master. This chapter explores how we have come to worship only wealth as productivity, paid employment, or inherited wealth becoming the measure of a good citizen.

We measure the wealth of nations (Smith, 1776) by the productivity of its people (GDP). Ever since Adam Smith defined the wealth of nations as the measure of the gross national product (GNP), paid employment connects citizenship with the direct contribution that citizen makes to the GNP (see Pateman, 1989, p. 184). That the amount of a citizen's contribution to the GNP was a measure of one's worth was practiced, for instance, in the amount of compensation that a family received after the 11 September tragedy—the calculation was based on the deceased person's yearly income times their working life expectancy. Thus, a stockbroker's or a lawyer's family was compensated much more than a secretary's or a paralegal's family was, and undocumented workers, such as a deli delivery person's family, went uncompensated. That women earn less than men for the same job 41 years after the Equal Pay Act was passed is well-documented—(white) women earn 74 cents to the male dollar,[2] and wages drop in fields that become predominantly female, such as family medical practioners. Unpaid work, such as caregiver to family members (children, disabled, and elderly), or volunteer work has been invisible in the GNP, and not valued, yet invaluable. While most measurements of production are measured on paid labor, productivity stands on the backs of unpaid labor. Unpaid labor includes child and elder care, yard (including maintaining small gardens) and housework, and volunteer work in the community—in the church or school, in the neighborhood—that helps to maintain civil society. Domestic work outside the home, until recently, was invisible. Laundry and farm workers were at first excluded from social security, legally, and many domestic workers, nannies and housekeepers, are excluded illegally. Food production relies on underpaid migrant farm workers and, invisible to most, food factory workers.

As Stevens noted in 2009, a contemporary form of feudalism supports the production of capitalism. This chapter will then look at the following three aspects of production—who we value in a capitalist society; minimum wage versus living wages; and the criminalization of poverty.

Hannah Arendt ([1958] 1999) said that we are a society of laborers who define ourselves by our jobs. Since we identify and value ourselves (and others) by our jobs and positions—plumbers are seen as working class though they make more per hour than the average lawyer, yet society values lawyers more than plumbers (until a pipe bursts or a toilet clogs). We relegate everything else as that might fully describe us as subordinate to our jobs. We work as a means of living, as a means of earning material consumables. Thus, we are what we do to earn a living, not as we are in community. Stiglitz (2012) takes this further, we are valued by our earnings: "Those with higher productivities earned higher incomes that reflected their greater contributions to society. Competitive markets, through the laws of supply and demand, determine the value of each individual's contributions" (p. 30).

The successful citizen is measured by what they are worth—or appear to be worth—courtesy of credit cards, school loans, and mortgages. We live in a material world. We do not question whether the money is earned or inherited; or luck, as the lottery commercials blare: all you need is a dollar and a dream. Research has shown that citizens, born and naturalized, have better economic opportunities available. But in truth, our laws and policies are meant to keep wealth sequestered and accessible only to the already wealthy.

We must travel back to John Locke's fifth chapter "Of Property" in *The Second Treatise on Government*. Here, we find Locke's definition of the individual in Section 27: "...yet everyman has a property in his own person; this nobody has any right to but himself." This clause has become a working definition of who may be a citizen—an individual. But Locke goes further in this chapter, describing labor and property, at first writing that one needs to mix one's own labor with what one is producing. "The labor of his body and the work of his hands, we may say, are properly his" (Section 27). But Locke realizes that property ownership and labor are not always the same thing. He further writes about the ability to accumulate more than one can use during his discussion of the accumulation of the fruits of the earth—the necessities of life—until they spoil (section 31). This problem is solved with the invention of money—the gold and silver, that does not spoil, yet does not sustain life unless from the consent of man we give it value (Section 50)—and develops the basic theory of unfettered capitalism. C.B. Macpherson (1962) writes that there is then a class difference that must exist between the property owners—the capitalists—and the laborers. In this economic relationship, these differences become an economic battle of the wills, where the property rights (ownership) are seen as economic gain, and those with the most do not have to subject themselves to the will of others. Macpherson calls this "Possessive Individualism," the economic freedom that humans in society crave. Wolin (2016) notes that Locke's articulation of individual, property, and rights, leads to the purpose of government: to protect the individual's property and rights, for all intents and purposes, this is considered to be the articulation of classical liberalism (p. 263). Laws, policies, and court decisions protect those with means and allows them to thrive and keeps those without means struggling.

Before the Depression, people who could not work relied on their families and charity to get by, the role of government was limited. The majority of Americans were Protestant, and during the period of the Second Great Awakening (1790–1840s), Protestant sects moved away from the stricter, puritanical Calvinist teachings and beliefs toward accepting human free will (the concept of individualism) and social reform. The strict Calvinist teachings had already become American catchphrases: "Cleanliness is next to Godliness"; "Work Hard to get ahead"; "God helps those who help themselves." These religious concepts along with the individualistic nature of self-reliance (autonomy) and America being the land of opportunity translated into viewing people living in poverty as immoral, lazy, and lacking a strong work ethic.

Tocqueville observed that Americans succumb to an excessive "passion for material well being" and that our culture promoted acquiring such. He continues to say that this might imperil democracy because those duties necessary to maintain democracy, such as political participation will be seen as burdensome, especially if they deflect energy and time from private economic activity. He goes on to state that in an aristocracy people are habituated to poverty, they do not aspire to material well-being because they do not think they can acquire wealth (Tocqueville, 2004, pp. 506–507). Today, this has changed, but the key is that those who aspire to wealth, yet suffer from income inequality, believe in meritocracy. The belief in those who deserve to have material wealth merit such, blinds all to structures that maintain the system. Mijs (2019) writes that those who this inequality impacts the most, do not see it because they are living and working in their milieu; thus, "they do not see the full extent of inequality in their society, nor develop an awareness of the structural processes shaping unequal life outcomes." Coupled with the strong belief in, and the popularity of, the meritocracy (p. 23) most people do not see the structural and institutional biases that lock inequality in place.

The idea that people rise to the top—economically, politically, socially—based on merit, allows us to view those who do not achieve "success" to be viewed as less than. The belief in society's meritocracy, that economic goods and political power are awarded to those with talent and to those who make the effort to achieve, hide the structural and institutional processes that maintain society. The rest of the chapter tries to articulate some of those processes that work to maintain economic inequality.

The Wealthy versus Workers

So, today we have unfettered capitalism in which the top three men,[3] on the 2018 Forbes 400 list, owned more wealth combined than the poorest half of Americans combined. The type of wealth these men, and others like them, hold is vastly different from the rest of the population. Their wealth is made of assets in stocks and mutual funds, or what Joseph Stiglitz (2012) calls rent seeking—making money off of money, rather than laboring to earn money. The rest of Americans are wage earners, and for most, their greatest asset is their home. The Census Bureau's data show the median net worth of the average white family at $132,000, Latino families have an average net worth of $12,000 just slightly higher than the African American family, which is the lowest at $9,000. The majority of these families are living paycheck to paycheck.

According to the Federal Reserve Board's *Report on the Economic Well-Being of U.S. Households* in 2017, released May 2018, 40% of adults could not cover a $400 emergency expense (this, though, is a 10% improvement since 2013). Still shocking is a quarter of the people report putting off or skipping medical care that they cannot afford (even those with health insurance experience medical bankruptcies).

Unfettered capitalism, which in today's world, allows for (the median) CEOs to make slightly more than 300 times their average (full-time) worker (Economic Policy Institute). Or in numbers, the median pay of a CEO is roughly $11,900,000 in 2017, of which in publicly traded corporations roughly 48% of that compensation is in stock. The idea behind this form of compensation is to tie the CEO's compensation to the company's performance. This leads to short-sightedness. The CEO can order layoffs and then rehire workers as contract workers at their same salary, which in reality, allows for the company to save up to 30%,[4] which they were paying in benefits, and shifts that burden to the now contract employee. The contract workers, who still have their jobs, are now responsible for their social security, health insurance, etc.; thus, their actual monies earned are diminished. The stock of said company goes up because labor costs have declined by 30%.

The idea of a corporation focusing solely on its core competencies has led to many companies and government agencies to contract out janitorial services and such. Contracting out such services allows the company/agency to focus on its main mission, but in doing so, puts the contract service worker at a disadvantage. For instance, the contracted janitor is usually an hourly (minimum) wage worker with little to no benefits, sick, or vacation leave offered from their company. In the case of government shutdowns, such as the one experienced over the Christmas/New Year's holidays 2018–2019, these workers along with the federal workers who are furloughed or working without pay. The difference between the two workers is, that once government resumes, the federal workers usually are recompensed retrospectively. The minimum-wage janitor, if s/he is not reassigned another job, is without a paycheck.

Hegel noted that unfettered markets lead to poverty, and it should be the state's role to prevent this. One such intervention would be via minimum wage, but the arguments against such basically have stagnated the federal minimum wage. For most people, working minimum wage and missing a paycheck is catastrophic since minimum wage is not a living wage; federal minimum wage is $7.25 as of 2019. A few states and municipalities have minimum wages that are higher—from Upstate New York's wage of $12.75/hour to Seattle and San Francisco's minimum wage of $15/hour. According to the *New York Times* (23 December 2018), a family earning $113,000 per year is considered low-income in San Francisco. (The median US household income in 2017 was $61,372.)

A living wage is calculated at $16.07 before taxes for a family of four. The ability to afford basic necessities such as food, childcare, health care, housing, and transportation varies based on geography. Housing and childcare costs are roughly 20% each of a household's take home (after taxes) pay. According to Nadeau and Glasmeier (2018), a single-parent household with two children earning the current federal minimum wage needs to basically work 138 hours per week to subsist; a two-parent family needs each adult to work 76 hours per weeks at minimum wage (Nadeau and Glasmeier, 2018).

The Federal Reserve Board report also noted that 30% of workers have variable monthly income, and this is not due to self-employment in the computer or internet-driven gig economy, but in such jobs as childcare and house cleaning, and now transporting others. Roughly 16% of workers work irregular schedules imposed upon them by their employers, some receiving their schedules less than a week in advance—this impacts planning for childcare and transportation.

The Foundation for Economic Education argues against minimum wage using Locke's concept of the individual owning his own labor. Their argument that maybe the seller of the (unskilled) labor would be better off selling their labor under the minimum wage so that they have a job, and they might want to take a second job to learn other skills (Mullen, 2018). This argument overlooks the true product of labor: profit. For example, in the early 1990s, IBM, which had based its computer empire on large mainframe computers, was economically floundering. The computing world was that of the personal computer (PC). IBM, in order to right its ship, laid off a large number of employees, hired them back as contract workers at the same salary, minus the benefits package and its ensuing cost (roughly thirty plus percent) (or they shipped the jobs to cheaper areas or offshore). Almost immediately the company's profits were reflected in their stock increases. Corporations are after all in business to make a profit.

Meanwhile, those now contract workers realized that they had lost in the transaction—they had to fund their own social security, health care, etc. from their salaries. This same model holds true when the public is used to augment workers' salaries, such as those minimum-wage workers at Walmart or Amazon, who need food stamps and other subsidies to exist. One report figured that American taxpayers underwrite the six-member Walton Family profits to a tune of $6.3 billion per year. The Waltons continue to reap the profit, as a family they sit at number one on the Fortune 500 list, and own more wealth than 43% of Americans. The 12,000 Walmart stores employ 1.5 million workers and have an annual revenue of $500.3 billion. So, if the six Waltons were laboring for their profit share, they would be doing so at roughly $1.56 million per hour. Even at $9 per hour, Walmart workers are limited to 34 hours per week (which Walmart considers full-time), which is less than $16,000 per year.

Another fallacy is that there is job mobility, or that people can just move to where there are better paying or more abundant job opportunities. Yes, there are jobs. Barbara Ehrenreich (2001), in her book *Nickeled and Dimed*, described the cost to move, live, and work minimum-wage jobs as a single person, and it is much harder if you have a family, children in school, and a partner who cannot easily uproot, or other family members who rely on you.

If only those who are poor worked harder, they could succeed. We blame the poor for their circumstances and do not look at the structural constraints that lock people in place. We are sold on the myths of Horatio Alger stories, but those rags to riches, and hard work with a good moral character everyone can grow up to be president or a founder of a technology company without needing a college education are myths. While there are exceptions to the rule, the idea that everyone can pick oneself up by one's own bootstraps is not only a physical impossibility, but a way to not extend the institutional tools necessary to all to be able to accomplish the impossible. These tools range from social security/welfare, nutrition to healthcare, from laws that open doors such as affirmative action, Title IX, or the Americans with Disabilities Act. Instead, we find school to prison pipelines and prisons with revolving doors.

The concept that all one needed to do was to work hard and one would be successful and be able to move up the socioeconomic ladder is built into the American dream. But there are many structural constraints—from laws and practices that limit what jobs women and others may take, to minimum-wage laws that entrench one in poverty. The structural problems and the laws that strengthen them are disguised as individual faults, and we blame the poor for their circumstances. But no matter how many minimum-wage jobs they may hold, they will still experience wealth inequality. Step back: Were we not all raised under the premise that if we just worked hard enough, we would succeed?

In 2017, the federal poverty threshold for a family of four was $24,858, 43.1 million; Americans were below this. A quarter of Americans earn less than $10/hour. A minimum living wage is $11.95/hour. If the minimum wage was adjusted for cost of living increases, it would be $10.41, and if pegged to executive income, it would be $23/hour.

Until the 1991 court case United Auto Workers (UAW) v. Johnson Controls, Inc., laws reinforced the type of positions and the hours that (middle-class) women could work. Muller v. Oregon (1908) limited women to 10 hours of work per day, and Radice v. New York (1924) limited the hours a female could work in a New York City restaurant to 6:00 in the morning to 10:00 at night. It should be noted that women of color and poor women worked jobs as household workers, cooks, and laundresses, and in factories and in fields with lax oversight. Until the 30 June 1966 picket of the *New York Times* by members of the National Organization of Women, including Kate Millett, the norm was that help-wanted ads were segregated by gender. Jobs for women were low paid and had no promotion ladders. A recent study of job ads found that feminine language of home health aides deterred men from applying for the positions, yet the masculine language of the fastest growing male dominated field—cartography—did not deter women from applying, probably because women are used to operating in a male dominant world, whereas men still feel the pull of masculine socialization and stigma of appearing at all feminine (Miller, 2017).

It should be noted that, until World War I left businesses bereft of secretaries, a secretary was an entry-level position for men in many corporations. When the positions were filled by women, who were seen as capable of handling office machinery (the typewriter), males did not want those positions back, and they became dead-end positions. Similarly, when women went into factories during World War II and were earning living wages, the federal government actually had to pass a law mandating that returning soldiers get their jobs back, also the federal government launched a campaign to return working women to the home and baby-making.

Protectionist, paternal laws provided special treatment for women, and practice allowed companies to hire women at lower pay rates, a 25% discount, because woman might, at whim, leave the job for marriage or to have babies. The UAW case lead to the prohibition of private sector companies from discriminating against women in hazardous jobs, which might expose their future offspring to health issues (birth defects and illnesses) but did not similarly protect male workers. Gendered hazardous jobs were made the higher-paid positions. The Bennington, Vermont, battery plant paid the males who worked with the lead batteries substantially more than those who did not work with the batteries. Women had to either be surgically sterilized or in menopause, with notes from their doctor to work in the higher-paid positions.

While the Equal Pay Act was passed in 1963, white women were earning 63 cents to the male dollar, unfortunately it was never enforced. Even after correcting for gendered choices of positions, coupled with women taking time to have children, as of 2017, there is not pay equity. White women earn 77 cents to the male dollar, black women earn 61 cents, and Latinas earn 53 cents. This varies from state to state, Louisiana has the largest gap, and California the smallest. This is important especially with the number of female heads of households, as in 2008 with the number of women whose salaries were supporting their families when men lost their positions, either in banking or construction, due to the financial crisis.

The Lilly Ledbetter Fair Pay Act of 2009 was a result of the unfortunate outcome of Ledbetter v. Goodyear Tire Co., 550 U.S. 618 (2007). Lilly Ledbetter found out that she was being paid substantially lower than male employees at the same level. Her 19-year career at Goodyear Tire had her regularly receiving lower performance reviews than her male colleagues. She sued the company for gender discrimination in violation of Title VII of the Civil Rights Act of 1964, winning her case in the lower courts. Goodyear Tire appealed to The Supreme Court citing a provision in Title VII, which requires such discrimination complaints to be made within 180 days of the initial infraction.

Like most employees, Ledbetter and her colleagues never shared pay information, so she never was aware of the discrimination until the end of her career. In a 5-4 decision, the court decided for Goodyear Tire and the 180-day window for filing discrimination complaints. The Lilly Ledbetter Act was put in place to counter this court decision and contains a retroactive clause to restore the intent of Title VII. Also, it prohibits sex-based wage discrimination based on men and women in the same location doing the same job. But in a closer reading, one can see that distinctions may still be made based on skills, responsibilities (amount of supervision required, which could be seen as subjective, for example), and working conditions (as per the Equal Pay Act).

Women in the "C" suites are rare. In the Fortune 500 companies, there are only 25 female CEOs. The higher echelons of corporate America are male. The Bureau of Labor Statistics reported that in 2017, of all the CEOs, only 28% are female, and 10% are non-white.[5] In other professions that have seen women entering graduate school at the rate as males, find that female practicing lawyers and doctors earn significantly less than their male counterparts. A similar look at females in academia found that, while they were entering graduate programs, their numbers were not reflected in the upper faulty ranks. Today, women and men may be offered similar jobs and salaries, but because men negotiate their starting salary, women end up at a $2,000 disadvantage. This disadvantage multiplies exponentially over the years in salary, and the difference is felt in social security and retirement benefits.

Rule of Law

"If men were angels, we would not need government," James Madison wrote in *The Federalist Papers* #51. We follow the rule of law, using laws to make sure the effects of the actions and consequences of actions undertaken by individuals and corporations are covered. As the majority decision in Lochner v. New York, 198 U.S. 130 (1922) pointed out, workers, in this case, bakery workers, do not need the protecting arm of the state to assert their rights. Yet in other decisions like the special treatment of women, "to protect the weaker sex," in the number of hours worked, these types of labor, protective, paternalistic laws were upheld, for example, in West Coast Hospital v. Parrish, 300 U.S. 379 (1937).

The rule of law should be designed to protect the weak against the strong, but as Stiglitz and others point out, those with wealth use their power as a political tool to design laws that advantage themselves, exploit others, preserve inequalities, and ensure that laws benefit those with economic power (Stiglitz, 2012, pp. 190–191). The Koch Brothers, along with other billionaires, through their charitable foundations (such as the Olins, Bradleys, and Scaife) and corporations helped to fund the American Legislative Exchange Council (ALEC). ALEC prepares model legislation for use and passage in state legislatures that benefit corporations (Mayer, 2016). One of the proposed draft legislation being pushed by ALEC is the Occupational Licensing Defense Act, which is couched in language that there is costly, burdensome, and a tedious amount of regulation, certification, and licensure, including continuing education requirements, that is driving up costs to consumers as well as acting as a barrier for those who want to enter occupations. This type of legislation is being pushed as an economic development tool necessary in a free market. Occupations that are or could be impacted range from professional engineers, to health workers and barbers. The implications are that certain workers might not be as well-trained; thus, they would not have to be paid as much, and they might not catch all the corners being cut in pipeline construction or food service.

ALEC also is pushing the end of inheritance laws on both the state and federal levels, the better to pass on wealth. These laws are not being called estate taxes since most Americans do not have "estates" to pass on to their heirs but are being called "death taxes" because after all we all die.

Based on what is known as the "Koch Network," ultra-conservative, big-money funders, along with issue advocates and constituency-builders have been pulling the Republican Party (and dragging the neoliberal centrist Democrats along) to the right (Skocpol and Hertel-Fernandez, 2016). This Network funds conservative candidates and works to unseat legislators who are anti-corporation and deregulation. The political agenda has been stacked with tax cuts for the wealthy, coupled with severe cuts to the social welfare safety net to pay for the tax cuts; bankruptcy provisions that favor the banks over the consumers, deregulation of industries from the banking industry to the coal industry, to programs that protected workers safety and those that protected our drinking water. This network pushes to deregulate environmental protections, expand offshore drilling (remember Sarah Palin's "Drill, Baby, Drill."), funds climate deniers' campaigns for elected and appointed office, and blocks clean-energy initiatives. The Koch Network also recruited the conservative evangelical church to help push their agenda, from equating environmentalism (once a nonpartisan issue) to the worship of a false god (Mayer, 2016, chapter 8).

It should also be noted that the Olin Foundation funds the Federalist Society for Law and Public Policy Studies. This is one of the many think tanks that the Koch Network funded and whose purpose it is to help influence political agendas, public debates, and train professional advocates. The Federalist Society is one that promotes original textual interpretation of the Constitution. The Federalist Society has a lot of power and influence in placing conservative lawyers in prominent clerkships, government positions, and in putting names of members into nomination for judgeships. The list of 30 potential nominees that President Trump has for nominations to the Supreme Court, for instance, has 25 members of the Federalist Society. The overall effect are decisions that favor corporations over individuals because corporations have the same standing as persons per the Santa Clara County v. Southern Pacific Railroad Company, 118 U.S. 394, 1886 headnote.[6]

A decision written by Justice Gorsuch, a member of the Federalist Society, concerning how two federal laws—the National Labor Relations Act and the Federal Arbitration Act—interact with signed employment contracts can legally relieve employees of their right to take outside class action suits in favor of individual arbitration of disputes (such as to overtime pay or sexual harassment or discrimination). In the past, the National Labor Relations Board might have sided with the employees, saying that the employee had the right to take a class action suit against a corporation. This case Epic Systems Corp. v. Lewis, 584 U.S. (2018), which consolidated three cases, decided that contracts with this clause were valid; employees can still be coerced to sign away their rights if they want the job, thus silencing many employees. Employees, thus, sign away their right to class action suit or they are terminated, giving the employer the advantage. Individual arbitration makes employers less accountable to all employees since most arbitration processes are not only individualized, but are conducted behind closed doors, and decisions usually have non-disclosure agreements. Justice Gorsuch wrote that individual arbitration is less costly than class action suits, and this decision actually makes the workers equal bargaining partners.

Another recent ruling, Janus v. American Federation of State, County, and Municipal Employees, Council 31, et al., 585 U.S. (2018), that bear the impact of the Federalist Society was one that Justice Alito writing for the majority and joined by Chief Justice Roberts and Justices Gorsuch, Thomas and Kennedy found that requiring non-union members to pay "shop fees" because they benefit from the collective bargaining by unions violates agency-shop agreements violate "the free speech rights of non members by compelling them to subsidize private speech on matters of substantial public concern." The impact of this will be to greatly undermine the finances of unions to undertake other political work. [One should note that unions were not always on the side of all workers; in the 1890s unions did not want to ally with women's groups, because the unions were more concerned with the male breadwinners ability to earn money, even if those men were not yet married or had families to support, the norm said they would.]

Elizabeth Anderson (2017) upends the liberal idea, and since the Industrial Revolution now myth, that John Locke and Adam Smith put forward that a free liberal market society produces not only a free and level society of equals but free the workers. Adam Smith, she reiterates, argued that equitable regulations should fall on the side of the workers (p. 122). The Industrial Revolution undermined the leveling effect of the liberal market, the factories and their norms leading to monopolies—from those of religion and media, to the rich controlling politics and policies to favor themselves, to men controlling all power in the family (ix). She articulates how in many, if not most, workplaces employees have little freedom, privacy, or rights. Employers are the most oppressive authorities on the job and off—regulating workers' attire and hairstyles, limiting or even eliminating political speech including the legal speech regarding forming a union, impacting their health from regulating when they can have toilet breaks when working in factories to medical testing, and regulating their use of alcohol and nicotine (and other recreational drugs) (pp. 38–40).

We see this when, in order to apply for a job at a big box store, one has to urinate in a cup to be drug tested as if, your use of (any) drug 24 hours or more ago, might impair your ability to stock shelves or ring up a customer at the cash register. We do understand the use of drug testing when it comes to jobs in which there are public safety concerns; surely we do not want our pilots or bus drivers to be impaired. By surrendering your urine, you also surrender your right to privacy—you have no control over the validity of the laboratory tests or for what is actually being tested. Even in states where marijuana is legal, the laws support both drug testing and not hiring or firing people to maintain a drug-free workplace.

Employment benefits also impact workers' ability to change jobs. For example, health insurance is tethered to about 60% of full-time work places. For many people who have preexisting conditions, this might also tether them to their workplace since the cost of health insurance plans are usually split between employee and employer. The cost of health insurance may be $250 per month for the employee and $600 for the employer: Kaiser Family Health calculates that employers pay 82% of single coverage, and 70% of family coverage. If the employee leaves, they may have to pay the entire amount until they find another job or another source of health insurance.

The Supreme Court case, Burwell v. Hobby Lobby, 573 U.S. (2014) found that in closely held for-profit corporations, the corporation could deny birth control coverage as part of its health insurance, if that offended the corporation owners' religious beliefs. Again, we see the impact of a conservative judiciary.

Criminalizing Poverty

Traffic laws should be enforced for public safety, but many communities make traffic stops a source of income to help balance their budgets. For the poor, these traffic stops and their ensuing traffic tickets, fines, and court costs escalate so much that those with little savings or discretionary monies enter our criminal justice system. These people either have to pay their fines or are remanded into jail, in what have become known as "pay or stay" schemes. Debtors prisons are thought to be a thing of the past, in fact, they were outlawed in 1833 in the United States, and in 1983, the Supreme Court decided in Bearden v. Georgia, 461 U.S. 660 that local jails could only imprison a person for "willfully" not paying a fine if they had the means to do so, thus, distinguishing between those who are too poor to pay and those who are not. Yet, today we have documentation that poverty has again become criminalized in which traffic fines, court costs, and other fees become too costly for many, thus, they are remanded to jail (Alexander, 2010; Law, 2012; Jerjian, 2016; Edelman, 2017). These "pay or stay" scenarios are common in communities of color and thus have become another factor in social control that keep people entrenched in poverty (Jerjian, 2016).

The cash bail system is another method of social control. If a person accused of a crime is deemed a flight risk or has prior convictions, the judge may set bail, sometimes without asking about family financial circumstances. Setting bail should be based on the type of crime; violent or nonviolent, property crime or misdemeanor. Studies have found that setting bail is raced, yet white persons released prior to trial were more likely to commit another crime than persons of color; 24% versus 2% of African Americans (Dobbie et al., 2018). A 2016 Bureau of Justice report notes that there were 458,600 unconvicted inmates in local prisons (Zeng, 2018). Even though we have the Sixth Amendment right to a speedy trial, many people are incarcerated pretrial because they cannot make bail, some for only one week, others for years, depending on the jurisdiction. In New York City, even when the bail is set at $500 or less, 85% of the accused cannot make bail (Wagner, 2015). Not making bail has other implications on the lives of the poor from lost wages to losing their employment all together. Losing income does not just affect the individual, but their family—the family may not be able to afford rent, car payments, and necessities such as food and medication. Society also will bear the costs via social welfare programs. We are not even considering the cost to the taxpayers for incarcerating these people, which has been estimated at $9 billion per year. Another consequence of not making bail is that there is a greater chance of the defendant being convicted (Dobbie et al., 2018). Low-income persons accused of low-level crimes also tend to either plead guilty or to plea deal, regardless of their innocence. As Peter Edelman wrote, "Rich people make bail…Regardless of actual guilt or innocence, poor people are criminalized for their inability to buy their way out of jail" (Chapter 3).

Summary

Being recognized as a productive citizen means you are worthwhile. Scan the shelves of a bookstore, listen to some TED Talks, and you will see many titles that tell you the "secrets" of successful people, they wake up early. We measure the social (and political) worth of a person by their bank accounts—without thinking about how they got their money—earned or inherited? Americans describe themselves by their jobs, not their families or hobbies. Those who labor without pay or do not work, tend to suffer from depression and feelings of worthlessness (Thompson, 2019).

We also demonize the poor for needing a social welfare safety net and look for ways to cut it. The Personal Responsibility and Workforce Act of 1996 makes work a requirement for benefits, and recipients are required to work 20 hours per week if they have children over the age of three, yet do not provide for childcare for those children. It only allows for people over the age of 21 to be on social services for a maximum of five years over their lifetime, and if they are females, mandate sexual abstinence training (more about this in the next chapter). With the cuts to the welfare safety net, we expect charity to fill in the gaps. For example, food pantries for when the Supplemental Nutrition Aid (SNAP) runs out, because at $27 per week per person for food items, non-food items (toilet paper, laundry soap, etc.) are exempt. This type of minimal government programming and minimal charitable programs allows for just enough relief so the poor exist, but do not thrive. Many people want to return to before the federal government had to step in and rescue the economy and families because of the Depression and the Dust Bowl. They think back to a voluntary civil society that uses charities and religion, instead of taxpayer dollars, when the rich under the guise of *noblesse oblige* provided for those misfortunates. But these rose-colored visions of the past overlook the realities that necessitated the government to step in, that the private voluntary systems were not enough to ensure security and protection for all. The government needed to step in and help stabilize civil society—from the first welfare programs and social security, to the 1960s Medicare insurance. The 2008 recession might have ended sooner if the government, instead of just bailing out the big banks, had spread some of that aid to tax-paying households. The federal government put $700 billion just to the Troubled Assets Relief Program (TARP), but there was a lot more. Nomi Prins (2010) clocked the actual cost of the bailout at over $14.4 trillion. In 2008, there were roughly 117,180,000 households. If the government had given each household say $100,000 to spend as they needed—to buy down their mortgages, pay for higher education or medical expenses, or even buying that new car or a washing machine, or if they had lost their jobs, had a cushion to do more than survive—the government would have invested roughly a billion dollars in its greatest resource, its citizens, and kept the economy working. Instead, people lived paycheck to paycheck, the unsold refrigerators sat at the big box stores, and the manufacturers did not produce more but laid off workers, and so the economy slid further into its recession.

As the Martin Luther King, Jr. quote at the beginning of the chapter states, we have socialism for the wealthy—the tax breaks for giving to their own personal family foundations or putting money into pension plans so that they can live off the interest when they are retired, for example. The federal government subsidized the canal companies, the continental railroads, and provided funding for research and development for our companies to invent new drugs, new materials, and so forth. We thought what was good for business was good for America. Even today we seem to be socializing the risk and privatizing the profit.

Former Speaker of the House, Paul Ryan was middle class when growing up. He was able to succeed because he went to a public high school and used the Social Security Survivor's benefits from his father's death to help pay his way to a public college education. Yet while he was in office, he wanted to privatize social security and cut back funding for education. The poor are told it is their fault for being poor, they have to pull themselves up by the bootstraps, that is the rugged individualism of capitalism, they get to barely survive.

People are told that if they are not successful, it is their own fault—they are not working hard enough, though one could have three full-time minimum-wage jobs and still be struggling (35 hours per week is full time, three jobs at $7.25/hour comes to less than $40,000 before taxes for a 52 week year (with no vacation). It is important because, if one is struggling to make ends meet, to meet the challenges of living in this material world, and raising a family, one is focusing on that. If a person is struggling to succeed but cannot get ahead because of the structural and ideological constraints, who is living paycheck to paycheck, where coming up with $400 in an emergency to make bail or pay fines, they lose access to the public sphere, and thus, their political agency. In short, when the majority of workers are surviving and not thriving, and the laws and courts are working to squelch their avenues to change, the end result is the creation of an obedient workforce and community, and that is NOT democracy.

Notes

1 See Campbell, the librarian of The Louis D. Brandeis School of Law at the University of Louisville attempted to track the source of this quote made by Nader when he accepted the Green Party nomination for President in 2000.
2 It took until 1 November 2018 for Chicanas' earnings to equal what white men had earned in 2017.
3 Amazon founder Jeff Bezos, Berkshire Hathaway Chair and CEO Warren Buffett, and Microsoft founder Bill Gates.
4 The BLS notes the average cost of employee benefits is $11.31/hour (2017) of the total employment per hour cost is $35.64—$24.33 is actual wages or benefits are 31.73%.
5 U.S. Department of Labor, Bureau of Labor Statistics, "Labor Force Statistics from the Current Population Survey." Accessed 10 March 2019, www.bls.gov/cps/cpsaat11.htm.
6 Santa Clara County v. Southern Pacific Railroad Company, 118 U.S. 394, 1886, headnote: "The defendant Corporations are persons within the intent of the clause in section 1 of the Fourteenth Amendment to the Constitution of the United States."

References

Alexander, Michele (2010) *The New Jim Crow.* New York: New Press.
Alson, Philip (15 December 2017a) "Statement on Visit to the USA, by Professor Philip Alston, United Nations Special Rapporteur on extreme poverty and human rights." Accessed 4 January 2019, www.ohchr.org/EN/NewsEvents/Pages/DisplayNews.aspx?NewsID=22533.

Alson, Philip (2017b) "Report of the Special Rapporteur on Extreme Poverty and Human Rights on His Mission to the United States of America." Accessed 4 January 2019, digitallibrary.un.org/record/1629536.

Anderson, Elizabeth (2017) *Private Governments*. Princeton, NJ: Princeton University Press.

Arendt, Hannah and Margaret Canovan (1999) *The Human Condition*, 2nd ed. Chicago, IL: University of Chicago Press.

Bearden v. Georgia, 461 U.S. 660 (1983).

Board of Governors of the Federal Reserve (2018) "Report on the Economic Well-Being of U.S. Households in 2017." Accessed 6 January 2019, www.federalreserve.gov/publications/files/2017-report-economic-well-being-us-households-201805.pdf.

Burwell v. Hobby Lobby, 573 U.S. (2014).

Campbell, Peter Scott. "Democracy v Concentrated Wealth: In Search of a Louis D. Brandeis Quote." 16 GREEN BAG 2D 251. Accessed 6 January 2019, http://greenbag.org/v16n3/v16n3_articles_campbell.pdf.

Davis, Elizabeth (14 October 2018) "How Much Does COBRA Health Insurance Cost?" Accessed 4 January 2019, www.verywellhealth.com/how-much-does-cobra-health-insurance-cost-1738554.

Dobbie, Will, Jacob Goldin and Crystal Yang (2018) "Future Crime, and Employment: Evidence from Randomly Assigned Judges." *American Economic Review* 108 (2): 201–240. Accessed 20 January 2019, www.aeaweb.org/articles?id=10.1257/aer.20161503.

Edelman, Peter (2017) *Not A Crime to Be Poor: The Criminalization of Poverty in America*. New York: New Press.

Ehrenreich, Barbara (2001). *Nickel and Dimed*. New York: Henry Holt.

Equal Pay Act of 1963. (Pub. L. 88–380).

Federal Arbitration Act of 1925. (Pub. L. 68–401).

The Federalist Society for Law and Public Policy Studies. Fedsoc.org.

Gramsci, Antonio (2011) *Prison Notebooks*. New York: Columbia University Press.

Habermas, Jurgen (1973) *Legitimation Crisis*. T. McCarthy (trans). Boston, MA: Beacon.

Hochschild, Arlie Russell with Anne Machung (1989) *The Second Shift: Working Parents and the Revolution at Home*. New York: Viking Penguin.

Holloway, Carson (2016) "Tocqueville on Christianity and American Democracy." *The Heritage Foundation*. Accessed 4 January 2019, https://www.heritage.org/civil-society/report/tocqueville-christianity-and-american-democracy.

Inequality.Org. "Income Inequality in the United States." Accessed 4 January 2019, inequality.org/facts/income-inequality/.

Inskeep, Steven with David Wessel (2018) "Why Wages Are Stagnating." 3 September 5:06 AM ET Heard on Morning Edition. Steve Inskeep talks to David Wessel. Accessed 4 January 2019, www.npr.org/2018/09/03/644260170/why-wages-are-stagnating.

Janus v. American Federation of State, County, and Municipal Employees, Council 31, et al., 585 U.S. (2018).

Jerjian, Olivia (2016) "The Debtors Prison Scheme Yet Another Bar in the Birdcage of Mass Incarceration." *New York University Review of Law and Social Change* 41 (2). Accessed 8 January 2019, socialchangenyu.com/review/the-debtors-prison-scheme-yet-another-bar-in-the-birdcage-of-mass-incarceration-of-communities-of-color/.

King, Martin Luther, Jr. (1964) "Speech on Problems in Our Economic System in Miami Fl." Accessed 4 January 2019, www.goodreads.com/quotes/691624-we-all-too-often-have-socialism-for-the-rich-and.

Knowlton, Alex (2018) "CEO Pay Trends." *Harvard Law School Forum on Corporate Governance and Financial Regulation*. Accessed 15 January 2019, corpgov.law.harvard.edu/2018/09/14/ceo-pay-trends/.

Law, Victoria (2012) *Resistance Behind Bars*. Oakland, CA: PM Press.

Lilly Ledbetter Fair Pay Act of 2009 (Pub. L. 111–2, S. 181). Lilly Ledbetter v. Goodyear Tire Co., 550 U.S. 618 (2007). Lochner v. New York, 198 U.S. 130 (1922).

Locke, John ([1690] 1952) *The Second Treatise of Government*. Thomas Peardon (ed.). Indianapolis, IN: The Liberal Arts Press.

Macpherson, Crawford Brough (1962) *The Political Theory of Possessive Individualism: Hobbes to Locke*. Oxford: Clarendon Press.

Mayer, Jane (2016) *Dark Money: The Hidden History of the Billionaires Behind the Rise of the Radical Right*. New York: Doubleday.

Mijs, Jonathan J.B. (2019) "The Paradox of Inequality: Income Inequality and Belief in Meritocracy Go Hand in Hand." *Socio-Economic Review* 1–29. doi:10.1093/ser/mwy052.

Miller, Claire Cain (16 January 2017) "Job Listings That Are Too 'Feminine' for Men." Accessed 25 July 2019, www.nytimes.com/2017/01/16/upshot/job-disconnect-male-applicants-feminine-language.html.

Modestino, Alicia Sasser, Daniel Shoag and Joshua Ballance (2019) "Upskilling: Do Employees Demand Greater Skills When Workers Are Plentiful?" *Unpublished Paper presented at American Economic Association Annual Meeting*, Atlanta, GA, 5 January 2019.

Mullen, Tom (4 December 2018) "The Best Argument Against Minimum Wage Laws: You Don't Own Other People." Foundation for Economic Education. Accessed 6 January 2019, fee.org/articles/the-best-argument-against-minimum-wage-laws-you-dont-own-other-people/.

Nadeau, Carey Anne and Amy K. Glasmeier (30 August 2018) "Bare Facts About the Living Wage in America 2017-2018." Accessed 25 July 2019, Livingwage.mit.edu/articles/31-bare-facts-about-te-living-wage-in-america-2017-2018.

Nader, Ralph (2000) "Acceptance Speech, Green Party." Accessed 25 February 2019, http://www.4president.org/speeches/nader2000acceptance.htm.

The National Labor Relations Act of 1935 (29 U.S.C. § 151–169).

Nessel, Lori A. (2017) "Instilling Fear and Regulating Behavior: Immigration Law as Social Control." *Georgetown Immigration Law Review* 31: 525–559.

Pateman, Carole (1989) *The Disorder of Women*. Palo Alto, CA: Stanford University Press.

Prins, Nomi (2010) "The Real Size of the Bailout." *Mother Jones*. Accessed 15 January 2019, motherjones.com/politics/2009/12/real-size-bailout-treasury-fed/.

Rawls, John (1971) *A Theory of Justice*. Cambridge, MA: Harvard University Press.

Santa Clara County v. Southern Pacific Railroad Company, 118 U.S. 394 (1886).

Shapiro, Thomas M. (2005) *The Hidden Cost of Being African American: How Wealth Perpetuates Inequality*. Paperback ed. New York: Oxford University Press.

Shierholz, Heidi with Anna Turner (25 February 2010) "The Effects of Citizenship on Family Income and Poverty." EPI Briefing Paper #256. Accessed 15 January 2009, https://www.epi.org/files/page/-/bp256/bp256.pdf.

"The Simple Truth about the Gender Pay Gap." www.aauw.org/research/the-simple-truth-about-the-gender-pay-gap/.

Skocpol, Theda and Alexander Hertel-Fernandez (2016) "The Koch Effect: The Impact of a Cadre-Led Network on American Politics." *Prepared for Presentation at the Inequality Mini-Conference*, Southern Political Science Association, San Juan, Puerto Rico, 8 January 2016. Accessed 8 January 2019, scholars.org/sites/scholars/files/the_koch_effect_for_spsa_w_apps_skocpol_and_hertel-fernandez-corrected_1-4-16_1.pdf.

Smith, Adam ([1776] 2016) *The Wealth of Nations.* New York: Bantam Classics.

Stevens, Jacqueline (2009) *States without Nations.* New York: Columbia University Press.

Stiglitz, Joseph (2012) *The Price of Inequality: How Today's Divided Economy Is Endangering Our Future.* New York: W.W. Norton.

Streib, Jessi (2018) "Class, Culture, and Downward Mobility." *SocArXiv.* doi:10.31235/osf.io/ws9gj.

Thompson, Derek (24 February 2019) "The Religion of Workism Is Making Americans Miserable." *The Atlantic.* Accessed 24 February 2019, www.theatlantic.com/ideas/archive/2019/02/religion-workism-making-americans-miserable/583441/.

Tocqueville, de Alexis (2004) *Democracy in America.* Arthur Goldhammer (trans). New York: Library of America.

U.S. Department of Labor, Bureau of Labor Statistics, "Labor Force Statistics from the Current Population Survey." Accessed 10 March 2019, www.bls.gov/cps/cpsaat11.htm.

Wagner, Peter (2015) "Jails Matter: But Who Is Listening?" Accessed 10 January 2019, www.prisonpolicy.org/blog/2015/08/14/jailsmatter/.

Weber, Max (1930) *The Protestant Ethic and the Spirit of Capitalism.* London: Allen & Unwin.

West Coast Hospital v. Parrish, 300 U.S. 379 (1937).

Wolin, Sheldon (2016) *Politics and Vision: Continuity and Innovation in Western Political Thought.* Princeton, NJ: Princeton University Press.

Zeng, Zhen (2018) "Jail Inmates in 2016." Department of Justice, NCJ 251210, 5 February 2019. Accessed 8 January 2019, www.bjs.gov/content/pub/pdf/ji16.pdf.

8

REPRODUCING CITIZENS

This chapter is about how citizenship gets reproduced, and who can reproduce citizens. The most obvious way that citizens are reproduced is through human reproduction. Kinship has been a norm for states identifying who is a citizen (Stevens, 1999, 2009), from early Sparta when a male citizen had to proclaim a child as his, to citizenship via *jus sanguinis* (by blood). The state has been very involved in who can reproduce through laws regarding sexual practices and behaviors including marriage and who can parent. Laws and norms regarding sex, marriage, and procreation are a means of controlling the sexual norm and hegemonic citizenship. Foucault (1978) unpacked sexuality as a discursively (socially) constructed as a means to transfer and consolidate power (p. 103), both social norms and political/legal norms reinforce this power construct. The current climate around reproductive rights removes women's autonomy and, in some cases, grants their rapist parental rights. The other way citizenship is reproduced and controlled is through immigration and naturalization. The last section of this chapter will look at immigration, naturalization, and denaturalization. In short, this chapter will explore how citizenship reproduction is controlled.

Sex and the Citizen

The state not only relies on kinship to mark citizens, it has controlled and limited non-procreational sex (sodomy), as well as trying to enforce abstention from sex for those who are not married or those receiving welfare benefits and trying to control sexual commerce (prostitution). Over the history of the United States, the government has regulated sexual activity, from the use of contraceptives and the right to an abortion (still a political issue), and sex acts including consensual sodomy between both heterosexual and same-sex couples; as well as regulated who could marry. The state and society both police sexuality so that it is both privatized and constructed, appropriate sexual practices happen in private, familial spaces.

Gender as a form of identity performance has also been regulated by the state, from the ordinances prohibiting wearing clothes not belonging to that of their own sex as early as 1848 in Columbus, Ohio, to similar laws existing in New York that were enforced as late as 2011. Stories abound of butch lesbians and men in drag having to wear at least two articles of clothing that were of their own sex when in the gay and lesbian bars of the 1950s and 1960s.

Similarly exposing female breasts, either for breastfeeding, sunbathing, or titillating others is seen as indecent, since the male gaze objectifies the female breast. In New York state, the law against women going topless was challenged in 1992 since no laws prohibit males from going topless (Glazer, 1993).

Regulation of sex work as a form of labor and commerce has been, since the early twentieth-century reformation movement, seen as a deviant behavior and criminalized in the United States, except for the regulated brothels in Nevada. It should be noted that the sex workers themselves are criminalized as are those who exploit or profit from their work (the pimps); as are now the consumers or the procurers. The arrest of the sexual activity procurers is a relatively recent phenomena, since the majority are white heterosexual male clients who were seen as just acting on their sexual desire. Some men, though, lost their status for such actions, the former Governor of New York Eliot Spitzer for example. The use of sexually trafficked women, who are forced to engage in sexual acts, has also changed the way the state treats sex workers. The Trafficking Victim Protection Law of 2000, and its various reauthorizations, considers women and children of sexual trafficking to be a form of slavery. There is training for law enforcement personnel and others, such as hotel workers, so that they might recognize and intervene appropriately. Socially, the sex workers are also stigmatized. With even the current awareness of sexual trafficking, and with sex workers beginning to form labor movements, the policing of sexual desire as a commodity and a deviant behavior is beginning to change (Bernstein and Schaffer, 2005; Grant, 2014; Davis, 2015; Myers, 2018).

The state has promoted heteronormativity including heterosexual sexual behaviors from public displays of affection to sexual intercourse. Despite the Lesbian and Gay liberation movements of the second half of the twentieth century, it was not until the 1990s in the United States when same-sex practices stopped being regarded universally as abnormal, highly penalized (from familial and societal shunning, to "corrective" psychological and medical practices, from electroshock therapy to aversion therapies), besides being illegal. Citizens who identified as lesbian, gay, bisexual, transgender, and gender fluid were also denied not only the legal ability to engage in sex acts, but were denied basic citizenship rights from employment nondiscrimination to housing nondiscrimination, from social justice to political rights.[1]

There were laws against sodomy, both heterosexual and homosexual acts, though it was gay male sexuality which triggered "the moral repugnance of the and disgust" the average man, or what Martha Nussbaum (2010) calls the "politics of disgust"—legislating restrictions based on a sense of morality that discriminates. The laws against sodomy stood until Lawrence v. Texas, 539 U.S. 558 (2003) overturned them. Same-sex marriage had been specifically outlawed by the Defense of Marriage Act in 1996 until Obergefell v. Hodges, 576 U.S. ___ (2015) allowed for marriage equality.

Healthy Procreative Sex, Only

The government (on all levels), as well as societal norms, preferenced procreative rather than recreative sex. In today's culture of #MeToo and the campus rapes, the norm has been to promote conscious awareness of consent for all parties engaging in sex. North Carolina legally allows men to finish the sex act even if a woman revokes her consent and even if the act becomes violent, State v. Way 297 N.C. 293 (1979). Until the 1990s, men did not have to have their wives' consent to engage in sex with them; since then, all 50 states have laws against marital or spousal rape or nonconsensual sex. Paternalistic laws and employer protectionist practices have, in the past, tended to protect women as reproductive vessels. Public health laws have also been used to regulate sexual behavior and practices.

In the United States, there have been public health agencies and policies for over 200 years, most concerned with protecting residents from contagious diseases especially in densely populated cities. When it comes to sexually transmitted diseases, public health policy has focused on protecting, at first, soldiers and then the general public from non-procreative sex, which might lead to the spread of venereal diseases. To protect the health of white men, San Francisco officials in the mid-nineteenth century tried to close all the brothels in Chinatown.

The American Plan was implemented across the United States to control venereal diseases (gonorrhea and syphilis), but in reality, it regulated poor women's bodies and their sexuality. From World War I to the 1960s, when the plan was operational, in the name of public safety and social hygiene, female citizens' rights and bodies were violated. Poor, single, working women were deemed "promiscuous"; thus, a threat to American citizens whether or not they were sexually active. The women were targeted by local police, and health officers were "enthusiastically warned that non-white women were less moral, intent on infecting soldiers and that blacks in particular were a 'syphilis soaked race'" (Stern, 2018, p. 98). The result of this plan was the harassment, loss of due process and other rights, and brutal medical treatment from forceful gynecological exams to mercury treatments, which were not only ineffective, but hazardous, and quarantining women in prisons because the government could not "trust" the women. This happened to tens of thousands of females (Stern, 2018).

While the American Plan was written as a gender-neutral policy, it only impacted women, and there were programs that focused on men, especially homosexual males and Black men. In 1919, the US Navy, under the guidance of Franklin D. Roosevelt who was then the Assistant Secretary of the Navy, waged a campaign against moral vice specifically same-sex friendship, desire, and intimacy in Newport, Rhode Island. Sigmund Freud had written in *Three Contributions to the Sexual Theory*, in 1910, that heterosexuality was natural and homosexuality as unnatural. What became known as the Newport Sex Scandal entrapped and persecuted homosexuals because the government feared "sailors were being 'corrupted' by local gay men, the Navy developed a program using sailors to entrap these men in sexual liaisons, whereupon they would be tried in a civil court of law" (Brenkart, 2003).

Homosexuality, male and female, was seen as a potential security risk as they might be blackmailed, on top of being seen as "unnatural," and thus they were prohibited from (openly) serving in the military (and if found serving dishonorably discharged) and in the federal government service. During World War II during a purge, then General Eisenhower was asked to identify the lesbians (and gay men) on his staff in order to purge them and passed this order to Sergeant Johnnie Phelps. Phelps replied her name would be on the top of the list. The General did not act on this order. Yet, in 1953, now President Eisenhower signed Executive Order 10450, which officially made sexual perversions grounds for exclusion from the federal government. This Executive Order stood until President Bill Clinton signed Executive Order 11479 in May of 1998 that called for sexual orientation non-discrimination in federal employment with military service exempted. The Don't Ask Don't Tell policy, adopted in 1993, allowed military personnel to serve as long as their sexuality was not found out and was repealed in 2011. During this time, more women were dishonorably separated from the military, even though they made up a smaller percentage of service personnel; this may have been due to lesbian-baiting when the women refused male colleagues' sexual advances (Myers, 2013).

The Tuskegee Study of Untreated Syphilis in the Negro male began in 1932, studying poor black sharecroppers in exchange for free health care and burial insurance. The study went on for 40 years, and none of the human male subjects ever received penicillin, an antibiotic which was available in 1940 to treat the disease.

Sexually transmitted diseases are a public health issue, but not all were treated the same. The first report of what would become "the gay cancer," which would become AIDS/HIV+ crisis, was on 5 June 1981. Since it affected mainly gay men, intravenous drug users, and Haitian immigrants, in the beginning, politicians, public health officials, and the Centers for Disease Control (CDC) ignored the crisis, even though the use of condoms may have curtailed the spread of the disease. The local municipalities and states shut down bath houses where gay men congregated and engaged in sexual acts. It was because of the activism of affected gay men and their allies in Act UP and other groups that research on AIDS would be undertaken at the CDC. In 19 states, there are laws that require HIV+ partners to disclose their status to their sexual partners (even if they have no viral load, and thus, cannot transmit the virus), and 9 states have laws requiring HIV+ persons who share needles to do the same. HIV and AIDS is still a scourge of those who are sexually active and/or drug users who share needles. In Indiana, for example, the opiate crisis has resulted in a spike of new HIV cases.

Employer paternalistic practices, known as fetal protection laws that acted to protect women's reproductive ability while also impacting their wage earnings, was also a way for companies to remove a future risk of suit by a future child. The case that ended this practice came before the Supreme Court stemmed from fertile women in a Bennington, Vermont, battery plant being prohibited from the higher-earning potential jobs unless they had a note from their doctors stating they had a tubal ligation or were in menopause. This case focused on women's reproductive capacity, but overlooked that fertile men, who were also exposed to the lead and produce sperm on a 24-hour cycle, also contribute to the birth defects and cancers of their children. The Automobile Workers v. Johnson Controls, Inc., 499 US.187 (1991) found Johnson Controls' policies to be biased against women since they did not have the ability to decide where to work in the battery production plant since lead is dangerous to the reproduction of all fertile workers and fetus protection is not the focus of the company.

Marriage and Citizenship

In the United States, marriage has been seen as the way the government passes rights and responsibilities to what it considers to be the building block of civic society: families. These rights and responsibilities encourage the couple to care for each other and to produce offspring—future citizens. We can see historically that marriage has been considered a privilege that not all people have. Slaves were denied the right to marry because they were considered chattel, and the master wanted control over the slaves and access to their bodies. Female slaves were seen as most valuable, as an economic asset, because they could reproduce more slaves. Thomas Jefferson wrote in a letter to John Jordan on 31 December 1805 that "I consider thee labor of a breeding woman as no object, and that a child raised every 2 years is more of a profit than the crop of the best laboring man" (Bridgewater, 2005). Incarcerated prisoners were not allowed to marry throughout the United States until 1987. Until Loving v. Virginia, 388 U.S.1 (1967) miscegenation statutes existed. States still deny marriage certificates to persons under the (state's) age of consent, which is 18 (except in Missouri where it is 21 and Nebraska where it is 19) without parental consent—with parental consent the age drops, though, and in some cases judicial consent is also necessary.[2] Same-sex couples got the right to marry in 2015. Marriage is now seen as a fundamental right, though states may prohibit marriages between generations within the same family or set marriage age as per their "police powers" (the right to make laws governing the health and welfare of their state residents). Polygamy, or as the members of the Church of the Latter-Day Saints refer to it as plural marriages, was banned in 1856.

Twenty-five states prohibit marriages between first cousins. This prohibition is to limit birth defects passed to the issue (offspring) of these marriages, exceptions are made to those marriages in which the cousins will not have children (Kentucky, Nevada, Ohio, and Washington), or if they are over the age of 65 and, thus, presumed infertile (Arizona and Utah). Certain close relatives are also denied the right to marriage; for instance, in New York, an ancestor and their descendent including uncles and aunts and their nieces or nephews. Until recently same-sex couples did not have the right to marry www.law.cornell.edu/wex/table_marriage.

The social normative goal set for most females is being a bride. This chapter will also explore the federal and state historic bans on civil marriage: the ban on slave marriages, miscegenation, prisoners, same-sex couples, and ban on intergenerational relatives. A fifth ban to marriage, which are state imposed laws against physically or mentally handicapped persons to marry, or if they marry to be sterilized so that they may not reproduce. At the same time, the goal of the 1996 Welfare reform law was to make poor women marriageable because, of course (not), marriage lifts people out of poverty. There are also deeper critiques of how conforming to the construct of marriage ignores other familial configurations and households.

Marriage also has an impact on citizenship beyond the children. Until the mid-twentieth century, American women, who married non-Americans, lost their citizenship; while males could bring in mail-order brides, and still do so.

Good Mother and Citizenship

Public welfare programs only consider jobs outside the home to be work, thus promoting the concept that unpaid labor is not worthy. "When assistance is available, programs are often used to control the lives of women, rewarding those who fit narrow definitions of 'good' or 'deserving' mothers while ignoring those who do not...definitions of 'good' mothers frequently exclude those who are poor, unmarried, immigrants, and people of color." From the turn of the twentieth century, there were programs that enabled mothers to "maintain suitable homes for the rearing of their children." These Mothers' Pensions according to President Theodore Roosevelt (1909) should only be for widows: "Parents of good character suffering from temporary misfortune and, above all, deserving mothers fairly well able to work but deprived of the support of the *normal breadwinner* should be given such aid as may be necessary to enable them to maintain suitable homes for the rearing of their children." The phrase "normal breadwinner" is italicized to highlight that only wives of good men were deserving, single mothers—either unwed or divorced women were not eligible. Only three states officially aided single mothers—Michigan, Nebraska, and Tennessee, and only a few women qualified. The same went for women of color (Law, 2017).

The Great Depression (1929–1939) led to many families breaking apart due to the financial hardships. Men were committing suicide or deserted their families they could no longer support; by 1932, one-fourth of the households no longer had an employed adult. If employed, wages had been cut by 40%, or if employed by the New Deal Work Project Administration (WPA), they were working far from the home. Children were sent to relatives or placed in orphanages as families no longer could afford to feed and clothe them.

The Social Security Act of 1935 included the program Aid to Dependent Children, which was meant to keep mothers and children intact as a family unit, without the mother having to work outside the house, by providing aid to the children themselves. Aid to Dependent Children became Aid to Families with Dependent Children (AFDC) in 1962, and this change allowed for caregivers to receive support as long as the homes were found "suitable."

Poverty and Children

Poverty and child welfare were the focus at the first White House Conference on the Care of Dependent Children (1909). The question on the table was "should homes be broken up because of poverty?" The ultimate answer was no: a family's economic state and their ability to raise a child or children were different:

> Home life is the highest and finest product of civilization. It is the great molding force of mind and of character. Children should not be deprived of it except for urgent and compelling reasons. Children of parents of worthy character, suffering from temporary misfortune, and children of reasonably efficient and deserving mothers who are without the support of the normal breadwinner, should as a rule be kept with their parents, such aid being given as may be necessary to maintain suitable homes for the rearing of the children.... Except in unusual circumstances, the home should not be broken up for reasons of poverty, but only for considerations of inefficiency or immorality. (cited in Bremner, 1971, p. 365 in Frame, 1999, p. 722)

This question, though, is still viable today. "'Suitable homes' is a means of behavioral regulation and caseload containment, as well as maintaining a critical link between the welfare and child protection systems" (Frame, 1999, p. 722). Fitness was tied to the mother being judged "as a proper person, morally, physically, and mentally, for the bringing up of her children…." (Frame, 1999, p. 725). Different states added specific criteria from the birth of an illegitimate child to the presence of brawling men or arrests for disorderly conduct (Georgia or Florida), or to be found in a "midnight raid" cohabitating with a man (for example in Washington or New York).

Today, women in prison, who are predominantly single heads of households, find it hard to be good mothers and tend to have their parental rights terminated, to losing custody of their children for abandonment. They are deemed unfit mothers because they are usually incarcerated more than 100 miles from their homes, and poverty coupled with the cost of visits becomes prohibitive. Male prisoners are not the responsible custodial parent and, thus, not subject to losing their parental rights (Law, 2012, pp. 43–58). In a unanimous decision, the Supreme Court upheld the Michigan Department of Corrections rule that limited prisoners' family visitations if the inmate had two or more write-ups for substance abuse, Overton v. Bazzetta 539 U.S. 126(2003) (see Myers, 2018).

AFDC was updated in 1996 by the Personal Responsibility and Work Opportunity Reconciliation Act P.L. 104-193 (PRWORA). This act reformed welfare or, as some stated, deformed it since it required recipients with children over the age of three to work, without a child care provision, placed a five year lifetime limit on benefits, excluded benefits for children born to mothers already on welfare, and enacted a lifetime ban on welfare benefits for people with felony convictions or who had violated probation or parole.

The purpose of PRWORA is straightforward in its findings: the family is the building blocks of a successful society:

> SEC. 101. FINDINGS. The Congress makes the following findings: (1) Marriage is the foundation of a successful society. (2) Marriage is an essential institution of a successful society which promotes the interests of children. (3) Promotion of responsible fatherhood and motherhood is integral to successful child rearing and the well-being of children….

Section 912, roughly 251 pages later, is the Section on Abstinence Education for not all the recipients of welfare, but those most likely to bear children out of wedlock (all the females who are pre-pregnant or not yet menopausal:

> …provide abstinence education, and at the option of the State, where appropriate, mentoring, counseling, and adult supervision to promote abstinence from sexual activity, with a focus on those groups which are most likely to bear children out-of-wedlock. "(2) For purposes of this

> section, the term 'abstinence education' means an educational or motivational program which—"(A) has as its exclusive purpose, teaching the social, psychological, and health gains to be realized by abstaining from sexual activity; "(B) teaches abstinence from sexual activity outside marriage as the expected standard for all school age children; "(C) teaches that abstinence from sexual activity is the only certain way to avoid out-of-wedlock pregnancy, sexually transmitted diseases, and other associated health problems; "(D) teaches that a mutually faithful monogamous relationship in context of marriage is the expected standard of human sexual activity; "(E) teaches that sexual activity outside of the context of marriage is likely to have harmful psychological and physical effects; "(F) teaches that bearing children out-of-wedlock is likely to have harmful consequences for the child, the child's parents, and society; "(G) teaches young people how to reject sexual advances and how alcohol and drug use increases vulnerability to sexual advances; and "(H) teaches the importance of attaining self-sufficiency before engaging in sexual activity.

The upshot of the PRWORA is to make women marriageable, because we know that marriage lifts women out of poverty, if they are Julia Roberts in Pretty Woman (1990) perhaps, but most women marry within their milieu. And, that poor women should not be having sex.

Many people believe that the poor should not have the same reproduction rights as all others, even though the average birth rate for a woman collecting aid is the same as that of a middle-class woman. The myth of the welfare mother having more children to increase her welfare payments is just that, a myth (on the other side of the coin, no one accuses middle-class women of having more children to take advantage of the tax breaks). But pregnancy prevention—regulating the sexual behavior and reproductive capacity of poor women is still a concern under the PRWORA as it was in the mid-twentieth century when there were bed checks that resulted in aid being denied to the mother for having sexual relations with any man (Frame, 1999, p. 731).

Sterilization was seen as a viable method to control undesirable populations and control welfare costs. Indiana passed the first state law authorizing sterilization in 1907. In 1909, California started a sterilization program that focused on Mexican, Japanese, and Chinese immigrants; by the 1930s, 33 state social welfare programs also operated as quasi-eugenics programs—some, such as the North Carolina Eugenics Board were not subtle. These programs determined who was fit to procreate and sterilized those deemed unfit. The women who were institutionalized in psychiatric hospitals, the disabled—blind, deaf, epileptic, or physically disabled, alcoholics, and those women who were too poor, women of color, or were Native American were sterilized, usually without their full knowledge or consent. Most of these programs became inoperative in the 1980s, but by then, over 65,000 women had been sterilized. In the South,

"Mississippi Appendectomies" were common practice to sterilize black women who transgressed societal norms. Government sterilization programs, though, continued through 2010 (www.uvm.edu/~lkaelber/eugenics/).

Two Supreme Court cases are critical to understanding forced sterilizations in order to protect society from inferior people (the poor and the feeble) or the dangerous (criminal): Buck v. Bell, 274 U.S. 200 (1927) and Skinner v. Oklahoma, 16 U.S. 535 (1942). Carrie Buck was sterilized in Virginia after she gave birth. Since her mother had been involuntarily institutionalized for her promiscuousness and feeblemindedness, it was assumed that Carrie (and her daughter, Vivian) had inherited these traits, and her foster parents had her committed as a "feeble-minded moral delinquent." Justice Oliver Wendell Holmes, in upholding the Virginia statute and, thus, legitimizing compulsory sterilization wrote: "It is better for all the world, if instead of waiting to execute degenerate offspring for crime, or to let them starve for their imbecility, society can prevent those who are manifestly unfit from continuing their kind. Three generations of imbeciles are enough." That Carrie and her daughter both had earned good grades in school was irrelevant. Buck v. Bell has not been overturned.

The compulsory sterilization laws that were upheld were gender-based is seen in the case Skinner v. Oklahoma. A 1935 Oklahoma statute provided for the sterilization of "habitual criminals" (defined as having two or more convictions). Jack Skinner, who had been convicted twice before for armed robbery, had been arrested and sentenced to be sterilized for stealing chickens. The law was found unconstitutional under the equal protection clause since it exempted white collar crimes (embezzlement). Justice William O. Douglas wrote in the majority opinion:

> The power to sterilize, if exercised, may have subtle, far-reaching and devastating effects. In evil or reckless hands it can cause races or types which are inimical to the dominant group to wither and disappear. There is no redemption for the individual whom the law touches. Any experiment which the State conducts is to his irreparable injury. He is forever deprived of a basic liberty.

The Skinner ruling was only applicable to the use of sterilization as punishment. In Gerber v. Hickman, 00-16494 (9th Cir. 2002), the United States Court of Appeals for the Ninth Circuit prohibited an inmate incarcerated for life from artificially inseminating his wife since:

> the right to procreate is fundamentally inconsistent with incarceration… [distinguishing this case from Skinner] By no stretch of the imagination, however, did Skinner hold that inmates have the right to exercise their ability to procreate while still in prison. The right to procreate while incarcerated and the right to be free from surgical sterilization by prison officials are two very different things.

When Norplant, a form of birth control surgically implanted in a woman's arm, was approved in 1991, many states saw this as a panacea to what they perceived as a welfare problem. Many judges started to offer women convicted of drug crimes or child abuse the choice between prison or this form of surgical birth control. State legislatures looked at laws to require or incentivize women collecting Temporary Assistance for Needy Families (TANF) to have Norplant implanted. The choice was just as coercive, exchanging welfare benefits for their constitutional right to reproductive choice. It also reinforces the idea that only women are responsible for birth control, pregnancy, and childrearing because men were not offered vasectomies as punishment for drug convictions or child abuse nor was sterilization a condition for their receiving public assistance (ACLU, 1995).

The Brookings Institute's Isabel Sawhill made a similar argument in 2015, when she proposed offering women under 30 access to the intrauterine device (IUD) form of birth control, since women under 30 are responsible for over half of unplanned pregnancies, and unplanned pregnancies are the slippery slope to poverty. Her thesis stated that reducing unplanned pregnancies would reduce child poverty and improve social mobility by allowing, for instance, the women to finish their education (Sawhill, 2015; Krause et al., 2017). Again, this reinforces women as being solely responsible for getting pregnant and the consequences thereof, allowing the male partner off the hook.

Recreational Sex Controls

That sexual acts were to be procreative can be seen by state laws that had prohibited the use of contraception drugs and devices. These laws were overturned with the 1965 case Griswold v. Connecticut, 381 U.S. 479, when the court decided that there was a right to privacy, and a right to make private decisions regarding family planning for "[i]f the right of privacy means anything, it is the right of the individual, married or single, to be free from unwarranted governmental intrusion into matters so fundamentally affecting a person as the decision whether to bear or beget a child." In 1972, Eisenstadt v. Baird, 405 U.S. 438 extended the right to contraception to unmarried couples.

While Bowers v. Hardwick, 478 U.S. 186 (1986) upheld the right to criminalize certain sex acts, such as sodomy—in Georgia such acts were prohibited to all, homosexual and heterosexual. Lawrence v. Texas, 539 U.S. 558 (2003) overturned this ruling, as Justice Kennedy stated: "Liberty presumes an autonomy of self that includes freedom of thought, belief, expression, and certain intimate conduct. The instant case involves liberty of the person both in its spatial and more transcendent dimensions." Thus, sexual acts need not always to be procreative ones, though there has been conservative pushback.

In some states, abstinence education is part of sex education in public schools, and it is required by those women who receive TANF. In Texas, the sale and possession of sex toys has been prohibited, the current law prohibits owning more than six dildoes. Localities are allowed to regulate adult sexual retail stores and adult sexual performance venues.

Reproductive rights are being curtailed. As of mid-2019, 13 states have passed "heartbeat" legislation that curtails abortion after six weeks from the woman's last menstrual cycle, regardless of when that fetus was conceived (in many cases, women do not even know they are pregnant at this point). Not only does this remove the woman's autonomy over decisions that affect her, it basically turns her into a reproductive vessel, especially in cases of rape or incest or the female being extremely young. Many of the states passing these laws also allow the father of the fetus to have parental rights, again regardless of whether the child was conceived via rape or incest.

Maternal Health

For poor women and minority women, reproductive health is being curtailed and defunded. Without access to reproductive health care, these women are being denied the right to not only control their bodies, but to healthy pregnancies that result in live births (Roberts, 1997; Flavin, 2009). Maternal and infant mortality rates in the United States are extremely high, even though we spend more on health care expenditures per capita, are double the Organization for Economic Cooperation and Development (OECD) average, and much higher than in all other countries. The first year that the United States started to keep infant mortality rates was in 1850, that year the reported black infant-mortality rate was 340 per 1,000 births; the white rate was 217 per 1,000 (Villarosa, 2018). The advent of hygiene and penicillin in the twentieth century has led to the 2016 infant mortality rate of 5.9/1,000, overall. That is misleading because black babies die at a rate of 11.4/1,000 to white babies' rate of 4.9/1,000 (CDC). Black mothers' mortality rate is worse today than 25 years ago, according to the CDC, the number of women who die during pregnancy are between 700 and 900 per year, of which black women are three to four times more likely to die from pregnancy complications. The cause of the high number of black women and infants dying, according to the medical establishment, is the "inescapable atmosphere of societal and systemic racism can create a kind of toxic physiological stress, resulting in conditions—including hypertension and pre-eclampsia—that lead directly to higher rates of infant and maternal death" (Villarosa, 2018). Research has also shown that for people of color, structural discrimination is inherent throughout the health care system; the mortality rate for black people is higher than that of white people, according to the Office of Minority Health (DHHS), for heart diseases, stroke, cancer, asthma, influenza, pneumonia, diabetes, HIV/AIDS, and homicide.

Raising Citizens

The reproduction and raising of new citizens is another important area since children are seen by the state as future citizens useful on two counts: to replenish the ranks of citizens that we have lost in war and to be productive citizens contributing to the nation's wealth as measured by paid employment. Yet who can have children and properly raises a political question—who can adopt children? Who is a good mother? Where are the fathers or other parents? What is the role of children born of immigrant parents?

Parents are key to political socialization, and they are the first educators of (good) citizenship. Children mimic their parents' politics—a check of your local elementary school's mock presidential election will mirror their parents' choices. Our nation wants the parents to care for the children, so the state does not have to do so.

But first the child and mother need to survive childbirth. The Centers for Disease Control (CDC) essentializes female health: a female may be pre-pregnant, pregnant, or menopausal. Depending on their status, the CDC proscribes how women ought to nourish and care for themselves because their goal is to birth babies, though, the site realizes that not all women do so, but it also notes that 50% of pregnancies are not planned. (It should be noted that males have access to erectile dysfunction drugs through the state—Medicare and Medicaid programs, but poor women do not have similar access to birth control or abortions, if needed.)

Some states are adopting laws that require notification of miscarriages, and if the miscarriage is deemed suspicious, the woman may be prosecuted. Indiana's SB 203, for instance, allows for criminal prosecution for murder, manslaughter, or feticide if the fetus dies at any point before birth. Other states are attempting to legislate fetus as person laws or fetal harm laws. In Indiana, fetal remains must be buried or cremated. These laws basically turn women's bodies into incubators, and the fetus's rights trump hers.

Research shows that black women and their babies are suffering from a mortality crisis, during pregnancy and at childbirth, at a rate of three to four times that of their white counterparts.

> The United States is one of only 13 countries in the world where the rate of maternal mortality … is now worse than it was 25 years ago… [and] For black women in America, an inescapable atmosphere of societal and systemic racism can create a kind of toxic physiological stress, resulting in conditions—including hypertension and pre-eclampsia—that lead directly to higher rates of infant and maternal death. And that societal racism is further expressed in a pervasive, longstanding racial bias in health care—including the dismissal of legitimate concerns and symptoms—that can help explain poor birth outcomes even in the case of black women with the most advantages. (Villarosa, 2018)

Adoption is another method of making a family, but recently, adoption agencies have been allowed to cite religion or sexual orientation as a reason to decline potential adoptive parents, though there are many children awaiting forever families. In Michigan, a same-sex female couple was denied a child, even though there are over 13,000 children awaiting adoption or fostering in Michigan's welfare system. The decision to deny the couple was made on a 2015 state law that allows state funded placement agencies to use religious criteria. Still other states, Kansas, Ohio, and Oklahoma are using religious liberty as the reason to deny adoption to parents who are not Christian (the potential adoptive parents might be Jewish or even Muslim). These laws are not in the best interests of children who need families.

Though not all marriages have issue—children—and to procreate one does not need to be married, the right to marriage equality underscores the importance of family and marriage to civil society. Obergefell v. Hodges, 576 U.S. ___ (2015) same-sex marriage equality and children quote Justice Anthony Kennedy writing for the majority in Obergefell v. Hodges, the case that gave the country marriage equality, framed his reasoning around the importance of a recognized committed couple to marry. He cited four reasons in support of same-sex marriages from the right of personal choice and importance of marriage as an unique commitment to the concept of the importance of the right to marry as fundamental and importance of, since like heterosexual couples, same-sex couples have children: [marriage] "safeguards children and families and thus draws meaning from related rights of child rearing, procreation, and education… [and] marriage is a keystone of our social order."

Same-sex couples have families in ways similar to heterosexual couples because they may have had children in previous heterosexual or same-sex relationships, via artificial insemination, surrogacy, or via adoption. But same-sex couples' marriages are not completely equal; states have had laws that prohibit same-sex adoptions, and while same-sex adoption is legal in all fifty states, there is still prejudice against same-sex couples raising children. Alabama, Colorado, Kansas, Oklahoma, Ohio, South Dakota, and Texas have pending legislation to allow adoption agencies to discriminate against same-sex couples, individuals or non-Christians, or to prohibit same-sex adoptions. Some religiously affiliated adoption agencies have actually dissolved and other not-for-profits have changed their focus and mission to avoid having to place a child with a same-sex couple (or a lesbian or gay individual). Others are using "religious liberty" arguments to deny adoption services to same-sex couples. Their reasoning is that homosexuality is not natural, against their religious morality, and children ought to be in heterosexual families.

In the case of one partner bringing a child or children into the relationship, not recognizing both parents' custody puts the child or children's future at risk, thus second-parent adoption is crucial. Couples may want to ensure custody rights and a legal connection with the non-birth parent if the legally recognized parent (birth parent) should die, the couple break up, or the other parent dies. In other cases, the couple may be childless and want to adopt a child (see Myers, 2013).

The Good Mothers and Fathers

In divorces, custody of most children is awarded to their mother. This is based on the tender years assumption that mothers are most maternal. UNLESS, the mother is deemed an unfit mother because of drug or alcohol abuse, mental instability, or a record of child abuse, which may include the child witnessing acts of domestic violence (the mother is supposed to protect the child).

Poor women, who are collecting welfare, do not adequately care for children (sometimes measured by number of cans of food in their pantry), or those who test positive for drugs may be deemed unfit mothers and lose custody of their children. Black women are more likely to lose their children because someone reported them to social services and have their children end up in the foster care system. In New Jersey, 14% of children were black, yet black children made up 41% of the children in the foster care system in 2013.

If a woman enters the prison system pregnant, but she desires an abortion, she is denied that, even though abortions are legal. If she becomes pregnant in prison or is already pregnant and gives birth while incarcerated, she does so shackled. Most prisons allow the child to stay in prison with their mother until the age of two. Most women in prison are single heads of households, and if there is no one to care for their children, the children are mandated into the foster care system. Many women have their parental rights terminated while they are imprisoned because they are seen as abandoning their children. The mothers are usually already impoverished and cannot afford the costs of visits, especially since the prison may be over 100 miles from their family home. Men do not suffer losing their parental rights since they are usually not the only responsible parent (Kennedy, 2012; Law, 2012, pp. 43–58).

Today, migrants seeking asylum at our Southern border are being separated from the children they are traveling with. This policy was announced in order to try and stem the flow of immigrants from Central America, but this threat is not worse than the conditions these people see in their home countries (drug and gang violence, for example). Nor is separating children from their families a new policy. Parents have lost their children historically if they were slaves or the mother was deemed unfit. Today, this separation is made more tragic since the agencies involved have no way of tracking and reuniting many of the children with their families.

Black fathers have been seen as derelict parents—absent from the home, irresponsible, and uncaring. The idea that black men do not marry their children's mother or support their children, causing the black family to be unstable and fragile, overlooks the part that extended family, church, and community play in supporting families ravaged by the poverty and the criminal justice system, besides overlooking middle-class intact black families (Moynihan, 1970; Davis, 2003; Conor and White, 2006; Alexander, 2012; Gates et al., 2012).

Immigration, Naturalization, and Citizenship

From the first indigenous peoples crossing the ice bridge to the New World to the colonists who came for religious freedom and economic gains, Americans have been taught that as a nation of immigrants we welcome all. With the words of Emma Lazarus's poem, "The New Colossus," emblazoned on the Statue of Liberty and ingrained in our American mythology, we were taught we were a nation of immigrants. Yet our immigration policies have not been as welcoming; in March 2018, the Trump administration changed the mission statement of the United States Citizenship and Immigration Services (USCIS) to reflect this, no longer was the phrase "nation of immigrants" visible:

> U.S. Citizenship and Immigration Services administers the nation's lawful immigration system, safeguarding its integrity and promise by efficiently and fairly adjudicating requests for immigration benefits while protecting Americans, securing the homeland, and honoring our **values**.

The majority of our immigration policy has from the first American laws to control immigration assumed that the immigrant was male. Since Great Britain had sent criminals to be indentured servants to Georgia and other colonies under the Transportation Act of 1717 (until the end of the American Revolution), the first two laws—the Naturalization Acts of 1790 and 1795—limited naturalization to free white men (and their children) if they were of good moral character, non-criminals, and non-drunkards, who had resided in the country for two years (1790) and revised to five years in 1795. Indigenous people, free black men, slaves, and indentured servants were excluded.

Chinese and Japanese women emigrated to the United States following their husbands who came as railroad laborers, or during the gold rush. The Page Act of 1875 prohibited prostitutes, felons, and forced laborers from emigrating; it was enacted to control both ethnicity of immigrants as well as their sexual conduct. Chinese, Mongolians, and Japanese women had to have proof before they left Asia that they were of good character or wives. The Immigration and Nationality Act of 1882 excluded Chinese laborers from emigrating. The Immigration Act of 1924 (Pub. L. 68–139, 43 Stat. 153, enacted 26 May 1924) extended the prohibition against Chinese to include all Asians and set quotas on Italians, Jews, Greeks, Poles, and Slavs (peoples from Southern and Eastern Europe). This discriminatory policy codified that poor immigrants are undesirable and undeserving to immigrate and importantly to be eligible to become American citizens. Because this policy did not have any specific criteria that included political refugees at this time, people who were being persecuted by Nazi policies were not allowed to immigrate to the United States. The policy at that time was anti-Semitic, and there was fear that the refugees might include spies, thus persecuting the victims (*see* Ruth Gruber, 1983 and Cook, 2016).

Undesirables were also prohibited from getting non-immigrant (tourist) and permanent (green card) visas. This category included gays and lesbians if they had a criminal record; in many countries, homosexuality was a crime, though some countries such as Great Britain only male homosexuality was in the criminal code. Prior to January 2010, foreign persons infected with HIV were prohibited from entry into the United States solely on their HIV status, and this meant that infected people could not seek medical treatment in the United States (Canaday, 2011).

While the United States does grant asylum for people who are persecuted—"persecution" as "the infliction of suffering or harm upon those who differ… in a way regarded as offensive" (Sangha v. INS); "Persecution by any other name remains persecution" (Pitcherskaia v. INS)—based on their sexual orientation, gender identity (including transgender), or HIV status; they need to have documented evidence per *in re Pitcherskaia* that they are targeted as a group. For lesbians and other women who are subjected to gender violence and harassment, many nations claim that this violence (including female genital mutilation) is not state sponsored but social-cultural norms. The law allows LGBT people and those living with HIV to apply for asylum as "members of a particular social group," if they have suffered past persecution or have a well-founded fear of future persecution in their home country based on their sexual orientation, gender identity, or HIV-status.

Women who married foreigners was seen as not capable of extending American citizenship to him—due to societal perception of women as being weak and subject to manipulation. When the Expatriation Act of 1907 passed, an American woman who married a foreigner forfeited her American citizenship and assumed that of her husband. If her husband then became a naturalized American citizen, she would then also have to take a loyalty oath, but if she naturalized, citizenship was not extended to her husband. The Cable Act of 1922 repealed this, allowing only women whose husbands could nationalize to retain their citizenship (this was known as the Married Women's Independent Nationality Act). Amendments to this act allowed divorced or widows the ability to regain their citizenship in 1936, and in 1940, a woman married to a foreign national could regain her citizenship via pledging her allegiance in district courts (Hacker, 2017). Men could then and now import mail-order brides, marry foreigners and not only not lose their citizenship, but be able to extend a pathway to citizenship via a green card to their spouses. Similarly, now, women and same-sex spouses can also sponsor their spouses for visas and citizenship, like men and heterosexual couples, as long as the marriage is bona fide. The Trump administration, as of October 2018 has denied visas to the unmarried, same-sex, or heterosexual partners of foreign officials, diplomats, and United Nations employees, marriage is required for a visa (note: not all countries allow same-sex marriages).

From January 2017, President Trump has worked to ban Muslims from traveling to the United States under the assumption that such a ban will be in the best interests of national security, citing the 11 September 2001 terrorist attacks on the World Trade Center and Pentagon (note: the nationalities of those terrorists were Saudi Arabia, Egypt, Libya, and United Arab Emirates). His first travel bans were not upheld in court. The policy currently called "extreme vetting" and focuses on seven Muslim-majority countries: Iraq, Syria, Iran, Libya, Somalia, and Yemen (there are 48 Muslim-Majority countries). The Supreme Court in June 2018 upheld the last version of the travel ban.

The President also closed the Mexico-United States border and shut the government (winter 2018–19), including Homeland Security, to get funding for a border wall. The refugees are coming from El Salvador, Guatemala, and Honduras. One of the policies implemented meant to stop families with children from seeking asylum is family separation.

Congressman Steve King (R-IA) underscored the politics of blood and soil for determining citizenship when separating children at the Mexico-United States border: "We can't restore our civilization with someone else's babies." This policy, Patricia Williams (2018) likens to that of the nineteenth-century separation of slave children from their mothers, or twentieth century removing poor children from unfit homes relies

> on rationalizations we encounter still: Certain classes of human beings are not "really" human; they do not feel pain to the same degree as "more civilized" classes; these "others" are incorrigibly predisposed to prevarication… This "they"-making obliterates due process, equal protection, and individual justice. It justifies racial and ethnic profiling and punishes people in the plural. (Williams, 2018)

This was written before two young children seeking asylum died in US custody in December 2018. Their deaths were met with just as callous othering—it was their parents' fault for making them trek to the United States, even though they were escaping the violence and sociopolitical chaos that the United States helped finance in the 1980s.

Deferred Action for Childhood Arrivals (DACA), or the Dream Act (2001, revised in 2007), is for undocumented young adults who were brought into this country before they were 16, have lived in the United States since 2007, have a high school degree (or are enrolled), and were never convicted of a serious crime. It was supposed to provide for these young adults, known as Dreamers, to stay in the only country they know (to not be deported) and have legal work permits. It is estimated that the 800,000 DACA applicants have paid $2 Billion in local and state taxes. DACA did not provide for a path to citizenship. This program was ended by President Trump, and new legislation has not been adopted.

The idea that foreign-born women enter the United States to give birth and give their children citizenship, what some are calling "anchor babies," is based on the concept of *jus soli*, or birthright citizenship found in the Fourteenth Amendment of the Constitution that *All persons born or naturalized in the United States and subject to the jurisdiction thereof, are citizens of the United States and of the State wherein they reside.* [The exceptions to this rule are found in U.S. Title 8 Aliens and Nationality. Children born to diplomats and other foreign government officials do not become American Citizens.] While we might talk disparagingly about Latinx anchor babies, there are other women traveling to the United States to give birth to an American citizen. In the Los Angeles, California, area there are reports of homes turned into Chinese hotels for pregnant women. In Miami Beach, pregnant Russian women are renting or buying homes so their babies will be Americans, too. The fear of anchor babies reaching back to their mothers and fathers and giving them citizenship is one that requires the parents to wait until the child is 18 years old.

Another way to citizenship is by the concept of *jus sanguinis*, by blood. If one or more of your parents are American citizens—no matter where you are born, you are a citizen. This process also applies to children acquired via adoption from abroad.

Family Reunification, a family-based immigration program, by which an adult citizen (including naturalized citizens) sponsors family members for their green cards (which allow for permanent residency), has also been derogatorily called "Chain Migration." It is also the way that Melania Trump's parents, who are native Slovenians, for instance, started the process that resulted in them becoming naturalized citizens on 9 August 2018.

Another way foreign nationals can become American citizens is through serving in the military. This perk of military service is especially important when the military recruitment of American citizens, even after waiving minor drug charges or physical impairments, falls short of the numbers necessary to maintain ready forces. The US Army needed 76,000 new recruits in 2018. The military has accepted roughly 7,000 foreign nationals annually to meet their numbers.

Foreign nationals have served in the American military since the Revolutionary War. Under Immigration and Nationality Act (INA) Section 328, people who have served in the US military, including the reserves, can file for naturalization with just one year of service and who are legal permanent residents in good standing when US Citizenship and Immigration Service (USCIS) reviews their application on Form N-400. For foreign nationals who have served during "hostilities," including any time after 11 September 2001, may make application with just one day of service. Once naturalized, they may sponsor their relatives for a green card.

The length of service was expanded in October 2017 to 180 days. In the summer of 2018 foreign nationals, who were recruited under the Military Accessions Vital to the National Interest program (MAVNI) because they had skills (language and/or medical that were considered crucial) and were told they then had an expedited path to citizenship, were discharged abruptly. Lengthy stringent background and security checks were instituted in 2012.

Denaturalization

The Supreme Court ruled in Schneider v. Rusk, 377 U.S. 163 (1964) that it is "impermissible" to assume "that naturalized citizens as a class are less reliable and bear less allegiance to this country than do the native born." Or, in short: naturalized citizens have the same rights and responsibilities as birthright citizen, that citizenship is a guarantee of security. Naturalization fraud existed in the nineteenth century (Weil, 2012). As early as 1906, fraudulently obtained citizenship became grounds to be denaturalized, though those persons were usually allowed to reapply (Wessler, 2018). But as Emma Goldman's (and 248 others) deportation in December 1919 as a radical alien under the Anti-Anarchist Act, citizenship for those naturalized is not that secure (Lind, 2018) and became politicized, acts of speech could lead to denaturalization (Weil, 2013; Wessler, 2018) Concerns about "un-American activities, and loyalty to America lead to the creation of a *conditional citizenship* for some categories of citizens—in 1907 it was women marrying foreigners, but in 1940 was extended to draft dodgers, those who joined foreign militaries or voted in foreign elections, or lived more than two years abroad. The focus on naturalized citizens remained not only for those who committed acts of fraud to achieve their citizenship, but included those who espoused radical and foreign ideologies" (Weil, 2013, pp. 56–57).

Today, the USCIS Application for Naturalization Form N-400, Part 12 question 22 line that asks you to list any crimes for which you have never been punished: "Have you **EVER** committed, assisted in committing, or attempted to commit a crime of offense for which you were **NOT** arrested? "(bolding is USCIS). It is a Catch-22. How many people have gone 20 miles over the posted speed limit? In most states, driving over the speed limit is considered reckless driving, a misdemeanor, and criminal offense (a regular speeding ticket and its fine are civil offenses).

Homeland Security Investigations, a unit of Immigration and Customs Enforcement has been working to identify people who have received citizenship under false pretenses such as having their birth certificates falsified. This program now called Operation Second Look was started as Operation Janus under President Obama's administration (Wessler, 2018). If one has obtained their citizenship illegally or they did not reveal something that was relevant to their application, the Department of Justice can start denaturalization proceedings against the alien citizen (Lind, 2018). USCIS has removed its mission form fulfilling "America's promise as a nation of immigrants...[to] securing the homeland" (Wessler, 2018, p. 40). The number of denaturalization cases have ticked upwards into the thousands between 2014 and today, leading to many naturalized citizens to be fearful and to be *conditional citizens.*

This politics of fear, and the fear of potential statelessness, has been used to keep immigrants and naturalized citizens obedient and silent. As Hannah Arendt wrote in *Human Condition*, statelessness is not only the expelling a person from one nation, but from humanity.

Summary

There are two general ways to reproduce new citizens: to birth them or to import them. This chapter looked at how and who can have children and then raise them, then who may cross our borders and become a naturalized citizen. The first way of reproducing or replenishing our citizens should be natural—sex happens—but the state has accentuated the sex and desire citizen. The polity and society, no matter how private the intimate act of sex is, is there in bed with the partners—from who and how to have sex, to who and when to marry. Raising the children, either because they were birthed by the parent or adopted, has state involvement if the parents fall out of the heteronormative classed and raced norms. The same norms hold fast for who may enter and stay in the country. The fear of being a majority minority country is making our southern border an entry point of contention. The misplaced fear of terrorism has also blocked entry into our country; brown immigrant bodies are seen as potential threats (though most acts of terrorism are committed by home-grown actors). Most undocumented residents have come into the country legally via our international airports and points of entry and have overstayed their visas; a majority of these people just blend into the community.

Notes

1 There are many excellent books on the Lesbian, Gay, and Trans liberation movements that examine the history and politics of the movements. From Duberman et al. (1990) to Brooks and Katz (2015). See also Shane Phelan (2001), Graff (2004), and Canaday (2011) among others on same-sex marriage, politics, and families.

2 family.findlaw.com/marriage/state-by-state-marriage-age-of-consent-laws.html.

References

Abramowitz, Mimi (2004) *Regulating the Lives of Women: Social Welfare Policy from Colonial Times to the Present.* Boston: Southend Press.

ACLU (1995) "Norplant: A New Contraceptive with the Potential Abuse." Accessed 28 December 2018, www.aclu.org/other/norplant-new-contraceptive-potential-abuse.

Alexander, Michelle (2012) *The New Jim Crow: Mass Incarceration in the Age of Colorblindness.* New York: The New Press.

Altman, Dennis (2001) *Global Sex.* Chicago, IL: University of Chicago Press.

The Automobile Workers v. Johnson Controls, Inc., 499 US.187 (1991).

Bamforth, Nicholas (2012) "Sexuality and Citizenship in Contemporary Constitutional Argument." *International Journal of Constitutional Law* 10 (2): 477–492.

Barker, Nicola (2013) *Not the Marrying Kind: A Feminist Critique of Same-Sex Marriage.* Basingstoke: Palgrave Macmillan.

Bedford, Kate and Janet R. Jakobsen (eds). (2009) "Towards a Vision of Sexual and Economic Justice." Accessed 15 January 2019, www.bcrw.barnard.edu/publication-sections/nfs/.

Bell, David and Jon Binnie (2000) *The Sexual Citizen: Queer Politics and Beyond.* Cambridge: Polity Press.

Bernstein, Elizabeth and Laurie Schaffner (eds). (2005) *Regulating Sex: The Politics of Intimacy and Identity.* New York: Routledge.

Bertone, Chiara (2013) "Citizenship across Generations: Struggles Around Heteronormativity." *Citizenship Studies* 17 (8): 985–999.

Bowers v. Hardwick, 478 U.S. 186 (1986).

Bowles, Nellie (18 May 2018) "Jordan Peterson: Custodian of the Patriarchy." *New York Times.* https://www.nytimes.com/2018/05/18/style/jordan-peterson-12-rules-for-life.html.

Brenkart, Benjamin (21 March 2003) "The Newport Sex Scandal, 1919–21." *The Gay and Lesbian Review Worldwide* 10 (2): 13–15.

Brooks, Adrian and Jonathan Katz (2015) *The Right Side of History: 100 Years of LGBT Activism.* New York: Cleis Press.

Brown, Wendy (2006) *Regulating Aversion: Tolerance in the Age of Identity and Empire.* Princeton, NJ: Princeton University Press.

Butler, Judith (2004) *Undoing Gender.* London: Routledge.

Calhoun, Cheshire (2000) *Feminism, the Family and the Politics of the Closet: Lesbian and Gay Displacement.* Oxford: Oxford University Press.

Canaday, Margot (2011) *The Straight State: Sexuality and Citizenship in Twentieth-Century America.* Princeton, NJ: Princeton University Press.

Center for Disease Control. "Infant Mortality What Is the CDC Doing?" Accessed 4 January 2019, www.cdc.gov/reproductivehealth/MaternalInfantHealth/InfantMortality.htm.

Centers for Disease Control. Accessed 16 November 2018, www.cdc.gov/reproductivehealth/WomensRH/index.htm.

Chambers, Clare (2007) *Sex, Culture and Justice: The Limits of Choice.* Philadelphia, PA: Penn State Press.

Cook, Blanche W. (2016) *Eleanor Roosevelt Volume 3: The War Years and After, 1939–1962.* New York: Viking.

Conor, Michael and Joseph White (2006) *Black Fathers: An Invisible Presence in America.* New York: Routledge.

Cossman, Brenda (2007) *Sexual Citizens: The Legal and Cultural Regulation of Sex and Belonging.* Stanford, CA: Stanford University Press.

D'Emilio, John (2000) "Cycles of Change, Questions of Strategy, the Gay and Lesbian Movement After Fifty Years." In: Craig A. Rimmerman, Kenneth D. Walld, and Clyde Wilcox (eds), *The Politics of Gay Rights.* Chicago, IL: University of Chicago Press, 31–53.

Davis, Adrienne (2015) "Regulating Sex Work: Erotic Assimilationism, Erotic Exceptionalism, and the Challenge of Intimate Labor." *California Law Review* 103 (5): 3. Accessed 15 February 2019, scholarship.law.berkeley.edu/cgi/viewcontent.cgi?article=4300&context=californialawreview.

Davis, Angela (2003) *Are Prisons Obsolete?* New York: Seven Stories Press.

Dean, James Joseph (2014) *Straights: Heterosexuality in Post-Closeted Culture*. New York: New York University Press.

Duberman, Martin, Martha Vicinus and George Chauncey (1990) *Hidden from History: Reclaiming the Gay and Lesbian Past*. New York: Penguin Press.

Duggan, Lisa (2002) "The New Homonormativity: The Sexual Politics of Neoliberalism." In: Castronova, Russ and Dana D. Nelson (eds), *Materializing Democracy: Toward a Revitalized Cultural Politics*. Durham, NC: Duke University Press, 175–194.

Duggan, Lisa (2003) *The Twilight of Equality? Neoliberalism, Cultural Politics, and the Attack on Democracy*. Boston, MA: Beacon Press.

Eggert, Nina and Isabelle Engeli (2015) "Rainbow Families and the State: How Policies Shape Reproductive Choices." In: David Patternote and Manon Tremblay (eds), *The Ashgate Research Companion to Lesbian and Gay Activism*. Farnham: Ashgate, 323–338.

Eisenstadt v. Baird, 405 U.S. 438 (1972).

Evans, David T. (1993) *Sexual Citizenship: The Material Construction of Sexualities*. London: Routledge.

Flavin, Jeanne (2009) *Our Bodies, Our Crimes: The Policing of Women's Reproduction in America*. New York: New York University Press.

Foucault, Michel (1978) *The History of Sexuality: An Introduction*. New York: Vintage Books.

Frame, Laura (1999) "Suitable Homes Revisited: An Historical Look at Child Protection and Welfare Reform." *Children and Youth Services Review* 21 (9–10): 719–754.

Fraser, Nancy (1995) "From Redistribution to Recognition? Dilemmas of Justice in a 'Post-Socialist Age'." *New Left Review* 212: 68–93.

Fraser, Nancy (1998) "Heterosexism, Misrecognition and Capitalism: A Response to Judith Butler." *New Left Review* 228: 140–149.

Gates, Henry Louis, Jr. Claude Steele, Lawrence D. Bobo, Michael C. Dawson, Gerald Jaynes, Lisa Crooms-Robinson, and Linda Darling-Hammond (2012) *The Oxford Handbook of African American Citizenship 1865–Present*. New York: Oxford University Press.

Glazer, Reena (1993) "Women's Body Image and the Law." *Duke Law Journal* 43: 113–147.

Grabham, Emily (2007) "Citizen Bodies, Intersex Citizenship." *Sexualities* 10 (1): 29–48.

Graff, E.J. (2004) *What Is Marriage For?* Boston, MA: Beacon Press.

Grant, Melissa Gira (5 March 2014) "Let's Call Sex Work What It Is: Work." *The Nation*. Accessed 15 February 2019, www.thenation.com/article/lets-call-sex-work-what-it-work/.

Gruber, Ruth (1983) *Haven: The Dramatic Story of 1,000 WWII Refugees and How They Came to America*. New York: Coward-McCann.

Hacker, Meg (2017) "When Saying 'I Do' Meant Giving Up Your U.S. Citizenship. U.S. National Archives." Accessed 15 January 2018, www.archives.gov/files/publications/prologue/2014/spring/citizenship.pdf.

Heaphy, Brian, Carol Smart and Anna Einarsdottir (2013) *Same Sex Marriages: New Generations, New Relationships*. Basingstoke: Palgrave Macmillan.

Hemmings, Clare (2012) "Sexuality, Subjectivity … and Political Economy?" *Subjectivity* 5: 121–139.

Hubbard, Phil (2001) "Sex Zones: Intimacy, Citizenship and Public Space." *Sexualities* 4 (1): 51–71.

The Immigration Act of 1924 (Pub. L. 68–139, 43 Stat. 153, enacted 26 May 1924).

Jefferson, Thomas (1805) in Bridgewater, Pamela (2005) "Ain't I a Slave: Slavery Reproduction Abuse and Reparations." *UCLA Women's Law Journal* 14 (1). Accessed 15 January 2019, /escholarship.org/uc/item/6vt8x3jj.

Joseph, Suad (1997) "The Public/Private – The Imagined Boundary in the Imagined Nation/State/Community: The Lebanese Case." *Feminist Review* 57: 73–92.

Kabeer, Naila (2012) "Empowerment, Citizenship and Gender Justice: A Contribution to Locally Grounded Theories of Change in Women's Lives." *Ethics and Social Welfare* 6 (3): 216–232.

Kaelber, Lutz (2011) "Eugenics; Compulsory Sterilization in 50 American States." Accessed 10 January 2019, www.uvm.edu/~lkaelber/eugenics/.

Kaplan, Morris B. (1997) *Sexual Justice: Democratic Citizenship and the Politics of Desire*. New York: Routledge.

Kaprielian-Churchill, Isabel (1993) "Armenian Refugee Women: The Picture Brides, 1920–1930." *Journal of American Ethnic History* 12 (3): 3–29.

Kennedy, Deseriee A. (2012) "'The Good Mother': Mothering, Feminism, and Incarceration." 18 Wm. & Mary J. Women & L. 161. Accessed 22 January 2019, https://scholarship.law.wm.edu/wmjowl/vol18/iss2/2.

Ko, Lisa (29 January 2016) "Unwanted Sterilization and Eugenic Programs in the United States." Accessed 26 January 2019, http://www.pbs.org/independentlens/blog/unwanted-sterilization-and-eugenics-programs-in-the-united-states.

Kollman, Kelly and Matthew Waites (2009) "The Global Politics of Lesbian, Gay, Bisexual and Transgender Human Rights: An Introduction." *Contemporary Politics* 15 (1): 1–17.

Krause, Eleanor, Katherine Guyot and Isabel Sawhill (8 November 2017) "Note to GOP: To Improve Women's Economic Opportunities Don't Cut Family Planning Expand It." Accessed 25 November 2018, https://www.brookings.edu/blog/social-mobility-memos/2017/11/08/note-to-gop-to-improve-womens-economic-opportunities-dont-cut-family-planning-expand-it/.

Law, Victoria (2012) *Resistance Behind Bars: The Struggles of Incarcerated Women*. Oakland, CA: PM Press.

Law, Victoria (17 July 2017) "What Makes a Good Mother, According to the Government?" *Bitch Magazine*, Accessed 24 December 2018, https://www.bitchmedia.org/post/what-makes-a-good-mother-government-rise-out-of-poverty-welfare-pension-history-racism.

Lawrence v. Texas, 539 U.S. 558 (2003).

Lind, Dara (18 July 2018) "Denaturalization, Explained: How Trump Can Strip Immigrants of Their Citizenship: A New 'Denaturalization Task Force' Raises Questions about Who Really Counts as American." www.vox.com/2018/7/18/17561538/denaturalization-citizenship-task-force-janus.

Moynihan, Daniel Patrick (1970) *Maximum Feasible Misunderstanding*. Detroit, MI: Free Press.

Myers, JoAnne (2018) "Justice System." In: Letizia Gugliemo (ed.), *Misogyny in American Culture* (2 volumes). Sacramento, CA: ABC-CLIO.

Myers, JoAnne (2013) *The Historical Dictionary of the Lesbian and Gay Liberation Movements*. Lanham, MD: Scarecrow Press.

Nussbaum, Martha (2010). *From Disgust: To Humanity.* New York: Oxford University Press.

Obergefell v. Hodges, 576 U.S. ___ (2015).
Office of Minority Health, Department of Health and Human Services. "Profile of Black/African Americans." The US Government. Accessed 25 January 2019, www.minorityhealth.hhs.gov/omh/browse.aspx?lvl=3&lvlid=61.
Olesky, Elżbieta H. (ed.). (2009) *Intimate Citizenships: Gender, Sexualities, Politics*. London: Routledge.
Pateman, Carole (1988) *The Sexual Contract*. Palo Alto, CA: Stanford University Press.
Phelan, Shane (1995) "The Space of Justice: Lesbians and Democratic Politics." In: Angelia R. Wilson (ed.), *A Simple Matter of Justice? Theorizing Lesbian and Gay Politics*. London: Cassell, 332–356.
Phelan, Shane (2001) *Sexual Strangers: Gays, Lesbians and Dilemmas of Citizenship*. Philadelphia, PA: Temple University Press.
Phillips, Anne (2006) *Which Equalities Matter?* Cambridge: Polity Press.
Plummer, Kenneth (2003) *Intimate Citizenship: Private Decisions and Public Dialogues*. Seattle, WA: University of Washington Press.
Plummer, Kenneth (2005) "Intimate Citizenship in an Unjust World." In: Mary Romero and Eric Margolis (eds), *The Blackwell Companion to Social Inequalities*. Oxford: Wiley Blackwell, 75–99.
Pretty Woman (1990) Dir Garry Marshall. Touchstone.
Puar, Jasbir K. (2007) *Terrorist Assemblages: Homonationalism in Queer Times*. Durham, NC: Duke University Press Books.
Puar, Jasbir K. and Amit Rai (2002) "Monster, Terrorist, Fag: The War on Terrorism and the Production of Docile Patriots." *Social Text, 72* 20 (3): 117–148.
Richardson, Diane (1998) "Sexuality and Citizenship." *Sociology* 32 (1): 83–100.
Richardson, Diane (2000) *Rethinking Sexuality*. London: SAGE.
Richardson, Diane (2004) "Locating Sexualities: From Here to Normality." *Sexualities* 7 (4): 391–411.
Richardson, Diane (2005) "Desiring Sameness? The Rise of a Neoliberal Politics of Normalisation." *Antipode* 37 (3): 515–553.
Richardson, Diane (2015) "Neoliberalism, Citizenship and Activism." In: David Paternotte and Manon Tremblay (eds), *The Ashgate Research Companion to Lesbian and Gay Activism*. Farnham: Ashgate, 259–271.
Richardson, Diane and Surya Monro (2012) *Sexuality, Equality and Diversity*. Basingstoke: Palgrave Macmillan.
Roberts, Dorothy (1997) *Killing the Black Body*. New York: Vintage.
Robson, Ruthann and Tanya Kessler (2008) "Unsettling Sexual Citizenship." *McGill Law Journal* 53: 535–571.
Roseneil, Sasha (2013) *Beyond Citizenship*. Basingstoke: Palgrave Macmillan.
Roseneil, Sasha, Crowhurst, Isabel, Santos, Ana Cristina and Stoilova, Mariya (2013) "Reproduction and Citizenship/Reproducing Citizens." *Citizenship Studies* 17 (8): 901–911.
Ryan-Flood, Róisín (2009) *Lesbian Motherhood: Gender, Families and Sexual Citizenship*. Basingstoke, UK: Palgrave Macmillan.
Sawhill, Isabel V. (21 August 2015) "Reducing Poverty by Cutting Unplanned Births." www.brookings.edu/opinions/reducing-poverty-by-cutting-unplanned-births/.
Segal, Lynne (2013) "Reluctant Citizens: Between Incorporation and Resistance." In: Sasha Roseneil (ed.), *Beyond Citizenship? Feminism and the Transformation of Belonging*. Basingstoke: Palgrave Macmillan, 66–88.

Seidman, Steven (2004) *Beyond the Closet: The Transformation of Gay and Lesbian Life.* London: Routledge.

Seidman, Steven (2009) "Critique of Compulsory Heterosexuality." *Sexuality Research and Social Policy: Journal of NSRC* 61 (1): 18–28.

Srinivasan, Amia (2018) "Does Anyone Have the Right to Sex?" https://www.lrb.co.uk/v40/n06/amia-srinivasan/does-anyone-have-the-right-to-sex.

Stacey, Judith (2012) *Unhitched: Love, Marriage and Family Values.* New York: New York University Press.

State v. Way, 297 N.C. 293 (1979).

Stein, Arlene (2001) *The Stranger Next Door: The Story of a Small Community's Battle over Sex, Faith, and Civil Rights.* Boston, MA: Beacon Press.

Stern, Scott W. (2018) *The Trials of Nina McCall: Sex, Surveillance, and the Decades-long Government Plan to Imprison "Promiscuous" Women.* Boston, MA: Beacon Press.

Stevens, Jacqueline (1999) *Reproducing the State.* Princeton, NJ: Princeton University Press.

Stevens, Jacqueline (2009) *States without Nations.* New York: Columbia University Press.

Stychin, Carl F. (2003) *Governing Sexuality: The Changing Politics of Citizenship and Law Reform.* Oxford: Hart Publishing.

Taylor, Yvette (2011) "Lesbian and Gay Parents' Sexual Citizenship: Recognition, Belonging and (Re)classification." In: Janice McLaughlin, Peter Phillimore and Diane Richardson (eds), *Contesting Recognition: Culture, Identity and Citizenship.* Basingstoke: Palgrave Macmillan, 144–165.

The Trafficking Victim Protection Laws of 2000 (106-386); 2003 (P.L.108-193); 2005 (P.L. 109-164) 2008 (P.L. 110-457); 2013 (P.L. 113-4).

Tremblay, Manon, David Patternote and Carol Johnson (eds). (2011) *The Lesbian and Gay Movement and the State: Comparative Insights into a Transformed Relationship.* Farnham: Ashgate.

Turner, Bryan S. (2008) "Citizenship, Reproduction and the State: International Marriage and Human Rights." *Citizenship Studies* 12 (1): 45–54.

United States Citizenship and Immigration Services (6 March 2018) "About Us." Accessed 22 January 2019, www.uscis.gov/aboutus.

Villarosa, Linda (11 April 2018) "Why America's Black Mothers and Babies Are in a Life-or-Death Crisis." *The New York Times.* Accessed 15 November 2018, www.nytimes.com/2018/04/11/magazine/black-mothers-babies-death-maternal-mortality.html.

Waites, Matthew (2009) *The Age of Consent: Young People, Sexuality and Citizenship.* Basingstoke: Palgrave Macmillan.

Warner, Michael (1999) *The Trouble with Normal: Sex, Politics and the Ethics of Queer Life.* Cambridge, MA: Harvard University Press.

Weeks, Jeffrey (1998) "The Sexual Citizen." *Theory, Culture & Society* 15 (3–4): 35–52.

Weeks, Jeffrey, Brian Heaphy and Catherine Donovan (2001) *Same Sex Intimacies: Families of Choice and other Life Experiments.* London: Routledge.

Weil, Patrick (2012) *The Sovereign Citizen: Denaturalization and the Origins of the American Republic.* Philadelphia, PA: University of Pennsylvania.

Wessler, Seth Freed (23 December 2018) "Denaturalized." *New York Times Magazine,* 36–53.

Williams, Patricia J. (20 June 2018) "The Generational Trauma of Separating Families." *The Nation.*

Wilson, Angelia R. (2009) "The 'Neat Concept' of Sexual Citizenship: A Cautionary Tale for Human Rights Discourse." *Contemporary Politics* 15 (1): 73–85.

9

WORKING TOWARD EQUALITY

Citizenship is essential in a liberal democracy, especially in a republic, since the key concept of democracy is that the people rule, that they not only formulate the public agenda but make public decisions (Dahl, 2000). In a liberal democracy, its members, the citizens, are presumed equal. We are taught that "one person one vote" allows all to take part in public decision-making and make their voices heard; if they do not take part, it is by their own choice. We are taught to pledge our allegiance and to obey the laws, we are taught that individualism is valued, but if we dissent to government actions, if we take a knee, we are no longer a patriot. We are taught that if you work hard, you will get ahead—that is the main tenet of the capitalistic meritocracy. Do we really have the same opportunities and potential? Many times, we see privilege and call it meritocracy or normal when it is, in fact, institutionalized privilege. We are all taught to tolerate the other, but we rarely see the other—we are cordoned off in our separate neighborhoods. Our nation, like all nations, wants and needs new citizens, but we do not value all. We do not see the hidden structural scaffolding, the institutionalized and legalized policies, along with the social norms that maintain the inequality of citizens. For example, we valorize the white middle-class mother who stays at home and raises her children, but the poor woman who is receiving temporary assistance for needy families *has* to work if her children are over the age of three. This book lays bare some of the intended consequences of social and political policies, making visible the invisible structural constraints. What is at stake when citizens are regulated and controlled by policies and norms so that some are not afforded full access to their civil rights is the survival of our liberal democracy?[1]

The purpose of this book is to expose how some citizens are controlled so that the status quo is maintained. The markers of good citizenship are a complex framework, a more intersectional model of how civil society—norms and myths—along with laws and policies reinforce those with (and without) privilege and entitlement. It is much easier to work with a docile citizenry than deal with the messiness of a democracy. But it is in the messiness in which we find the essence and potential of the noble experiment that is American Democracy.

The argument that citizenship is either a binary—you either belong or you do not—or that it could be this nuanced spectrum of belonging and that one's access to rights is marked by this nuanced spectrum. How do we assimilate and to what ideal? Can we all reach that ideal, or is there a limit? How do we tolerate differences in a multicultural society, one quickly becoming a majority minority one? The key is to realize that we all belong, we the people all have a stake in this expanding mulipolyglot of a democracy. We need to work to ensure all have the equal opportunity to be good citizens and to be part of the whole.

This chapter will articulate a practical path to counter this and achieve equality. Without correction, not only is democracy and the promise of equality a false hope, but we may consider the noble experiment that is the United States a failed one. The attitude of democratic Calvinism can easily shift from one of tolerance and avoidance to a politics of disgust and aversion. We need to rethink this selfish individualism, that only a few may enjoin democracy. Over the course of our history, we have seen the expansion of enfranchisement, the expansion of opportunity. We must once again embrace this ever expanding potential. We must recognize that if we all have the opportunity, if we all can participate fully, then we will have a richer more robust nation.

Democracy is messy, without the ability to achieve true equality or the markers of good citizenship, people can easily slide into the status of other. From this othered status, it is a slippery slope into an entrenched status from which there is no recovery, with no one else really noticing, because they are trapped in their own situation. It is important to restate that the average citizen in Germany was busy minding their own lives as the laws started to shift German citizens who were Jewish into a second-class citizenship, and as they were further scapegoated, into noncitizen, from there it was easy to make them into non-humans.

If equality is key to citizenship (Marshall, 1964; Rawls, 1993; Heater, 1999), how may we best achieve this? The previous chapters have shown that while there may be supposedly a formal legal equality, that is not the lived reality of citizens who get marked—they lose access to their political voice, their constitutional rights, their privacy, and in some cases their lives. Michelle Alexander (2012) illustrated how even with the Voting Rights Act and Civil Rights Act of the mid-1960s, society and the governments use the war on drugs to incarcerate black men. The Black Lives Matter (BLM) movement was founded to focus society's attention on how police officers summarily judge unarmed black men, women, and children as mortal threats, yet are able to capture alive most white mass killers.

In response to the BLM, Blue Lives Matter and All Lives Matter sprung up. The Blue Lives Matter says that police lives are endangered. This movement even spawned addition federal legislation, "The Protect and Serve Act" to increase the sentence of people who knowingly assault law enforcement officers causing bodily injury, even though there are already substantial state and federal laws that exist. Around the country, 128 law enforcement officers lost their lives in 2017; that same year, 987 persons were killed by the police of which over 50% were people of color, which is proportionally greater than their demographics (Khazan, 2018; *Washington Post*, 2018). It is also to be noted that the name of this proposed bill is misleading, and law enforcement is supposed to "Protect and Serve" *all* the people. The police use the Public Duty Doctrine when deciding what incidents receive priority, allowing them administrative discretion. The Supreme Court has upheld the use of this discretion in cases where the police did not enforce mandatory arrest requirements when orders of protection are broken because they deemed there was no property interest.[2]

While all lives do matter, the importance of Black Lives Matters is to underscore the law of due process in the summary killing of people of color. The police use of deadly force against persons of color is not only a miscarriage of justice, it underscores the privilege that white people enjoy.

One of the main purposes of government is protection from threats from outside our borders and from within them. Our government over the course of our almost 250-year history has used fear and national security to protect us; we, the people, knowingly give up more of our rights for this protection. A prime example is after the 11 September 2001 attacks Congress readily passed the US Patriot Act (the full title is the Uniting and Strengthening America by Providing Appropriate Tools Required to Intercept and Obstruct Terrorism Act of 2001). Sold to the public as an anti-terrorism tool for law enforcement, it tramples on First and Fourth Amendment rights, handing law enforcement agencies the ability to gather information without court warrants and allows for "sneak and peek" warrants, which allow for officers to raid a suspect's residence without notification (in some cases, the suspect is not notified until after the raid) and view evidence on home computers. The Act basically replaced all the investigative procedures the police had lost under the Warren Court. The Act has primarily been used against environmentalists, drug cases, fraud cases, and organized crime. As Ben Franklin (1969) is often quoted: "Those who would give up essential Liberty, to purchase a little temporary Safety, deserve neither Liberty nor Safety." Political theorists point to Machiavelli's advice to the Prince and Thomas Hobbes' *Leviathan* regarding using fear and security to govern.

The use of fear in the name of national security not only makes us wary of foreigners, but of strangers who are fellow citizens.

We might give these citizen strangers the title of citizen, but if we do not see them as good citizens, we do not afford them respect or full inclusion on our civil society (Conover et al., 2004). Conover et al. note in their study that

> Despite the successful institutionalization of civil, political, and social rights, this ideal remains elusive, for the law has proved more progressive than has society. Many minorities are still routinely ignored, excluded, patronized, and not regarded as full members of the political community. Denied equal standing, they are denied equal citizenship. ... From a liberal viewpoint, it is further desirable to distinguish clearly between "citizens" and "good citizens," because the latter concept layers on assumptions and stereotypes that favor predominant groups. To be regarded as a fully authentic citizen, as an equal citizen, "basic" citizenship should be sufficient. (pp. 1061–1062)

Their conclusion is relatively pessimistic, that the normative ideal of equal citizenship may not be achievable because it is unrealistic to separate culture and citizenship. Citizenship as an ideal is deeply rooted in both its abstractness as a concept and the biases of citizenship as a "desirable activity"—the concept of good citizen. They continue that these liberal interpretations also color the motivations of national civic identity (p. 1063).

Citizens and the government theoretically view citizenship as the liberal individualistic concept of treating all the same without taking in their differences formally as per Rawls (1993). The purpose of government is to protect, adjudicate fairness, and distribute and redistribute resources as needed. "Citizenship is intended to buffer its members against the vagaries and inequalities in social systems, with methods for redistributing resources as needed" (Yoder and Verzijl in Rosales, 2018, p. 35). In practice, we are all trying to assimilate to that hegemonic ideal good citizen, unfortunately not all of us succeed. Not all of our differences can remain private, and as the markers of good citizen show, there is structural discrimination that constrains many. In reality, the liberal democratic practice is a selfish form of individualism (What is in it for me? Does it affect me?) based on the unfettered capitalism and property rights of Locke.

Rousseau would point to the abdication of citizens' full responsibility to participate in public decision-making to an elected representational government that they, the citizens, do not pay attention to in between elections. But, the citizenry does not even go to the polls—only 80% of the population eligible to vote are registered to do so. Voter turnout indicates that we do not like to exercise this right, the highest voter turnout for a presidential election was 63% in 1960, the second highest was the 2008 election of Barack Obama versus John

McCain when the voter turnout was 56.8%. Off-year federal elections have a voter turnout of under 40%, turnout for local elections are as low as 7%. Those turnout rates are by people who have registered, who can vote; there are still existing obstacles to enfranchising all citizens—from voter identification laws to polling places that are inaccessible.

The local community is the site of participation, production and the rights of citizens as both Tocqueville (2002) and Rosales (2018, p. 4) proclaim, yet as the voter turnout numbers above show, we do not pay attention on the local level to those local decisions that impact us the greatest. How may we achieve the equality that liberal democracy needs? How do we challenge this individualistic, selfish, content model of citizenship?

A multiculturalist view of citizenship, which recognizes and accepts cultural differences, is promoted by thinkers such as Will Kymlicka (2001), Bhikhu Parekh (2002), and Iris Marion Young (1990). This pluralistic citizenship allows for the citizens to believe they are valued for their difference, and such a belief would connect them to the larger democratic project, overtime all will develop shared values. The cosmopolitan view of citizenship promoted by Seyla Benhabib and Abdullahi An-Na'im is that we are all global citizens and political, social, and economic rights should be attached to the citizen and thus portable as we cross boundaries and borders, rights should not be granted by the state.

The ideal form of citizenship would be to enable all to be committed and act with a duty toward the best public good for all. If we make public decisions in the best public interest—with the idea that if people have living wages they will be able to spend more money, and the economy will prosper. If all had access to affordable health care and sick leave, workers would not come to work sick and sicken others, thus lowering productivity for all. And, so on. We should not have as Martin Luther King, Jr. often said: "Socialism for the rich and rugged individualism for the poor." We should not be privatizing profit, while putting the costs of potential and future risks on the backs of others. The issue is how to attain this, where all citizens have agency to act and are viewed as equal. One way would be to recognize that without those we tend to ignore or denigrate, we would not have the quality of life we aspire to—think of how difficult life becomes when there is a sanitation or subway worker strike, or the cost of food when gas prices rise? What happens when we are inconvenienced by power outages? How do we achieve equality in a pluralistic society?

Leap of Faith: Pluralistic Democracy and Equality

This book has focused on how public policy and societal norms entrench citizens in a second-class citizenship from which they cannot escape, nor is it noticed by others because it does not affect them. The five markers identified are subtle yet damning if marked as not being a good citizen to be patriotic, own property, participate or be productive, or to be able to reproduce citizens.

Citizens "tolerate" others, individualizing others' problems and blaming them for what is, in reality, structural processes that discriminate. If only they did "X," they would not be poor or live in crowded housing, for example. We have taken John Stuart Mill's liberal individual to the extreme, except when we are essentializing them as a group (Brown, 2006).

How do we recover and deliver on the concept of equality, democracy, and human rights in a pluralistic diverse society?

We have made the leap from natural rights to individual rights. Individual rights have been translated into individualism and self-centeredness. Even corporations have the standing as citizens, they have individual rights courtesy of Santa Clara County v. Southern Pacific Railroad, 118 U.S. 394 (1886), a case that dealt with the taxation of railroad property, BUT a comment made before oral arguments by the then Chief Justice Morrison Remick Waite that "the court does not wish to hear arguments in the question whether the Fourteenth Amendment to the constitution… applies to these corporations, we are all of the opinion it does" became recorded precedent, and not challenged (there were more cases concerning corporations than humans as citizens in the late nineteenth century). Most recently, corporations as citizens with First Amendment rights of political expression has been heard by this Supreme Court session Citizens United (Hillary the Movie) v. FEC.

And, most recently, we have seen (closely held) corporations such as Hobby Lobby be able to lay claim to having a religion, whose morality was offended by having to extend birth control as part of their health insurance benefits to their employees. Corporations are persons, with a political voice and a morality. We have lost the original concept of corporations giving back to the public good.

But what of human citizens—their rights and responsibilities? What about their connection to the public good, to the polity? Over the past 50 years we have been losing this connection.: that is the tension between self-interested individual rights and the public good.

Where once we made sacrifices, and "ask not what your country could do for you, but what you could do for your country" (Kennedy, 1961). Have we now have abandoned the public for our material well-being—for our consumerism to buy happiness a la John Stuart Mill? And if we can be happy with our goal to own seven houses while others are homeless, so be it.

Individualism also affected religion giving birth to the Protestant Reformation where the individual no longer needed the church to interpret God's word, and the polity separate from the church. With the US Constitution, we had the separation of church and state best articulated by former NY Governor Mario Cuomo (1984) at a talk at the University of Notre Dame on Religious Belief and Public Morality:

> I protect my right to be a Catholic by preserving your right to believe as a Jew, a Protestant, or non-believer, or as anything else you choose.

> We know that the price of seeking to force our beliefs on others is that they might someday force theirs on us.
>
> This freedom is the fundamental strength of our unique experiment in government. In the complex interplay of forces and considerations that go into the making of our laws and policies, its preservation must be a pervasive and dominant concern (13 September 1984).

The role of religion inched its way into the public debate during the Reagan administration. By the early 1990s, the evangelical religious right began to distribute voter guides to churches and ran stealth campaigns for boards of education, reframing public debates around family values. The insecurity and unsureness after the attacks on 11 September gave rise to a stronger fundamentalist movement—followers became even more removed from the polity—homeschooling, for example, increased. How people understand and know reverted from the scientific rationalism of the Enlightenment back to faith-based gnosticism. Creationism became valid theory; the science of climate change shares the public forum with climate deniers. Facts do not seem to matter. In the past 50 years, we have become the epitome of Hofstadter's anti-intellectual, leave no child behind has left those in public schools able to memorize for tests rather than critically think or use their imaginations—which renders them silent in the public square. They no longer can imagine or debate policy and its consequences. In third grade, most students used to learn to write cursive; today that is no longer required. Those students will not be able to read original documents or early deeds. Those with funding or vouchers to go to private schools, parochial or even public charter schools, are given more latitude, and they are not forced to regurgitate facts. Our governments—local, state, and national—are more concerned with assuring our students will have jobs, so much so that we are tending to illiberal educations—to professional training, not the liberal arts education that Jefferson and Dewey thought necessary to nurture our democracy. Derek Thompson (2019) says we suffer from *workism* "the belief that work is not only necessary to economic production, but also the centerpiece of one's identity and life's purpose; and the belief that any policy to promote human welfare must *always* encourage more work." So, we pass laws that demand work, we work hard to stay in place, acknowledging the culture of meritocracy that allows some to succeed, and the wealth gap has become a chasm (Mijs, 2019).

We have become Marcuse's *One Dimensional Man.* Marcuse stated, "The requirements for profitable mass production are not necessarily identical with those of mankind" (1964, p. 244). We have misconstrued Adam Smith's (2015) *The Wealth of Nations* into thinking that we need to earn the most without paying for the privilege of living in a democracy. The United States is considered to be one of the wealthiest nations, and its population holds a lot of wealth, yet in terms of citizen's own assessment of their well-being, the country is number 18 out of 156 countries surveyed for the United Nations' World Happiness Report.[3]

Can we recover? Or have we become such a passive, individualistic society that we "Let Go and Let God" and have forsaken the potential of liberal democracy?

Might there be another measurement for successful government other than Gross National Product? Might there be another mark of a good citizen? Since 2012, the United Nations has been issuing an annual "World Happiness Report" ranking the 156 nations' citizens' happiness as a measure of well-being. The report measures strong community support, trust in government, and how much freedom the citizens have. In turn, citizen well-being has a positive effect on civil society including political participation.[4]

John Rawls (1971) had proposed that policy makers use a "veil of ignorance" when making decisions that would lead to a more just society. This process would lead to policies and programs that would not benefit just one population to the detriment of another, because theoretically the policy maker would not know if they might be impacted, thus would want the best policy for all. If, coupled with this, the policy makers also coupled in the goal of happiness and well-being.

It's Time for Another Leap of Faith—From Individual Rights to Human Rights

Eleanor Roosevelt helped lay out the precepts of human dignity in the Universal Declaration of Human Rights in 1948. But Mrs. Roosevelt and the others didn't go far enough—there is still room for liberal states to be illiberal, still room for laws and practices that restrict the poor and women (though by all means these are not exclusive terms), and still opportunities for religious leaders who influence the secular world by imposing their world view on others.

The world is not homogeneous, we live in a multicultural bazaar—so why can't we choose the best bits of all cultures and leave the distasteful ones on the proverbial plate? Look at how our palates have expanded, we have done so with food—Taco Tuesdays, Pizza, Chinese Takeout, Sushi. Let us do that with other differences.

We also need to recognize that all cultures are progressive, and they are not frozen in a cultural glacier. Uma Narayan (1997) sets forth her personal story of when women got married in her family, and over the generations from her grandmother on, the marrying age increased, but the Indian culture did not falter. Narayan then turns the lens on female genital mutilation and how that has changed over time due to sociocultural pressures. Kwame Anthony Appiah (2006) does the same with tracing how the Chinese ended foot binding, and how it was an issue of community honor to end that tradition. Other cultures are used as an example here because it is sometimes easier to look outward when we begin to be reflective of the change we need to ask of ourselves. The failure of including human rights in our domestic policies is both a failure and a threat: civil rights are for citizens and organized at the legal level; human rights are organized at the human level states (An-Na'im, 2017). The failure is thinking that others "out there" need human rights, and we do not. Every one of us a multiplicity of identities that we are negotiating and mediating, and one includes being part of the global civil society. An-Na'im goes further and calls the United States a rogue state since we use the cover of the threat of terrorism to invade other states, yet we do not observe human rights domestically. For instance, the death penalty is still enforce, and the basic tenets laid out in the opening Preamble of the Declaration of Human Rights: "Whereas recognition of the inherent dignity and of the equal and inalienable rights of all members of the human family is the foundation of freedom, justice and peace in the world"; we do not afford all people dignity. The United States and Somalia are the only countries that have failed to ratify the Convention on the Rights of the Child, 20 years after it was written (1989); Somalia has not signed because it does not have a recognized functioning government. The United States shows its indifference to human rights by not ratifying all the conventions. The failure to connect human rights and civil rights is a radical failure for all Americans because all need dignity for their humanity and to achieve equality (An-Na'im, 2017).

So, one of the first transformative steps would be to demand that our country accept and practice human rights. Human dignity and civil rights are human rights, but if we can diminish someone's citizenship via invisible structures and processes, then we will not achieve equality and will keep people entrenched in second-class citizenship. If we just tolerate some people, it is still a power relationship; if we can manipulate their citizenship for whatever reasons, they are not full citizens.

We should demand that the country abide by the values set forth in the Declaration of Independence: the right to life, liberty, and the pursuit of happiness. One of the goals of government should be to help all achieve happiness. There are public policies that can be put forth to allow all Americans to be happy—safe and subsidized child (and elder) care, health care that does not bankrupt people, public education that teaches all children critical-thinking skills and civics; and subsidized higher education for those who want or need more education.

The key is that we need to teach all citizens (and people) about working in the best public interest, for the public good. The most radical and transformation idea to begin to teach others about our shared values and goals would be a mandatory gap year at the completion of secondary education. In an ideal world, all people would have this opportunity to become active citizens. The gap year would be fulfilled by military service, or a version of Americorps or the Civilian Corps that was developed as part of the New Deal. This year of public service, which moves the young adult out of their comfort zone and allows them to make their way in a new community where they help others build housing, maintain trails, or work in a non-profit (for example), will demonstrate the need for a focus on the community's needs and not on their own. The immediate goal would be to empower the collective, to demonstrate the shared values, and to help achieve equality. We will be relearning and living "we the people." Seventy years after President John F. Kennedy's admonishment to ask what we can do for our country, we will be able to answer by our actions.

The ultimate goal would be to achieve a liberal and just democracy were there were no second-class citizens, and we would all be evolved and involved good citizens. As An-Na'im and others have stated, none of us have monolithic identities, we all have multiple identities, but what we all have in common is that we are all human.

Notes

1 It needs to be noted that this model of citizenship, the five markers that are used to police, control, and regulate citizens were conceived long before "birtherism" was even a political notion. The need to make visible the invisible constraints that allow for is even more crucial today, when we cannot keep track of the changes to state that are made under cover of another crisis that appears more important in the media. But this administration will pass and another one take its place, and if we do not pay attention to the processes, we will find ourselves further into the quicksand where we will not be able to recover our democracy.
2 Castle Rock v. Gonzales, 545 U.S. 748 (2005).
3 Helliwell et al. (2019).
4 Ward, George. Chapter three: https://worldhappiness.report/ed/2019/happiness-and-voting-behavior/.

References

Abramowitz, Mimi (2004) *Regulating the Lives of Women: Social Welfare Policy from Colonial Times to the Present.* Boston: Southend Press.

Alexander, Michelle (2012) *The New Jim Crow: Mass Incarceration in the Age of Colorblindness.* New York: The New Press.

An-Na'im, Abdullahi (25 October 2017) *Dialectic of Civil Rights and Human Rights in the Law and Policy of the USA.* Emory University, video. Accessed 6 November 2018, scholarblogs.emory.edu/aannaim/2017/11/11/dialectic-of-civil-rights-and-human-rights-in-the-law-and-policy-of-the-usa-video/.

Appiah, Kwame Anthony (2006) *Cosmopolitanism: Ethics in a World of Strangers.* New York: W.W. Norton and Co.

Appiah, Kwame Anthony (2011) *The Honor Code: How Moral Revolutions Happen.* New York: W.W. Norton and Co.

Bauer, Lauren (3 January 2019) "Who Was the Poor in 2017?" Accessed 3 January 2019, https://www.brookings.edu/blog/up-front/2019/01/03/who-was-poor-in-the-united-states-in-2017/?utm_campaign=Brookings%20Brief&utm_source=hs_email&utm_medium=email&utm_content=68735259.

Benhabib, Seyla (2004) *The Rights of Others.* New York: Cambridge University Press.

Benhabib, Seyla (2011) *Dignity in Adversity.* Cambridge, UK: Polity Books.

Brenkert, Benjamin (21 March 2003) "The Newport Sex Scandal, 1919–21." *Gay and Lesbian Review Worldwide.*

Brown, Wendy (2006) *Regulating Aversion, Tolerance in Age of Identity and Empire*. Princeton, NJ: Princeton University Press.

Burwell v. Hobby Lobby, 573 U.S. ___ (2014).

Castle Rock v. Gonzales, 545 U.S. 748 (2005).

Citizens United v. FEC, 558 U.S. 310 (2010).

Conover, Pamela Johnston, Donald Searing and Ivor Crewe (2004) "The Elusive Ideal of Equal Citizenship: Political Theory and Political Psychology in the United States and Great Britain." *The Journal of Politics* 66 (4): 1036–1068.

Convention on the Rights of the Child (1989) Accessed 15 January 2019, www.unicef.org/rightsite/237_202.htm.

Cuomo, Mario (13 September 1984) "Religious Belief and Public Morality: A Catholic Governor's Perspective." University of Notre Dame. Accessed 28 December 2018, http://archives.nd.edu/research/texts/cuomo.htm.

Dahl, Robert (2000) *On Democracy*. New Haven, CT: Yale University Press.

Franklin, Ben in Johnny Rossen (1969) *The Little Red, White & Blue Book [Revolutionary Quotations by Great Americans]*. New York: Grove Press.

Freud, Sigmund (1910). *Three Contributions to the Sexual Theory*. Ithaca, NY: Cornell University Press.

Gooden, Susan Tinsley (2003) "Contemporary Approaches to Enduring Challenges." In: Sanford F. Schram, Joe Soss, and Richard C. Fording (eds), *Race and The Politics of Welfare Reform*. Lansing, MI: University of Michigan Press.

Graber, Ruth (2010) *Haven: The Dramatic Story of 1,000 World War Two Refugees and How They Came to America*. New York: Open Road Media.

Hacker, Meg (2017) "When Saying 'I Do' Meant Giving Up Your US Citizenship." Accessed 10 March 2018, www.archives.gov/files/publications/prologue/2014/spring/citizenship.pdf.

Heater, Derek (1999) *What Is Citizenship?* Maldon, MA: Polity Press.

Helliwell, J., Richard Layard and Jeffrey Sachs (20 March 2019) "World Happiness Report-2019." Accessed 5 May 2019, https://worldhappiness.report/ed/2019/.

Hobbes, Thomas and Edwin Curley (1994) *Hobbes Leviathan*. Indianapolis, IN: Hackett Publishing Co.

Huntington, Samuel P. (2005) *Who Are We? The Challenges to America's National Identity*. New York: Simon and Schuster.

Kennedy, John F. (1961) "Inaugural Address." Accessed 30 January 2019, www.jfklibrary.org/learn/about-jfk/historic-speeches/inaugural-address.

Khazan, Olga (8 May 2018) "In One Year, 57,375 Years of Life Were Lost to Police Violence." *The Atlantic*. Accessed 26 January 2019, www.theatlantic.com/health/archive/2018/05/the-57375-years-of-life-lost-to-police-violence/559835/.

Kymlicka, Will (2001) *Politics in the Vernacular: Nationalism, Multiculturalism and Citizenship*. Oxford, UK: Oxford University Press.

Locke, John and Jonathan Bennett (2017) "The Second Treatise of Government." Accessed 15 January 2019, www.earlymoderntexts.com/assets/pdfs/locke1689a.pdf.

Lombardo, Paul (2008) *Three Generations, No Imbeciles*. Baltimore, MD: The Johns Hopkins University Press.

Lopez, Ian Hanley (2006) *White by Law*. New York: New York University Press.

Machiavelli, Niccolo and E.R.P. Vincent (eds). (2008) *The Prince*. New York: Signet Books.

Mackert, Jurgen and Bryan S. Turner (eds). (2017a) *The Transformation of Citizenship, Vol 1: Political Economy*. New York: Routledge.

Mackert, Jurgen and Bryan S. Turner (eds). (2017b) *The Transformation of Citizenship, Vol 2: Boundaries of Inclusion and Exclusion*. New York: Routledge.

Mackert, Jurgen and Bryan S. Turner (eds). (2017c) *The Transformation of Citizenship, Vol 3: Struggle, Resistance and Violence.* New York: Routledge.

Marcuse, Hebert (1964) *One Dimensional Man.* Boston, MA: Beacon Press.

Marshall, Thomas Humphrey (1964) *Class, Citizenship and Social Development*. Garden City, NY: Doubleday.

Mijs, Jonathan J.B. (2019) "The Paradox of Inequality: Income Inequality and Belief in Meritocracy Go Hand in Hand." *Socio-Economic Review* 1–29. doi:10.1093/ser/mwy052.

Mill, John Stuart (2010) *On Liberty.* Accessed 30 January 2019, www.gutenberg.org/files/34901/34901-h/34901-h.htm.

Molina, Natalia (2006) *Fit to Be Citizens?: Public Health and Race in Los Angeles, 1879–1939.* Los Angeles, CA: University of California.

Myers, JoAnne (2018) "Justice System." In: Letizia Gugliemo (ed.), *Misogyny in American Culture* (2 volumes). Sacramento, CA: ABC-CLIO.

Narayan, Uma (1997) *Dislocating Cultures.* New York: Routledge.

Nussbaum, Martha (2010). *From Disgust: To Humanity.* New York: Oxford University Press.

Parekh, Bhikhu (2002) *Rethinking Multiculturalism: Cultural Diversity and Political Theory.* Cambridge, MA: Harvard University Press.

Rawls, John (1971) *A Theory of Justice*. Cambridge: Harvard University Press.

Rawls, John (1993) *Political Liberalism*. New York: Columbia University Press.

Rosales, Rodolfo (ed.). (2018) *Community as the Material Basis of Citizenship*. New York: Routledge.

Rousseau, Jean Jacques and Jonathan Bennett (2010) *The Social Contract*. Accessed 30 January 2019, www.earlymoderntexts.com/assets/pdfs/rousseau1762.pdf.

Santa Clara County v. Southern Pacific Railroad, 118 U.S. 394 (1886).

Smith, Adam (2015) *The Wealth of Nations*. New York: Simon and Brown.

The Protect and Serve Act, H.R. 5698. Accessed 26 January 2019, www.congress.gov/bill/115th-congress/house-bill/5698 and www.govtrack.us/congress/bills/115/s2794/summary.

Thompson, Derek (24 February 2019) "The Religion of Workism Is Making Americans Miserable." *The Atlantic*. Accessed 24 February 2019, www.theatlantic.com/ideas/archive/2019/02/religion-workism-making-americans-miserable/583441/.

Tocqueville, Alexis de (2002) *Democracy in America, Volumes One and Two.* Pennsylvania State University Electronic Classics Series Publication. Accessed 25 July 2019, seas3.elte.hu/coursematerial/LojkoMiklos/Alexis-de-Tocqueville-Democracy-In-America.pdf.

Universal Declaration of Human Rights (1948) Accessed 15 November 2019, http://www.un.org/en/universal-declaration-human-rights/.

US Patriot Act, Uniting and Strengthening America by Providing Appropriate Tools Required to Intercept and Obstruct Terrorism Act of 2001. P.L. No: 107-56.

Washington Post (2018) "Fatal Force." Accessed 26 January 2019, www.washingtonpost.com/graphics/national/police-shootings-2017/.

Young, Iris Marion (1990) *Justice and the Politics of Difference*. Princeton, NJ: Princeton University Press.

INDEX

Note: Page numbers followed by n refer to notes.